Psychology for social workers and counsellors

Library of Social Work

General Editor:
Noel Timms
Professor of Social Work Studies
University of Newcastle upon Tyne

John Hough

Psychology for social workers and counsellors

An introduction

Carole Sutton

School of Social and Community Studies
Leicester Polytechnic

Routledge & Kegan Paul
London, Boston and Henley

First published in 1979
by Routledge & Kegan Paul Ltd
39 Store Street, London WC1E 7DD,
Broadway House, Newtown Road,
Henley-on-Thames, Oxon RG9 1EN and
9 Park Street, Boston, Mass. 02108, USA
Set in Times English
and Printed in Great Britain by
T. J. Press (Padstow) Ltd, Cornwall
Reprinted with corrections in 1981

British Library Cataloguing in Publication Data

Sutton, Carole

Psychology for social workers and counsellors.—
(Library of social work ISSN 0305-4381).
1. Social service
2. Psychological research
I. Title II. Series
361'.007'2   HV41   79-40089

ISBN 0 7100 0297 1
ISBN 0 7100 0298 X Pbk

To my family, for their patience and encouragement, and to the staff and students of the School of Social and Community Studies of Leicester Polytechnic, with whom it is so rewarding to work.

Contents

Contents

Contents

Preface

My objective in writing this book has been to draw attention to the relevance of the vast amount of information emerging from the field of psychological research to the everyday practice of social work and counselling. I trained as a social worker at the London School of Economics in the 1960s, and for the first few years after that, attempted to put into practice the theoretical principles which I had been taught there; I do not think that I was very successful. Yet I should still be trying to practise, and even teach, those same principles had I not come upon experimental psychology, a discipline which certainly existed in the 1960s but which was not represented in any way within the course of training which I experienced.

It was with relief, mixed with initial ambivalence, however, that I encountered the more critical and rigorous discipline and methods of psychology, and since at the time I was studying I was also in part-time social work employment, I was able to try out in practice some of the concepts which were presented to me in my academic studies. It was astonishing to discover the breadth of material available from the research literature of psychology, and astonishing too, to realize the immediacy of its relevance to social work and counselling. Yet it seemed to be barely represented in the writings by and for social workers. I have tried to fill something of this gap.

As will be apparent, I have had to be highly selective in my choice of material for so short a book but I have chosen the areas which seem to me to be of special relevance to social work and counselling. It is distressing to find so many deeply committed members of the social work profession so disillusioned by the impossibility of their task: I venture to suggest that one reason for this (though only one) is that practitioners are using, and students are being taught, theories of practice which are inadequate to the task they are asked to do. Perhaps in the 1960s there was a shortage of theory relevant to the social work task: that is no longer the case, and social work teachers and trainers have at least some responsibility for familiarizing themselves with a little of that which is available. This book is written in the hope that it may make the task of a few social workers and counsellors a little easier, and their contribution more effective.

Carole Sutton

Acknowledgments

The author and publisher are grateful to Marie T. Gilbert and *Nursing Times* for permission to reproduce Mrs Gilbert's article 'Behavioural approach to the treatment of child abuse'.

I want to know, to understand, to experience and to give . . . .

Roger Sim

Introduction
Why do we need
theory?

What theory is about

There are a great many people, helping a great many other people, who never bother with theory at all. In any community, in any country, there are those who provide practical help, comfort and strength to individuals or to families in need from their own personal concern and resources; to many of these the concept of a 'theory of helping' would probably seem irrelevant.

If contributions from spontaneous helpers are of such indisputable value, what is the need for professional training and the study of theory? Why do social workers and counsellors have to engage in months of academic work, involving attendance at lectures, hours of reading, essay writing and participation in discussion groups? These are valid questions, when there is so much which can be achieved without recourse to theory at all.

There are several answers. One is that when one moves within a society beyond the provision of the basic essentials for maintaining life and health to such fields of human relationships as mental health, the care of children and the prevention of crime, the helpers soon begin to disagree. They disagree about who should be helped, how much they should be helped, and how they should be helped; they disagree about why the problem arose in the first place and about what they are trying to do to rectify it; further, they disagree a-bout who should do the helping, and about the very nature of 'help' itself. These are profound issues, with political and philosophical implications, but our society has now reached a stage of sophisti-cation where extremely complex questions are being asked: How can we best help brain-damaged children? What causes schizophrenia?

Can we cure alcoholism? Is there such an entity as the psychopathic personality? Slowly, very slowly, by means of scrupulous and painstaking research, some tentative answers to some of these questions are emerging; similarly, we are also beginning to understand better the nature of 'help' in the field of human relationships.

A second answer is that social workers and counsellors do not work alone but in co-operation with many professions—doctors, psychiatrists, teachers and health visitors—many of whom are trained in the understanding and use of research findings—medical, psychological and sociological; it is important that we share a language with them. The contribution which we can make as colleagues and team members will be diminished if we cannot share the theoretical understanding given to other workers in the field. If a psychiatrist, for instance, with whom social workers are statutorily required to work on occasion, refers to his intention to use 'a behavioural approach, based upon learning theory' in a given case, it is very important that we should know what he is talking about, and that our training should have equipped us with this knowledge.

A third answer, and there are many more, is exceedingly important: counsellors and social workers, particularly the latter, constantly find themselves invested with the necessity for making predictions: Will these parents be likely to injure their child if he is not taken into care? Is this boy likely to respond to intermediate treatment? Will this couple prove suitable as adoptive parents throughout the years to come? Almost all action, by social workers or anyone else, is taken on the basis of an anticipated outcome, and social workers, by virtue of their claim to be 'professional', are expected to be better than most at predicting outcome. As we know from the distressing and tragic experiences in which children have died during the last few years, the press and the public expect considerable accuracy in prediction, and are very harsh towards those who err in their forecasting. Reliable prediction, however, is rooted in sound theory, and herein lies the necessity for those who seek to be effective in their role as professionals both to be acquainted with theory, and to be able to use it to advantage in their work. For this is the ultimate test of theory: its capacity to predict.

What does 'theory' mean?

The Greek word 'theoros' is translated as 'spectator': the word 'theory' then has links with this meaning as a way of looking at or surveying a field of evidence with a view to extracting principles from it. Different spectators will extract different principles, at higher or lower levels of complexity: one onlooker may see, or think he sees, small sequences which appear to repeat themselves time and again; another may consider the overall pattern and the way its parts relate one to another. If the first viewer's perceptions are seen and endorsed by others, we may say that he has isolated a fragment of theory, a principle which, for the time being at least, links two or more of the phenomena of our world. (An example of such a fragment might be that talking frequently and clearly to young children appears to have an effect of raising the children's verbal ability, at least in the short term, as measured by the intelligence quotient, and by comparison with young children not so stimulated. The same sequence has been observed sufficiently often by different spectators in many different settings for this theoretical fragment to have become extremely valuable: it may be used predictively.) The second viewer's perceptions are of a different order: inasmuch as he is looking at the overall field the validity of the patterns which he detects, and which he teaches to his children, may hold sway for generations before that validity is questioned. The popular Greek view of the role of the 'gods' in the course of events, so apparent to the original 'theoros', is not held by many theoreticians nowadays, and few people would use Greek mythology as the basis of their attempts to anticipate the future.

For the most part we have, within the field of human development and behaviour, just a few fragments of theory which have predictive capacity. Hopefully, within the years to come, these fragments will interlock with others so that we have a network or assembly of principles in terms of which we may understand more and more of the phenomena of our world. Within other disciplines, particularly those of the physical sciences, much progress has already been made: it was because of the predictive capacity of their theories that physical scientists were enabled to send man to the moon. In the human sciences we are as yet able to predict only very little of use in either the field of education or of family relationships.

Later in this chapter I propose to consider in more detail how theoretical ideas are formulated, as possibilities or 'hypotheses' and then researched—to be supported or rejected. First, though, I wish to highlight the effect which the public's desire for accurate prediction has upon the providers of services. To be able to anticipate the future is for most of us extremely gratifying, and we seek more and more foreknowledge, in order to take appropriate action. We usually only take medicines which have been pronounced reliable on the basis of repeated laboratory testing; we usually travel only in cars and aeroplanes which engineers have assured us 'will be safe'; and we even take our macs or leave them at home according to the predictions of the men who compile the weather forecast. We live, then, in a society in which people have come to expect accuracy in prediction, and in many situations, particularly those touched upon by the physical sciences which have developed a vast number of predictive tools and techniques, this accuracy is forthcoming.

The human sciences, however, are in their infancy; serious and systematic research into human development, thought and behaviour began only a few decades ago and there is as yet no widely accepted bed-rock of knowledge about people from which more sophisticated ideas may emerge. There are, it is true, many fragments of theory available, of the kind I mentioned earlier, but these are by no means integrated one with another and are likely to remain fragments for many years to come. Perhaps the greatest problem is that the object of one's research does not, in the human sciences, remain constant; an aeroplane wing or a motor-car engine is likely to be broadly the same phenomenon, and to yield the same results, whether it is examined early in the morning or late at night—assuming that the air temperature has not changed—and to anybody who cares to be present at the examination. The same is not true of a human being: the time of day, what has happened just before, who does the examining, and who else is present at the examination are just a few of the variables which have to be taken into account when attempting to introduce scientific techniques to the study of people and their behaviour.

The subtlety of some of the influences which affect human behaviour and interaction are only just beginning to be appreciated, as psychologists attempt to tease out the intricate relationship between cause and effect—an exercise which proves exceedingly difficult and which, as I have said above, has so far yielded only a few fragments of reliable theory. Few psychologists feel confident of making more than very limited predictions about human interaction on the basis of present understanding.

And yet, because the public has become so used to accurate prediction from other disciplines, and because large sums of money are involved in the provision of public services, it is naturally expected that those who call themselves 'professionals' will make accurate predictions. Social workers are expected to be able to forecast whether parents will neglect or injure their children, whether those who have offended in the past will offend again and whether a given type of court order will prove effective or not. How can they possibly tell?

The irony is that, lulled by the confidence brought by having good intentions and, if they are fortunate, a two-year training behind them, they are willing to make or be party to such predictions. They collude with, and thus often become the victims of, public expectation: those who train social workers and counsellors have the responsibility of pointing out the tentative nature of much of that which is often dispensed as 'knowledge' and of warning against the uncritical acceptance of dubious theory. Questions which are usually appropriate are: What is the evidence that the teaching you are giving us is theoretically valid? and How does it help us make predictions?

An example of the way in which it has now been recognized at central government level that it is vital to use theoretical knowledge based upon research findings is given by the reliance placed upon the computer by Home Office psychologists working in conjunction with parole boards. It has been found that the probability of another offence being committed by an offender released from prison is governed by many variables, including whether he has a job to return to, whether he has a family who actively wants him back, whether he has stable accommodation, and so on. Each of these probabilities, if isolated, is separate and distinguishable, but in real life of course they interact, so that a man has a family but no job, or accommodation, but with divorce pending; in other words the subtlety of the interaction effects is so complex as to demand a computer to predict whether a given man is a good candidate for parole.

If in this field computers are called for, how can we allow young and inexperienced workers to take decisions and assume responsibility for the lives and well-being of both individuals and whole families while providing them with inadequate resources, inadequate training, or even no training at all? What of the quality of the training: how many courses attempt to introduce their students to the critical appraisal of theory, or indeed to explore with students the origins of theory?

An unresolved theoretical issue: maternal deprivation

An excellent example of the difficulties encountered in establishing a sound basis for prediction and decision is offered by the search for knowledge of the effects of maternal deprivation. I choose it because this is an area of particular importance for those working with families in the attempt to provide healthy surroundings, physical and emotional, for the optimal development of young children, and an area therefore in which the pronouncements of those who undertake research in the field are listened to extremely attentively.

In 1948 the Social Commission of the United Nations decided to make a study of the needs of homeless children, and the World Health Organization offered to look at the mental-health aspects of the problem. John Bowlby was asked to compile the report, and this appeared as *Maternal Care and Mental Health* in 1951. Then in 1953, Penguin published Margery Fry's abridged version, *Child Care and the Growth of Love,* which sold widely and which proved extremely influential among the policy-makers of children's departments—the local authority bodies then responsible for the welfare of children in need—and among the general public. The essence of the book was the examination of the evidence for a link between early childhood deprivation of maternal care, and subsequent mental ill-health. In the chapter 'What observation has shown', the author writes:

The evidence suggests that three somewhat different experiences can each produce the affectionless and delinquent character:

(a) Lack of any opportunity for forming an attachment to a mother-figure during the first three years.
(b) Deprivation for a limited period—at least three months and probably more than six—during the first three or four years.
(c) Changes from one mother-figure to another during the same period.

In the following chapter, 'Theoretical problems', the writer draws attention to key periods of development in the child's capacity for human relationships, and summarizes the conditions required for health:

if mental development is to proceed smoothly, it would appear to be necessary for the unformed mentality to be exposed, during certain critical periods, to the influence of the psychic organizer—the mother. . . . In broad outline, the following are the most important:

(a) The phase during which the infant is in the course of establishing a relation with a clearly identified person—his mother; this is normally achieved by five or six months of age.
(b) The phase during which he needs her as an ever-present companion; this usually continues until about his third birthday.
(c) The phase during which he is becoming able to maintain a relationship with her in her absence. During the fourth and fifth years such a relationship can only be maintained in favourable circumstances and for a few days or weeks at a time; after seven or eight the relationship can be maintained, though not without strain, for periods of a year or more.

Now the role of the good mother was defined 'scientifically': she should be an 'ever-present companion' to her young child, until he was three. Moreover, clear guidelines had been set, 'scientifically', for children's departments: a first priority was the keeping together of young children and their mother under almost any circumstances. For the message of the evidence was clear: deprivation in the early months was 'scientifically' linked with mental breakdown or disorder in adolescence. The theory was accepted as tried and true, and strong enough to bear prediction.

The theory, or fragment of theory, as then pronounced has not been validated, i.e. later studies have by no means found that a clear link exists between the experience of deprivation as defined by Bowlby (1953) and subsequent mental disorder. The World Health Organization published in 1962 *Deprivation of Maternal Care. A Reassessment of its Effects,* which acknowledged that 'While the practical effects of Bowlby's monograph in the realm of child care have been universally acknowledged to be wholly beneficial, his theoretical conclusions have been subjected to a considerable amount of criticism.' This uncertainty had the valuable effect of promoting a large number of research projects into the subleties of what occurs within the over-inclusive concept of 'maternal deprivation', and two fairly recent publications, *Maternal Deprivation Reassessed,* by Michael Rutter and *Early Experience: Myth and Evidence,* by Ann and A. D. B. Clarke, attempt to review the mosaic of evidence linking separation of mother and child, in many different sets of circumstances, and later mental or emotional disorder. What has emerged is that a very large number of separate variables, length of separation, reason for separation, the circumstances of the separation, and many others, all have to be taken into account as distinct influences and that the unitary concept of 'emotional damage' has also to be defined more accurately—in terms of short- or long-term effects, in terms of differing results according to differing temperaments of children, and in terms of the behavioural effects themselves, as well as the possibility of such effects being reversed or 'cured'. It is now to be anticipated that as clearer findings emerge isolating which particular circumstance of deprivation, or which circumstance interacting with which others, do presage problems in adolescence, then these more subtle influences may be brought to the attention of students in their training and taken into consideration together with other factors when deciding during their professional life whether a child should be taken into care or not. Clearly, a computer is desirable to deal with so many variables but computers are not readily available in departments of social service.

For example Rutter (1972) distinguishes between long- and short-term effects. His research has led him to the conclusion that separation between mother and child is stressful and has undesirable effects in the short term, but he has found that the cause of the separation appears to be much more important than the separation *per se* in determining long-term effects. His results show for example that delinquency rates are nearly twice the normal for boys whose parents had divorced or separated, where there is likely to have been considerable tension and unhappiness within the family, but that the rate among boys who lost a parent through death was only slightly raised.

It is by this process of inquiry and research, of one investigator attempting to support or refute the findings of another by re-examining the original inquiry or conducting others, that fragments of theory are constructed. Few psychologists would consider that the research relating to maternal deprivation is yet sufficiently cohesive for the field to be dignified with the term 'theory'; there is no serious 'theory of maternal deprivation', the subtleties of the interacting variables have yet to be teased out. It is quite possible, indeed probable, that the conclusions reached by Bowlby, (1953) and the different ones reached by Rutter, (1972) will all be over-turned by the findings of some future investigator who may test out his hypothesis that some as yet unrecognized variable has vital implications, and be proved right. It is in this way that researchers gain greater and greater approximations to 'reality'.

Meanwhile, readers will say, we have no computers, and life has to go on. This is so, and because of public expectation of accurate prediction and the enthusiasm which counsellors and social workers have to be seen as 'professionals' we have foolishly let ourselves be seen as able to make predictions. It is scarcely surprising that we are often wrong and that public confidence in us is waning. Compare the medical profession: a general practitioner, after six years of intensive training, and supported by regular information concerning research findings, still cannot be held responsible for mistaken clinical judgement *per se*.

What reliable theoretical material is available?

Just as the publication of Bowlby's work in 1951 had an extremely influential effect on the new children's departments established by local authorities in 1948, with the result that it coloured important policy decisions, so the dissemination of the ideas of Freud and his followers in the post-war period had a powerful influence on the teaching given to social workers at that time. When I was a student in the 1960s we received a weekly lecture on Freudian developmental theory from a psychoanalyst. This was the backbone of our course. The books we read reflected this approach, and we were encouraged to think in psychoanalytic and psychodynamic terms when working with families or individuals. My early years of attempting to use these ideas in practice were uncomfortable ones: I found them useful when trying to understand situations, and see how they might have come about, useful, too, in the initial stages of a contact when people needed to talk openly and freely, but I found them much less useful when that stage came to an end. I had understood from my training, perhaps incorrectly, that once one had enabled a person to have 'insight' (an understanding of why it was that he was feeling or behaving in a way which brought him no happiness) this understanding would enable him to feel or behave more appropriately. This did not seem to happen; the more I looked at the psychodynamics deeper and deeper was the water in which I found myself.

My personal discomfort with the theoretical ideas which I had been taught was not sufficient, however, to lead me to question them; I felt rather that it was my inexperience in handling them and relating theory to practice which accounted for the poor results I achieved. Indeed, it did not cross my mind that the theory might have flaws: I had received it from a psychoanalyst at one of the foremost academic institutions in the land. How insensitive and misguided appeared the supporters of Barbara Wootton (1959), who challenged the psychoanalytic approach, and the sociologists who claimed that social circumstances might be as important in causing delinquency among young people as individual psychopathology. With our new-found wisdom, such ideas seemed to be 'rationalizations' or 'projections'.

The psychodynamic approaches, however, do seem to have lost ground, first as the impact of sociological studies on social work training increased their effect, as community work developed and as successive fashions for therapeutic endeavour reach us from across the Atlantic. Client-centred therapy has proved very influential and Rogerian techniques are still widely used; but transactional analysis, gestalt therapy and, more recently, family therapy have all gained their adherents and are training their own counsellors and practitioners. All these therapies have their theories, usually rather elaborate constructions, each with its own jargon and its own self-coherence. *But do the theories have predictive capacity?*

As we have seen earlier it is all too easy to conclude, in good faith, that one has isolated an irreducible principle of human living, to teach this to others and yet to be only partly right or even wholly wrong. But as we have also seen, and had demonstrated to us in the press in the last few years, the public demands that with regard to the safety of children at least, social workers will always be right. *There is no theory available with this degree of predictive capacity.*

Olive Stevenson (1976), Professor of Social Work at Keele University, has spoken recently of the 'shifting balance between sociology and psychology and between individual work and community work', and said that 'she rejoiced in this eclecticism'. But she also said, 'we should be masters of theory for practice, that is, in the

9

selection and use of theory for a professional purpose.' These are fine words, but as we look round counselling agencies and social services departments, how often do we recognize the active selection and use of theory for a professional purpose? How often indeed is there time even to think of theory?

What reliable theory is then available? In the sense of there being an integrated, fully understood body of knowledge, on the basis of which one can make confident predictions, there is none. All we have are a few fragments of theory, not integrated one with another, and which may yet be challenged. But some fragments are becoming increasingly capable of bearing prediction. This book is about some of those fragments.

The next part of this Introduction is devoted to an examination of ways in which methods of psychological research contribute to the formulation of theory; it shows how an idea is first set out as a hypothesis or possibility on the basis of certain findings, to be subsequently attacked by others who question the findings, and how this process of repeated attempts to verify and refine ideas gradually contributes to the bank of psychological theory.

The contribution of psychological method to establishing a body of theory

Psychology, which is broadly the study of human development, thought, feeling and behaviour, is an extremely young science— barely forty or fifty years old. It has been able, however, to make use of the methods of investigation developed by the older, mathematically based, sciences for its own inquiries and is having considerable success in introducing a disciplined way of looking at the shifting scene of our world and ourselves. One of the main objectives of this young science is to search out some of the irreducible principles of living which manifest themselves in us; if this is possible we may then be able to take these principles into account both in trying to meet the needs of others and in management of our own lives.

There are, however, at least three main difficulties which researchers encounter when investigating psychological processes.

Some difficulties encountered by psychologists

Choosing a representative cross-section (problems of sampling)

Since it is impossible to investigate an entire population when carrying out research it is customary to select a small sample which one hopes will be representative of the whole. But how does one choose such a sample, and having chosen it how does one enlist the co-operation of the individuals concerned? If one has a captive audience and wishes, for example, to examine the stability of a characteristic such as intelligence in the growing child, it is usually possible for an educational psychologist to select, say, every tenth child in a school and conduct an intelligence quotient test with those same children every three or four years. This will give some indication, provided one uses a 'valid' test (one which actually does test the intelligence quotient) and one which is 'reliable' (one which gives roughly the same results whoever administers it), of the stability of this characteristic.

There are, however, few captive audiences and thus the problems of sampling become considerable. People who are approached in the street and asked to take part in a psychological experiment may be extremely reluctant to do so; sadly any word beginning with 'psych-' seems to promote anxiety—perhaps because of inevitable associations with psychiatry and the implications of mental disorder. Researchers are therefore obliged to fall back on volunteers, which at first seems fitting and desirable—except that further research into who are the people who volunteer to take part in psychological experiments has shown that volunteers tend to be less conforming, rather more intelligent and more likely to come from professional backgrounds than a random sample of the general population. Furthermore the difficulty often experienced in obtaining volunteers has led to a strong tendency to use college students as subjects for research, and few people would concede that these constitute a representative sample of society as a whole.

This problem of finding a fair cross-section of the public is common of course both to sociologists and to psychologists, and the inaccuracy of the forecasts of the opinion-survey agencies demonstrates the difficulties involved. If one's initial sample of subjects is biased how can one have any confidence that what may be true for that sample is still true for the population as a whole? Such are the problems of establishing irreducible principles which constitute the theoretical foundation of a discipline.

Distorting the situation merely by investigating it

Just as one cannot be sure that by enlisting the co-operation of volunteers to act as the subject of one's investigations, one is not contriving or manipulating a situation, so one is bound to take account of the fact that the mere presence of an investigator changes that situation. We are all familiar with the discomfort of being assessed or examined, and it seems that however detached or neutral the researcher may claim to be, people do not behave in the same way in the company of an observer as they do without him. The age, sex and race of investigators have all been found to have discernible effects upon the outcome of inquiries, and other social variables such as the extent to which the observer smiled or his tone of voice when speaking seem also to affect results. If these effects, which are often completely unintentional, are so marked how much more influential are likely to be the effects of the observer's expectation.

Inevitably, most psychologists who undertake research do so with a hypothesis in mind; they have noticed, or believe they have noticed, a link between two phenomena, which might be a link between cause and effect, and their inquiry is designed to examine whether their hypothesis can or cannot be supported by evidence. It is natural that their very wish to establish this link, and their enthusiasm for their hypothesis, will convey itself non-verbally to the subjects of the inquiry and colour the results. Smale (1977) has shown the powerful effect which the expectation of the helping person of the outcome of his intervention in the life of his client has on that very outcome. If the helper feels pessimistic, that pessimism is likely to be conveyed non-verbally to the client despite the best intentions of the helper, and is influential on the result. The significance of this realization for the work of counsellors and social workers is of vital importance.

The problem of arriving at shared meanings

When discussing what occurs when we look at a field of vision, psychologists who have studied perception suggest that we 'make a visual hypothesis' of what is 'out there'. The human brain appears to be so constructed that it tries to make sense of visual data, usually in terms of our past experiences. Other people may be making a different sort of sense of the visual data, according to their past experiences, for many visual perceptions have emotional associations which colour the percept. One can compare their activity to seeing pictures in a fire; as when two or three people look into a glowing fire they see different things, so in day-to-day life we believe we go along with a general consensus about what is 'out there', but it seems increasingly that we live in a world composed of personal subjectivities and personal meanings. Some sociologists have gone as far as to suggest that we construct reality, i.e. that there is no ultimate knowable reality, but only interpretations of sensory data by individuals. Since these interpretations are in many cases shaped by culture, and take place within a social context, we do share many personal meanings, but many we do not share and so truth has many faces. To seek to establish the truth in an interpersonal dispute is likely to be a fruitless exercise: there are often as many truths as there are people involved.

If this is so, and it is of course itself a debatable idea, then theory must use the currency of shared meanings. A chemist, talking to another chemist, can be fairly sure that when he speaks of calcium carbonate, then the other will know precisely what he has in mind: can any one social worker be sure what another means by even such common terms as casework or group work?

The importance of arriving at shared meanings within a discipline which is attempting to introduce rigour into the study of man is therefore all the greater. It is alarming how casually counsellors and social workers bandy about such concepts as 'regression', 'projection', 'defensiveness', and 'treatment', presumably under the impression that their listeners understand not only what the speaker means by the term but have the same meaning as himself. Furthermore, the proliferation of 'therapies' arriving here from the USA all lead to more jargon and more possibilities of misunderstanding. (A glance at the Forthcoming Events page in a popular journal notes meetings on primal therapy, gestalt therapy, transactional analysis and transpersonal psychosynthesis, all to be held by separate organizations and each with its own distinctive terminology.) There seems to be a decreasing, rather than an increasing likelihood of shared meanings in general psychological parlance over the next few years, and it is therefore all the more important for the research psychologists to be absolutely clear that their meanings are tightly defined and described.

Some principles and methods central to research in psychology

Techniques of careful planning of experiments, meticulous observation and recording of what happens and the employment of mathematical and statistical techniques in order to evaluate results have now been introduced into the study of human thought and behaviour. These approaches attempt to take into account the difficulties inherent in such study which I have described above, namely problems of sampling, of changing situations merely by investigating them and of shared meanings; extremely subtle methods have been devised to tease out fundamental principles despite these difficulties. Readers who are interested in the techniques of conducting experiments and drawing conclusions based on the results from experiments are recommended to read David Legge's *An Introduction to Psychological Science* (1975). Although the application of these techniques to the study of man has been practised for only two or three decades they have brought a rich harvest of information from which the theoretical fragments can be tentatively drawn out. The advantage of this approach is that, should another inquirer, in any part of the world, doubt the accuracy of the methods or the conclusions of one researcher's investigation he is at liberty to challenge these by conducting his own inquiry and attempting to reproduce the findings. If he obtains different results he may well publish these, claiming to show the errors of the original inquiry and putting forward his own revised view of the principle involved—to be followed by others attempting to refine and improve it further. For theory is inevitably based on retrospective investigations; but the goal of researchers is usually prediction—the use of detected patterns of human experience, perceived retrospectively, in order to anticipate the future. This is manifestly so in medical research: it is equally true in psychological research.

Consider, for example, the mental disorder schizophrenia: researchers interested in the genetic basis for this disorder have been able to predict since the work of Slater (1968) that there is a 9-16 per cent probability of a person developing schizophrenia if one of his parents suffered from the disorder, and a 35 per cent probability of his developing it if both parents suffered from it. These figures have been supported in many later studies throughout the world and bear predictive capacity on a genetic basis. More recently, though, work with a psychological emphasis by Vaughn and Leff (1976) has indicated the role which family and social factors appear to have on the course of psychiatric illness in a study based on meticulous research and bearing some predictive capacity, i.e. using their techniques it has become increasingly possible to anticipate which patients with schizophrenia will relapse following discharge from hospital, Gradually, then, a clearer picture of schizophrenia is emerging: it appears that both genetic and social factors are involved, and indeed interact; armed with this knowledge we may be able to take steps to take the genetic factors into account and to minimize the effect of the social factors.

Below are some of the principles to which psychologists are trained to adhere: (by 'psychologist' in this context I refer to those qualified to apply for membership of the British Psychological Society).

Very clear definition of terms

In an attempt to be as accurate as possible in their communication, and to arrive at shared meanings, psychologists try to convey explicitly what they understand when they use a term—particularly when reporting their experimental work. They are trained to be aware that by a simple word such as 'learn' there may be as many different understandings of the word as there are people encountering it, and that bitter disputes and factions can arise from such misunderstandings. Thus within experimental psychology terms and concepts are often given an 'operational definition' i.e. an exact description of the phenomenon under investigation, how it is to be recognized and how measured, so that there shall be as little room as possible left for confusion. This does not mean that the term cannot be used in a different way by a different investigator, but that in the particular circumstances of that inquiry it is being used in the tight and exact way specified. It is by such methods, for example, that psychologists and psychiatrists are at last moving towards a shared understanding of what constitutes schizophrenia; investigations have been bedevilled by the fact that the term has been so loosely applied as to make it almost meaningless as a diagnosis, but at last by increased refinement of the criteria employed, specific symptoms have been isolated as typifying schizophrenia. (These are already published in the journals of psychiatry and abnormal psychology, but years will pass before the general public has a shared understanding of them.)

In the fields of social work and counselling many psychologists would feel impatience towards the vagueness and woolliness of the language employed, and towards the assumption that there exists a common definition and understanding of the terms used. We have, for instance, seen over the past few years an increase of interest in T (training) groups and posts are created and workshops held as a result of the belief among the helping professions that such groups are useful and beneficial; expressions such as 'they promote human growth' tend to be put forward to substantiate the claims made for them. Now, many psychologists would want to know exactly what is meant by 'promoting human growth' and how it can be shown that it has occurred; and if a given person reports that after attending a T-group he 'feels better' does he mean some or all of the following possibilities?

He has a wider social circle.

He feels increased confidence.

He is more accepting of himself.

He is more aware of and alert to other people.

He is more aware of how other people perceive him.

He is more accepting of other people.

He can manage his life more as he wishes to.

And so on.

And when these answers have been received there are other questions to be asked:

Do other people endorse the improvement that this group member reports?

Does it persist or wear off within a few days or weeks?

15

Did all other members experience the same improvement?
Was this related to the composition of that particular group?
Was this related to the leadership of that particular group?
Do all people who go to all T-groups experience improvement?
If not, which people do 'improve' and which do not?
And so on.

These questions may seem over-academic and quibbling, but they are in fact extremely important. Several studies of T-groups by psychologists have been carried out: Campbell and Dunnette (1968) found that 30—40 per cent of those who attended a T-group improved in terms of their ability to communicate, their understanding of themselves and of human behaviour in general and their sensitivity to the needs of others: however, 10—20 per cent of a control group, who went to no group at all, improved in the same way over the same period. Furthermore, in an earlier study by Underwood (1965) it was found that for every two people who became more effective as a result of T-group experience one became less effective. A summary of this and other relevant research indicates that 30—40 per cent seem to benefit, about 50 per cent are unaffected, while up to 15 per cent deteriorate as a result of their participation.

It is not that psychologists are trained to be critical or destructive: it is rather that they are trained to be as exact and accurate as they possibly can—to approach the 'scientific' position as nearly as is possible when the object of their investigation is people, in all their intense variety and individuality. Thus it is not that they do not believe T-groups are helpful, but that they require empirical evidence of their usefulness in order to reach an opinion.

Systematic methods of testing hypotheses

In their attempts to discover cause—effect relationships, on the basis of which prediction may be made, psychologists emulate the natural scientists both in their use of disciplined techniques of experiment or observation and in their tendency to measure numerically the outcome of their inquiries. This readiness to employ mathematics when investigating human behaviour offends some people, but it has yielded a rich harvest of information and does not of itself invalidate alternative ways of viewing human experience.

The two main techniques of investigation are as follows:

The experimental method This approach requires the experimenter to arrange that the influence (variable) which he wishes to study should affect one group of people or animals (called the 'experimental group') but that it should not affect a second group of people

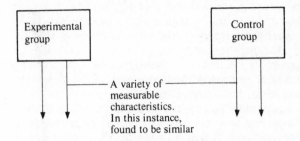

Pre-test situation: two matched samples, chosen to be as similar
upon as many different variables as possible: e.g. age, sex

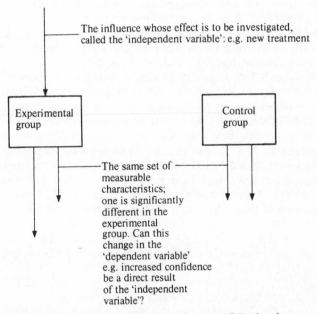

Test situation: the same matched samples tested following the
application of a specific influence e.g. a new drug, or a new
form of treatment

Figure 1   *Independent and dependent variables in a controlled
experiment*

or animals similar in every other respect to the first (called the 'control group'). Then if the first group shows evidence of some change while the second group does not, and if this change is greater than one might attribute to the chance factors which may be operating, the experimenter may feel justified in claiming that the influence he is studying has had a discernible effect upon his experimental group. If the effect is significant he will probably repeat the experiment to attempt to substantiate his findings and then, if the nature of the experiment is of sufficient interest to others in that field he may publish his results and the implications of these results in one of the major psychology journals. If he is successful and his paper is published it will be read by those who will be impressed by the methods and accept his findings, as well as by those who will carry out further investigation on the same theme with the desire either to confirm, refute or refine the original results. This is the laborious way in which the theoretical fragments I described earlier (pp. 5-8) are established.

A Home Office study published in 1976 (Folkard, Smith and Smith) illustrates this approach well; for the previous fifteen years or so an investigation had been taking place into the Intensive Matched Probation and Aftercare Treatment project—abbreviated to IMPACT. Probation officers had for many years been claiming that because of the size of their case-loads their efforts to bring about a beneficial change in their clients were spread so thin as to be valueless. In an attempt to evaluate this claim, a number of probation officers throughout Britain were selected as an experimental group and allocated considerably smaller case-loads than the control group —in order to allow them much more time to work individually with offenders. Therefore the hypothesis to be investigated was broadly that the amount of time which a probation officer spends with an offender has a beneficial effect upon the offender's behaviour.

The influence being studied (known technically as the independent variable) was the amount of contact-time available to the probation officer and the offender, and the effect of this influence might become apparent in some outcome or result (known technically as the dependent variable, since it 'depends' on what has gone before). In this exercise the dependent variable was a simple and obvious measure: the reconviction rate of offenders. This rate was compared in the two groups, i.e. the rate for those in the experimental group, who were randomly selected and for whom increased time with their probation officers was made available, was compared with the rate for offenders in the control group, who were also randomly selected but who received no increase in contact time.

Sad to tell, the hypothesis that increased contact-time between probation officer and offender results in a smaller reconviction rate was not upheld by the results; the actual reconviction rate of those who experienced increased contact was 4.5 per cent higher than that of the control group. The authors report that even when the effect of the probation officers on typical problems of work, accommodation and family relationships was examined, 'there was no solid evidence found to support the claim that experimental treatment produced more beneficial results than control treatment.' Indeed, although the 4.5 per cent higher reconviction rate of the experimental group may be attributed to chance (technically, it was 'statistically non-significant') there is clearly no evidence at all from this study that more probation officers, using their traditional methods of work, ought to be employed in order to allow smaller case-loads. As I have explained (p. 18) these results will no doubt be challenged and flaws in the experiment will be detected, but inasmuch as American studies are yielding very similar kinds of evidence and inasmuch as IMPACT was a carefully designed and conducted study, a good deal of attention is likely to be paid to these results. Probation officers may well find that the Home Office points firmly to these findings when complaints about large case-loads are registered.

The observational method This approach, which includes studies of the same group of people or particular subjects over time, as well as surveys and field studies, characteristically considers much larger samples and does not usually set out to investigate a particular influence. Such studies may examine the development or degree of certain behaviours or characteristics at different periods, e.g. the consistency of the intelligence of a sample of children as measured by the intelligence quotient, or note how regularly certain features or events occur in conjunction with other events. When a conjunction is found, a link or correlation can sometimes be established between the two features under examination (thus there is a correlation between the increasing height of a growing child and his weight); but care has always to be taken not to attribute causality between two phenomena found to be associated. Occasionally one feature is found to be the cause of the effect, but in most circumstances this assumption cannot be made.

One of the best-known British observational studies is that being carried out by the National Children's Bureau on 11,000 children born in one week in 1958. The children's progress in terms of their physical development, health, family circumstances, school experience and, as they grow older, their employment, has been followed in great detail over the intervening years and several reports and publications have been produced from the data gathered. These include *From Birth To Seven* (Davie *et al.,* 1972), *Born to Fail,* (Wedge and Prosser, 1973), *11,000 Seven Year Olds* (Pringle *et al.,*

1966) and *Britain's Sixteen Year Olds* (Fogelman, 1976). Such a study is of course at one and the same time both a sociological and psychological inquiry, since the observational approach is common to both disciplines.

The use of statistical techniques to evaluate findings

In my brief description of the Home Office inquiry IMPACT (p. 18) I referred to the higher reconviction rate of the offenders in the charge of those in the experimental group as statistically non-significant. All this means is that this higher rate could have occurred because of chance factors which could not be taken into account when compiling the experimental and control groups, and therefore no significance can be attached to it.

The use of sophisticated methods of analysing the findings from investigations and of determining whether importance can or cannot be attached to the findings (whether they are 'significant' or 'non-significant') is now standard practice among experimental and research psychologists, and it is this ability to demonstrate that their conclusions are founded not upon personal impressions and hearsay but have a firm mathematical foundation which demands our attention.

Consider, for example, the absorbing controversy, still not fully resolved, which arose between Eysenck and his opponents in the 1950s and 1960s. Eysenck caused a storm when his paper 'The effects of psychotherapy: an evaluation' was published in 1952; this indicated that, on the basis of published evidence, there was no justification for the belief that counselling and psychotherapy had beneficial results. Eysenck claimed that a very high proportion of people with so-called neurotic symptoms get better without any treatment at all ('spontaneous remission' of the disorder) and therefore argued that psychotherapy, in order to justify itself, must improve upon the spontaneous rate. There was, of course, outcry from the proponents of psychotherapy, and other papers were published, for example by DeSharmes, Levy and Wertheimer (1954) and by Sanford (1954), criticizing Eysenck's conclusions on the basis of his having included questionable data and his having indiscriminately pooled data from reports with differing criteria for treatment and improvement. Eysenck replied with another paper 'The effects of psychotherapy: a reply', in 1955, and this controversy provoked a valuable flurry of research—using mathematics and statistics to support claim and counter-claim. Frank, for example, suggested in 1961 that statistical studies consistently reported that about 60 per cent of neurotic patients improve immediately after psychotherapy, regardless of the form of therapy received, but that the same improvement rate had been found for comparable patients who had not received psychotherapy.

This use of research methods, involving closer definition of terms used and detailed monitoring of results, has yielded absorbing new material which is of immediate relevance to anyone engaged professionally or otherwise in counselling. Inquiries into the detail of what occurs in counselling increased throughout the 1960s and culminated in the publication of a major book, *Towards Effective Counselling and Psychotherapy* by Truax and Carkhuff, in 1967. This is both an exhaustive review of most of the previous research on psychotherapy and counselling and an account of their finding, based on this review, that in order to be effective, counselling should manifest certain key features which arise not from the characteristics of the client but from the person of the counsellor. This work is the focus of chapter 2 of this book. Briefly, their review supported Eysenck's claim, but detected a greater subtlety reflected in the figures than was appreciated by Eysenck—namely that different counsellors consistently produced different results.

It is this increasing use of tight mathematical and statistical techniques which gives credibility to the research results emanating from psychology, and with which trainers and practitioners ought to be familiar. There is now available in the literature a substantial body of information, fragments of theory, which is of major importance to those who attempt to help others and particularly to those who claim to be professionals. To those, for instance, who claim that a 'relationship', the traditional tool for promoting beneficial change within clients, cannot be measured or quantified the psychologist would answer that since the work of Truax and Carkhuff (1967) this is no longer so; the blanket concept of 'the therapeutic relationship' has been refined and its beneficial components have been distinguished. This work, and its implications for training and for predicting who will be effective counsellors are essential knowledge for those employed in the selection and teaching of those in the helping professions; yet here in Britain, a decade and more after the publication of this work it appears almost unknown.

One final point: should later investigators have reason to question the conclusions of Truax and Carkhuff (1967) or indeed of any investigators who have preceded them on grounds, say, of faulty sampling or lack of experimental rigour, they are at liberty to do so; they can highlight weaknesses, and indicate that data which they have gathered leads them to a different conclusion. Then someone else will come along and criticize their work—and so on. This is the way in which theory is developed: by teasing out increasingly accurate approximations to irreducible principles of human living and behaviour.

Introduction

The selection of theoretical material for this book

A considerable number of fragments of theoretical knowledge concerning man, his development, his thinking and behaviour are now available within psychology. They are not, however, integrated within a single 'view of man' and this is because almost any activity of man can be considered from a number of different points of view; thus, when a person greets a friend one can examine the event in terms of physiological and neurological happenings occurring within his body, in terms of his intentions towards his friend, in terms of his emotions about his friend, in terms of how someone watching sees him behave, and so on. Because of this richness of ways of conceptualizing man, it has become customary to adopt a variety of 'models', or 'approaches' towards him; in this way man's complexity and subtlety can be represented, and a large amount of the theoretical fragments which we now have concerning man can be accommodated. Some of the most frequently used models are these:

(1) The physiological approach.
(2) The psycho-analytic and psycho-dynamic approach.
(3) The social learning and behavioural approach.
(4) The cognitive approach.
(5) The humanistic approach.

Although it would be possible to attempt within this book to convey to the reader some of the main research findings concerning human interaction as they fall within these five models, I have chosen not to do so. Instead I have been guided in my choice by two principles: first, the desirability of keeping abreast of the research which is published month by month in the psychology journals and which seems relevant to the fields of counselling and social work; and second, the practical, day-to-day usefulness of the concepts themselves to people in the helping professions. These principles are reflected in the divisions within the chapters; for the most part the earlier section of each chapter contains the theoretical material, and the later section concerns the practical application of the theory.

On reviewing my selection, I find that I have chosen material which in my view is seriously under-represented in current social work and counselling literature; thus I offer no space to psycho-analytic theories, not because I consider them of no value or because I am not able to conceptualize my work sometimes in psychoanalytic terms, but because they have already received an enormous amount of attention from other writers. Similarly I make little reference to systems theory, for although I recognize the contribution that this can make to our understanding of a situation, psychologists are only just beginning to be able to accommodate the multiplicity of variables which such a theory implies. My emphasis throughout is upon ideas and theoretical material current within mainstream psychology which are of day-to-day relevance to the practice of social work and counselling. If these professions are to retain their credibility they urgently need some ways of understanding situations, and some tools and techniques of helping change them, which, used aright, will inform their practice.

I have, therefore, deliberately based my choice of theoretical material on empirical research, and have attempted to bring to a wider audience evidence and information which have profound implications for practice. References to the original published papers or books are given, and I hope that readers may feel stimulated or provoked into referring to these primary sources. It is time that we looked much more closely at the theoretical foundations of what we are doing, since if these are askew then many of our assumptions and techniques may well be inappropriate. Since psychology, because of its empirical approach, offers a means of building sound foundations for practice, I make a plea for the incorporation of more of its theory, albeit still fragmented, into the teaching and training of social workers and counsellors.

Part one

Effective counselling
and social casework

Chapter 1

What contributes to effective counselling and social casework?

The various activities associated with counselling and social casework share enough common ground to warrant considering them together. Although marriage-guidance counsellors and school counsellors, for instance, may wish to distinguish their role very clearly from that of social caseworkers who tend to be tied fairly closely to a legal framework and to have their work delineated by statute, these differing emphases often seem to obscure how much those who work with people have in common, particularly when one looks at the principles and ethics of the various services. It is my intention to draw attention to similarities rather than differences between those in the helping professions.

A second reason for so choosing, and an even stronger one, is that when I came to examine the research data which is to form the backbone of this chapter I found that almost all those who carried out research into helpful relationships had themselves apparently been unable to distinguish between the roles of different professionals, be they psychologists, counsellors, therapists or case-workers and as a result tended deliberately to blur distinctions between roles by using the terms interchangeably. It appears that what is important is not so much what the helping person calls himself or herself, but rather the sort of person he is and how he goes about his work. It is for these reasons, therefore, that I shall in this chapter and through-out the book use the terms 'counsellor', 'social caseworker' and even 'therapist' in a somewhat loose way, intending thereby to refer to the common component of their work.

I am aware, however, that this decision on my part may plunge readers straight away into the problem mentioned in the first chapter: that of shared meanings. Almost every person taking up this book will have his own understanding of the terms 'counselling', 'social case work', and 'psychotherapy' and each will be an understanding or concept rich in associations—some positive and some perhaps negative. For some people these associations may be so negative as to make the very use of the word, say, 'counsellor', difficult for them; they will be likely to use the word seldom and not at all in relation to the work which they themselves do; others will identify themselves fully with the concept of 'counsellor' and understand the term in a positive light. This response is also likely to be true of their potential clients; one person who is offered the opportunity of 'going to see a counsellor' will accept gratefully; another will feel insulted.

In order to be as clear as possible upon the meanings of terms, I have been looking at some of the definitions of counselling offered by writers on the subject. Here is a small selection: Brammer and Shostrom (1964) view counselling and psychotherapy from the standpoint of therapeutic psychology:

> Therapeutic psychology applied through counselling and psychotherapy is primarily a process of building understanding, integrating disparate elements of the personality, and enabling the client to utilise his good judgment, social skills, problem-solving and planning abilities.

Halmos (1965) writes:

> Basically and essentially all the practitioners of counselling . . . have a common origin and aim; their common ancestor is the giver of spiritual solace and their common aim is health, sanity, a state of unspecified virtue, even a state of grace, or merely a return to the virtues of the community, adjustment . . . . Above all, all counselling procedures share a method: they are all 'talking cures', semantic exercises; they all attempt treatment through clarification of subjective experience and meanings.

Morea (1972) draws attention to the importance of the individual's perception of reality, and sees counselling as

> a process by which a counsellor helps an individual to grow in his adjustment to himself and his environment, and through growth helps him to make personal decisions. In counselling we are concerned with experience. Information and data have little value and relevance in themselves; it is how they are perceived and experienced by the individual himself that proves significant. The position is in a sense phenomenalist; reality consists simply in what we perceive and experience.

Patterson (1973) emphasizes the professional status of the counsellor, but does not distinguish his role from the psychotherapist's:

> Counselling (or psychotherapy) is a relationship, involving verbal interaction, between a professionally trained person and an individual or group of individuals voluntarily seeking help with a problem which is psychological in nature, for the purpose of effecting a change in the individuals seeking help.

Clearly there is no shared meaning.

A discussion paper 'Developments in Counselling' prepared by Packer (1974) suggests that the Standing Conference for the advancement of Counselling appears to be fully aware of this lack of consensus upon a definition of counselling, and reports that in the usage of that body counselling is understood as a practitioner—client relationship defined with reference to the boundaries provided by the agency offering the service, or the professional reference group of the counsellor, or his training or supervision. This relativism seems commendable, in that it allows freedom and opportunity to accommodate both different theoretical positions as well as different methods of practice, but it does not help us towards arriving at a shared meaning. Since, however, I have the responsibility for making clear the way in which I am using terms I prefer, rather than propose yet another definition, to bring to wider public awareness the simple explanation of this core component of counselling, therapy or social casework offered by Truax and Carkhuff in 1967: *Counselling or psychotherapy is aimed at producing constructive behavioural and personality change.*

I have deliberately chosen this description because it is at a very low level of abstraction, and couched in very general terms; it can thus embrace different theoretical allegiances and different styles of training or practice and I hope that social workers and counsellors, to whom this book is addressed, may find it broadly acceptable as a working description. It represents what I myself found to be the common component in my own work, both as social worker and as trainee marriage-guidance counsellor, but it also represents what I believe I see as the common core of the work of counsellor and social work friends and colleagues about me.

One cannot assume, however, that this core is common to the bewildering array of individual and group therapies which flows to Britain from the USA. As already mentioned anyone seeking 'encounter' or 'personal growth' has an astonishing range of proffered experience to choose from, each with its own theory, techniques and terminology: psychodrama, gestalt therapy, transactional analysis, primal therapy, logotherapy, family therapy, transpersonal psychosynthesis, regression therapy and so on. The relative usefulness of these many and different approaches to helping people has not yet, as far as I am aware, been systematically researched, so it is not yet possible to supply the reader with findings as to the value of one approach by comparison with another; few appear to have yet reached a level of theoretical sophistication which makes it possible to use their theory predictively; and that, as I explained in the first chapter, is a central test of any claim to theoretical validity.

What *have* been researched, however, are the more traditional approaches to helping people, known generally as one-to-one or casework, and inasmuch as this is still a central component of much social work, and of much school-, marriage- and employment-based counselling, it is these findings which now call for attention.

Psychological research on effective counselling

I have described on page 20 the challenge posed to therapists by Hans Eysenck when he published 'The effects of psychotherapy: an evaluation' (1952), in which he reviewed, in statistical terms, the effectiveness of this type of intervention as revealed in studies published up to that time. His claim that the figures indicated that the average effect of psychotherapy was nil provoked a storm of protest from practitioners who felt that their efforts were effective. This claim stimulated a great deal of valuable research. Since one of the attacks levelled against Eysenck was that he had brought together and 'averaged out' the results of a number of very different studies which employed different ways of measuring 'improvement', other researchers attempted to avoid this serious weakness by undertaking major inquiries, designed with great care, using large numbers of subjects and with a clear definition and a shared meaning of 'improvement' clarified beforehand. The apparently unitary concept of 'relationship therapy' and the assumption that it produced beneficial results whoever engaged in it, and in whatever circumstances, was completely undermined as a mounting tide of research was addressed both in the UK, where Eysenck had launched his attack, and in other countries particularly the USA, to disentangling the many variables which interact in psychotherapy. This process still continues.

For instance, one major study, already drawing to its conclusion at the time of Eysenck's paper, was reported by Teuber and Powers in America in 1953; this is known as the Cambridge—Somerville youth study and involved comparing 325 potentially delinquent boys who received supportive counselling or psychotherapy with 325 untreated boys who formed a control group. Over a ten-year period the writers found no overall average differences between the two groups in terms of what had been previously agreed would indicate improvement. This strong support for Eysenck's position has, however, as I have already indicated, been counterbalanced by evidence from other studies and inevitably, because researchers are seldom, despite their best intentions, wholly disinterested observers, conflicting evidence has accumulated. Both schools of thought — the 'counselling-is-effective' and the 'counselling-is-not-effective' — are able to point to research findings to substantiate their claims; much heat has been generated between the factions.

The reader may well question how, if bona fide researchers employing sophisticated experimental and statistical techniques reach divergent conclusions, any confidence may be felt in either position? The answer lies in the emergence of a number of fragments of theory concerning counselling and therapy which are emerging increasingly clearly from a great many of the investigations being undertaken and reported in the psychology and counselling journals. For in the last two decades there seems to have been a change of emphasis in research studies—a movement away from preoccupation with 'outcome' associated with this or that particular theory of human development or interaction, and towards distinguishing and defining what appear to be variables of far greater importance, linked to such subtleties as client and counsellor motivation, personality characteristics, shared expectations of what happens in counselling and whether client and counsellor like each other.

It is quite impossible to give adequate consideration to all the aspects of psychotherapy and counselling which have been and are being researched in this latter half of the twentieth century, and I have therefore chosen the expedient of selecting from the now wide literature upon the subject three categories of research findings which seem to me to demand attention:

1 Ideas about counselling or casework for which there is a measure of empirical support.
2 Ideas about counselling or casework for which there is considerable empirical support.
3 Ideas about counselling or casework for which there is strong empirical support.

I wish to draw attention immediately to the subjectivity of my selection; inasmuch as I am an individual person with limited knowledge and limited time, it is inevitable that I should have missed what another writer may consider crucial material; inasmuch, too, as I have come to certain opinions and conclusions as a result of my own life experience and my professional practice, these too may be reflected in my selection. All I can offer is my attempt to reflect the weight of categories of research, and if a reader criticizes my choice, I shall endeavour to be open to correction. This, as I have said elsewhere, is how a body of theory is built up.

Ideas about counselling having a measure of empirical support

It can be helpful if a counsellor speaks now and then of his own experience

Traditionally, it has been thought desirable that counsellors should avoid almost all reference to their personal lives in their discussions with those who seek their help. This idea, however, is now being questioned in studies on the effect upon counselling of 'counsellor self-disclosure'; work by Jourard (1971) and Bundza and Simonson (1973) suggests that such a rigid rule is not in fact most helpful to clients and that counsellors can very appropriately, on occasion, reveal aspects of themselves, their lives or their feelings. They point out that since we expect clients to reveal intimate aspects of their lives to us, it can be a useful modelling experience if they can experience counsellors who, in their turn, can reveal something of themselves without shame or embarrassment. A counsellor who occasionally refers to his own experience also decreases the 'distance' between himself and his client. While Weigel and his colleagues (1972) questioned the usefulness to clients of self-disclosure there seems to me to be a heavier weight of evidence supporting the view that occasional reference to personal feelings or circumstances in the lives of counsellors has a beneficial effect. The reason for such reference would in no circumstances be to shift the focus of the discussion to an examination of difficulties experienced by the counsellor, but rather to illustrate the reality of the counsellor and his world, enabling him thereby to reveal himself as a genuine and empathic person.

Certain client characteristics are associated with a positive outcome

The evidence concerning the characteristics of patients or clients who seek help and who are likely to show positive change is very confused. At one time age and length of disorder were thought to be accurate indicators, with a poorer prognosis for older people and for those with many years of distress behind them, but the picture is apparently not as clear as was once thought. Wood, Rakusin, Morse and Singer (1962a and b) studied both the degree of illness and the diagnosis of psychiatric patients, and found that neither was related to outcome. Cabeen and Coleman (1962) also found that intelligence and age were not accurate indicators of therapeutic outcome in their inquiries into group therapy.

In attempting to review this very confused and sometimes contradictory array of research findings, Truax and Carkhuff (1967) surveyed much of the available literature upon accurate indicators of improvement and found that while there were some apparent inconsistencies in the evidence there was a general indication inherent in the data that the patient or client with the greatest 'felt' disturbance (i.e. a personal sense of emotional distress) and with the least 'overt' disturbance (i.e. behavioural disorder as rated by others) were those who subsequently showed the greatest improvement. Thus the shy isolated person may be easier to help than the extrovert prone to violent tempers.

Therapists high in persuasiveness have beneficial effects

Truax, Fine, Moravec and Millis (1968) found that clients seemed to make greater improvement if their therapists were high in persuasiveness. This finding, which seems to cut at the very roots of 'client self-determination'—a dearly held principle of social work and counselling for many years—is nevertheless very challenging and needs careful consideration before it is discounted. Even if there is as yet only modest empirical support for its validity, it seems to indicate the attention which one ought to give to the subtlety of the counselling process and indeed of human interaction in general. For, even though the social worker or counsellor is deliberately and consciously holding fast to the principle of 'client self-determination' it seems increasingly probable that because of the role and inherent status of the counsellor and because of a straightforward need for an opinion, some clients search their counsellors' faces for non-verbal indications of 'what he is really thinking' and find them. Bednar (1970) has reviewed recent findings relevant to the persuasibility of clients and points out the very different levels of suggestibility which exist among people and the importance therefore of fostering an optimistic approach towards existing difficulties. As Woody (1971) writes, on the same theme, 'It would therefore be important to the outcome efficacy for the counsellor-therapist purposefully to instill in the client an expectation that he will improve as the result of the treatment.'

The situation perhaps becomes clearer if we can distinguish between the importance of cultivating a generally positive and optimistic approach towards a client's difficulties, which increasing amounts of research suggest is very important, and actively directing a client's decision-making. When people are actively and deliberately trying to change their behaviour, as in stopping heavy drinking or learning to control violent behaviour, persuasiveness can be seen more clearly to have a place.

It is valuable for a counsellor to have an eclectic theoretical position

The word 'eclectic', from the Greek *eklektikos* (*eklego*: I pick out), means one who borrows freely from various sources and who is not exclusive in his adherence to any particular doctrine or school of

33

thought. There is some, and increasing, evidence that such an attitude, assuming it is backed by knowledge and ability, is of value to one's clients in counselling and therapy. It was Fiedler (1950) who found that a therapist's school of psychotherapy, be he Freudian, Jungian, Adlerian or whatever, was less critical to achieving an 'ideal therapeutic relationship' than was his expertise, i.e. there was no clear association between a therapist's own theoretical position and his client's improvement. This early suggestion has now received further backing, particularly from Thorne (1969a) who, considering accumulating research studies, concluded that therapy based on any single theoretical system revealed major inadequacies; he called for the adoption of a more flexible and eclectic approach to both training and practice.

The clients who most need our help in fact receive the least

The preferred client for many helpers, be they counsellors, social workers, doctors or psychiatrists is what Schofield (1964) calls the YAVIS patient—young, attractive, verbal, intelligent and successful. We may be amused by, or may perhaps reject this assertion, but sadly there is mounting evidence, from the USA if not from this country as yet (because the research has not been carried out) that counsellors and others in the helping professions spend more time with and feel more committed to helping those in the higher rather than the lower socio-economic groups. There has been awareness for some time of the clustering of multiple problems round specific low-income families, and every social services department probably has such families at whose name everyone groans during the allocation meeting.

It is not surprising that this should be so; in terms of social exchange theory, to be described in chapter 3, dealing with a single, localized difficulty is likely to be easier, in that it offers more chance of the social worker's feeling satisfaction than attempting to deal with multiple problems when many others before oneself have tried so hard. Middle-class people tend to be better educated and more willing to sit down and discuss intellectually the difficulties they face; this in itself can be very rewarding to the worker, particularly if he has been trained by the 'what we have to do is to promote growth and insight' adherents in our schools and departments of social work. These impressionistic comments are backed by research: Williams (1956) in his paper on class differences and psychiatric patients, McMahon (1964), in a paper on a similar theme, and more recently, Goldstein (1973), have all concluded from their investigations that the most needy receive proportionately less help than the less needy.

Ideas about counselling having considerable empirical support

It is important to clarify clients' expectations concerning counselling

This finding has emerged rather unexpectedly from many research studies, but it has emerged unequivocally and repeatedly, thereby demonstrating the value of different workers attempting to replicate the investigations of others. This means that the finding that it is important to clarify the expectations of one's clients is not just an artefact of one particular experimenter's inquiry, but a real and persistent variable, which is of considerable importance in successful counselling. The elicitation by the counsellor early in their relationship, and probably within the course of their first meeting, of what the client hopes to gain from their meetings (assuming these are to be regular and more than just a single occasion) and how he anticipates the counsellor's ability to help him, can remove misunderstandings which may otherwise bedevil the relationship at a later stage; this discussion can also enable the counsellor to explain what he thinks he may really be able to offer. Frank and his colleagues (1959) were among the first to draw attention to clients' expectancies as factors affecting improvement in psychotherapy, and this was supported by Goldstein and Shipman (1961) in their paper on patients' expectancies in psychotherapy.

Heine and Trosman (1960) obtained findings which were also strongly supportive of the importance of clarifying expectations, since they found that when therapist and patient do not agree on the aims or methods of help then the patient tends to discontinue treatment quickly. This work also offers indirect evidence of the importance of eclecticism and flexibility in the counsellor since, as it is he who claims to be the 'expert', it is he who should be able to adapt to the client rather than insist rigidly upon the correctness of his particular theoretical position or viewpoint.

Therapist 'commitment' to clients is a predictor of outcome

Lerner and Fiske (1973) examined the attitudes of therapists towards the prognosis for clients from lower socio-economic groups and with severely disturbed backgrounds. They found that where therapists had absorbed the view that work with these clients was more difficult and had a poor prognosis, the outcome in a majority of cases was indeed poor; by contrast, where therapists had been relatively unimpressed by such a view and had sustained their feeling that they could help whatever the circumstances, they had in fact been able to help. Here is a beautiful example of the self-fulfilling prophecy; where a counsellor feels pessimism he is likely to convey hopelessness to his client by all the subtlety of non-verbal communication; it seems that where the counsellor anticipates little satisfaction from the outcome of the relationship, he is willing to invest less of himself and his enthusiasm in the relationship. The 'committed' counsellor, however, convinced that he has something to offer even to the most unpromising of those who seek his help and anticipating satisfaction, manages by his very attitude and the non-verbal messages which accompany it, to bring about optimism in his clients and hence, beneficial change.

This finding by Lerner and Fiske tends to confirm the conclusion reached by Swensen (1972) in his investigation of key therapist variables; it was Swensen whose statistical techniques allowed him to isolate a variable which he labelled 'commitment', and although other writers have pointed out that this has not yet been adequately defined in terms of actual practice, there are, I believe, strong associations in most people's minds between 'commitment', enthusiasm, perseverence and concern for the other person. These characteristics would be easily recognized by any person seeking help from a counsellor or social worker and would readily contribute to a positive and optimistic approach towards meeting problems.

This should not be taken as implying that the counsellor is at any time right to lose sight of the reality factors of a situation, or to give false reassurance that things will be all right, or that he, the counsellor, can bring about improvement in an almost magical fashion. Rather it is that by displaying 'commitment' the counsellor conveys to the client that he cares about him and will do his best for him, and it is this attitude which is so restorative and productive of optimism. The caring of the counsellor enhances the self-concept, and this itself may give a person confidence to try new ways of coping with difficulties.

Counselling (even when non-directive) is a social influence process

This may be a difficult pill for some readers to swallow. The implication of the term 'social influence' is that merely by being, by existing, I influence people; in ordinary day-to-day human interaction my words, my facial expression and my actions are impinging upon people for good or for ill—as theirs are impinging upon me. Some of the time we speak or act deliberately, aware of attempting to bring about a certain type of influence, but most of the time we neither behave nor respond in such a self-conscious and planned fashion—and yet we are having an effect upon others all the time. Who has not felt snubbed or put down by apparent lack of recognition, only to learn later that this was entirely unintended?

If there is such an effect in casual, everyday encounters how infinitely greater is likely to be the influence of one who assumes the title and role of counsellor with all its ancient connotations of wisdom and mystery—especially if he sits in a room with COUNSELLOR painted on the door. Once inside the door the client experiences the counsellor both as a model, good or bad, and as a source of social rewards and penalties and also perhaps as the person who reminds him of his headmaster and who therefore seems rather alarming. All these events are occurring at the same time as the actual process of counselling; how can counsellors then deny that the social-influence approach ought to be taken seriously?

Gerard Egan, in his book *The Skilled Helper*, writes of social-influence theory in the following terms:

> We live in a society charged with social influence attempts. All of us from time to time involve ourselves in social-influence attempts, overtly or covertly, knowingly or unwittingly. Since the laws of social influence operate both in the transactions of everyday life and in helping situations, it is only natural to study helping and interpersonal relating from the viewpoint of the principles of social influence so that we can use these principles creatively instead of becoming their victim.

Egan goes on to describe the model of helping which he feels is appropriate to those who, like him (such as Strong (1968) and Dell (1973)) find it impossible to ignore the elements of influencing which they detect in counselling but which, because of its subtlety, seems so far to have escaped popular notice:

> The model, in its simplest form, states that in Stage 1 the helper establishes a power base or influence base with the helpee through perceived expertness, trustworthiness and attractiveness and in Stage II uses this influence to help the client change both his attitudes and his behaviour to more constructive patterns.

If this is unacceptable to some readers, as it was to me initially, then I sympathize with their dilemma; if I were to fail to report this viewpoint, however, I would be deviating from my task of attempting to present research on ideas in counselling which have considerable support in the literature. It is perhaps appropriate to add that when I reflected upon my own on-going work as a counsellor and realized how, merely by taking up one topic and letting another drop, I was in fact influencing both the situation and my client, I then began to accept the validity of the social-influence theorists' viewpoint; once again it was the subtlety which had eluded me. So now I am willing to see myself at least partially as a person with influence, but strive both to know what I am influencing and to what end—if possible to one already agreed with the client. Now that I am more aware of what I am doing, I have the responsibility for using my influence constructively.

Lay counsellors can be as effective as professionals

This is another viewpoint which is continuing to receive strong empirical support both in Britain and in the USA. I hope, if this is not already common knowledge, that this will be encouraging information for Britain's National Marriage Guidance Council.

In 1964 Truax, Carkhuff and Douds designed a training programme which sought to improve the quality of counselling given by both professionals and lay counsellors, and which incorporated both an information-giving and an experiential component; the characteristics they sought to foster in the trainees were accurate empathy, genuineness, and non-possessive warmth; they then compared the levels of therapeutic effectiveness of these lay counsellors with those of a group of post-graduate clinical psychology trainees, and with those of a group of experienced therapists. They subsequently reported:

> After slightly less than 100 hours of training. . . the levels of accurate empathy communicated to patients were not significantly different between the three groups. . . there were no significant differences between the three groups in terms of the levels of non-possessive warmth. . . . With respect to therapist's genuineness, however, the experienced therapists showed a significantly higher level of genuineness or self-congruence than did the lay trainees. . . . These data suggest that these ingredients can be learned, by both professional and non-professional persons.

A year later, in 1965, Carkhuff and Truax went on to confirm this conclusion with an examination of the differential functioning of lay and professional helpers; when working with hospitalized patients he found the lay counsellors, after appropriate training of the order of 100 hours, as effective as the professionals. Further, Guerney (1969) drew attention to the valuable roles which non-professionals, teachers and parents can play in offering counselling-type support, while the major achievement, reported by Varah (1973) of the volunteers of the Samaritan organization in Britain in contributing to the fall in numbers of those committing suicide seems also to reflect the effectiveness of lay people, perhaps with little training but with high motivation and commitment. A further notable British testimony to the value of the contribution made by volunteers is the study of Hadley et al., (1974).

Ideas about counselling having strong empirical support

It has been possible to isolate a major factor or variable in successful counselling: counsellor personality

The application of methods of psychological research to counselling gathered momentum in the USA in the 1950s; it has scarcely even begun elsewhere. Earlier in this chapter I reported that in 1950 Fiedler had found that a counsellor's theory of therapy was of less importance than his own personal expertise, and this type of inquiry, using rigorous indexes of 'improvement', as noticed both by the person seeking help and by observers, has continued with increased momentum. Thus, researchers have considered the effects of such variables as age, length of period of distress before seeking help, sex, and expectations of type of help; they have also investigated characteristics of counsellors in terms of personality profiles, counselling styles, theoretical allegiances and attitudes towards different client groups; they have even looked at features of the actual counselling process in terms of the type of relationship which developed between counsellor and client, the focus of their discussions, and the correlations which emerged between any of these features and the client's sense of having been helped.

It may come as a surprise to many readers that sophisticated tests of this kind exist and are used regularly in counselling research in many universities and institutions in the USA. While the use of tape-recorders and television equipment to produce material from counselling sessions which can subsequently be analysed would probably strike us as intrusions upon the counselling process (as they undoubtedly are), investigators in the USA have nearly three decades of detailed research upon which to draw. Thus although it is undoubtedly true that recordings of this kind must distort the nature of the interactions between client and counsellor, researchers have learned to control for this effect or to take it into account. If much of the material upon which I draw is American, it is because other material is not available in the quantities required.

The publication by Eysenck of his challenging paper, 'The effects of psychotherapy: an evaluation', in 1952 gave impetus to the application of research methods; in 1955, for instance, Strupp was able to show from his study of possible differences in techniques employed by psychiatrists, psychologists and social workers that there was in fact a 'considerable degree of similarity' between them. He concluded that the professional affiliation, i.e. whether the therapist is a psychiatrist, psychologist or social worker, 'exerts a relatively minor influence upon the kinds of technique used'. The following year Betz and Whitehorn (1956) published research showing a significant statistical relationship between the personality type of therapists and the success of their psychotherapy with schizophrenics, and in 1958 the American Psychological Association held the first of a series of conferences on research in psychotherapy. Papers presented at this meeting and at the second conference in 1961 drew increasing attention to the role of the personality of the counsellor as a major variable in successful therapy.

Meanwhile there had been published, in 1951, a book by Carl Rogers, *Client-centred Therapy*, which marked the founding of a new theoretical school of counselling, which soon became extremely influential in America and, as its central ideas became disseminated, in other countries too. Its success seems to be linked partly to the fact that Rogers had researched the validity of his ideas widely before attempting to claim that he had developed a new and effective method of counselling; not only did this commend his methods to the experimental psychologists who sought empirical support for claims to effectiveness, but it became apparent that Rogers really had a basis for his claims when his methods were seen to work. Patients experiencing client-centred therapy, whether individually or in groups, with Rogerian-trained therapists, actually found that it was effective and reported that it was effective in the research studies that were carried out. Moreover, independent observers using objective rating techniques, pronounced the methods effective.

In 1957 Rogers published another major piece of work, a paper entitled 'The necessary and sufficient conditions of therapeutic personality change', and this was followed by a succession of other writings both on the therapeutic relationship, the personal characteristics of the counsellors able to offer such relationships and how to train would-be therapists to acquire and display these characteristics. Meanwhile, of course, other theoretical positions and methods of practice were being explored and researched by a wide range of investigators, and this continued throughout the next decade and is still in progress.

Every so often, when a subject provoking great interest has become confusing because of the wealth of claim and counter-claim, and people have lost their way in a mass of detail and conflicting evidence, a major paper or book is published which reviews the issue from a more detached and comprehensive standpoint. This overviewer attempts to adopt a much broader perspective than is usually available to the individual researcher in his hospital, counselling centre or university and, hopefully, he can discern trends and detect patterns which may hitherto have passed undetected. Such a review was published in 1967 by Charles Truax (a colleague of Carl Rogers) and Robert Carkhuff, in their major work, *Towards Effective Counselling and Psychotherapy*.

What contributes to effective counselling and social casework?

Truax and Carkhuff explain that their book, which in my view ought to be a key reference text for every trainer of social workers and counsellors whatever his ideology, had 'grown out of the human and therefore selective readings of literally thousands of articles and countless books and chapters.' In it they attempt to grapple not only with the major challenge posed by Eysenck, but also with the positive findings of researchers in certain areas, notably in client-centred therapy. The essence of their review of the literature is extremely disturbing: on average, psychotherapy and counselling prove harmful as often as helpful.

The authors write:

> After a careful review of the relevant research literature, it now appears that Eysenck was essentially correct in saying that *average* counseling and psychotherapy as it is currently practiced does not result in average client improvement greater than that observed in clients who receive no special counseling or psychotherapeutic treatment.

and they go on:

> However, some other relatively well-controlled studies show that certain counsellors or therapists do produce beneficial effects beyond that observed in equivalent control groups.
>
> Putting together these two bodies of evidence, it logically follows that if psychotherapy has no overall average effect, but that there are valid specific instances where it is indeed effective, then there must also be specific instances in which it is harmful. That is, to achieve this average, if some clients have been helped, then other clients must have been harmed. This suggestion *that psychotherapy and counselling can be for better or for worse* is the major starting point for the present approach to practice and training.

When Truax and Carkhuff turned their attention to the detail of the counselling situations in which beneficial outcomes had been reported, they found that these situations had in common not a particular theory of human development or method of working with clients but counsellors who were characterized by certain clearly definable personalities. It appeared that those counsellors or therapists whose clients benefited from their meetings were endowed with, or had learned, certain specific attitudes or traits. These characteristics may be described as (my paraphrases):

Genuineness or sincerity: the conveying of 'realness', of 'being themselves', as distinct from adopting a role or being defensive in their dealings with clients.

Non-possessive warmth: the attitude of caring, conveyed by a friendly and concerned approach to their clients.

Accurate empathy: the capacity to 'feel with' those who seek help, so that clients 'feel understood'.

As Truax and Carkhuff themselves openly acknowledge, many writers before themselves had recognized the importance of the above characteristics within the therapeutic relationship, but few seem to have appreciated the centrality of these components. I say 'few' because, as I have attempted to show earlier, so often difficulties arise because writers or therapists have arrived at a shared concept, but have expressed it in different terminology. In this case, for instance, many readers will probably feel that 'non-possessive warmth' is surely synonymous with Carl Rogers's 'unconditional positive regard' and Truax and Carkhuff would probably agree with them; all they have done is to introduce the amendment 'non-possessive' in order to draw attention to the readiness of successful counsellors to retain a measure of detachment and to seek no personal emotional involvement from the relationship. In fact, these writers attempt to trace, via Carl Rogers and Otto Rank (who was a student of Freud) the growing awareness of the importance of therapists's personality from its first unformulated origins within psychoanalysis to its present central position within the whole field of therapy.

These findings by Truax and Carkhuff have been substantiated by many researchers since 1967, and have been used to design training programmes in human relations applicable not only to counsellors but to all the helping professions. A paper by Lambert *et al.* (1978), while calling for even greater precision in sampling and rating therapy sessions, nevertheless confirms modest support for the consistent effectiveness of therapists demonstrating the characteristics described above. The implications will be discussed in the next chapter.

While the conditions of therapeutic personality change may be necessary, they do not, however, appear to be sufficient

When Carl Rogers published his paper in 1957 on 'The necessary and sufficient conditions of therapeutic personality change' which claimed effectively that the therapeutic ingredients of unconditional positive regard, accurate empathy and genuineness on the part of the therapist were enough, of themselves, to promote if not actually accomplish a cure of personality disorders, he inevitably attracted further researchers eager to test the validity of his ideas. As I have explained in the previous section, many investigators were able to uphold the centrality of Rogers' 'ingredients' as having primary importance within counselling, but there have also been critics of Rogers' apparent claim that he had found a universal panacea to the emotional and behavioural ills of mankind. As Martin (1972) writes:

> The criticisms of Rogers have fallen roughly within two general areas:(1) the efficacy and breadth of applicability of his therapeutic techniques and (2) theoretical under-pinnings of his approach.
>
> Critics have said that Rogers' approach to therapy is naive and superficial, and although the conditions he describes as necessary and sufficient may be desirable conditions for psychotherapy, they certainly are not *sufficient* for any but mild neurotic problems (Thorne (1944, 1957), Ellis (1959), Menninger (1963), Wolberg (1967)).

The key question appears to be whether 'growth' or 'self-actualization' is as intrinsic and predictable a tendency as Rogers would have us believe; for Rogers has made this theory the central notion in his theory of how therapy works, saying that the therapist's role should be to create the right conditions within which the client's self-actualizing tendency can blossom. As I have said explicitly in the previous section Rogers, and Truax and Carkhuff have powerful evidence that the offering of a relationship characterized by genuineness, unconditional positive regard and accurate empathy is usually extremely beneficial, but this does not of itself validate Rogers' claim that what he is doing is to be viewed as 'promoting growth' or enabling self-actualizing tendencies to flourish. Many other writers, while recognizing Rogers' achievement, feel obliged to question whether Rogers' view of therapy as 'growth' is adequate (we are into a situation in which definition is absolutely central) and suggest that a better, more accurate way of describing 'growth' is 'the capacity to learn'. Shoben (1949), for instance, writes:

> Rogers describes the therapeutic process as a freeing of the 'growth capacities' of the individual, which permits him to acquire 'more mature' ways of reacting. If 'growth' in this context means (as it must) something more than physiological maturation . . . it must refer to the client's acquisition of new modes of response. Such new modes of response are 'more mature' because for a given patient they are less fraught with anxiety or conflict. Thus Rogers is actually talking about psychotherapy as a learning process.

Dollard and Miller (1950) write:

> We agree with Rogers that faith in the patient is a most important requirement in a therapist. But we would describe

it as a belief in a capacity to learn rather than one in a capacity to grow because 'growth' suggests physiological models which we do not believe are as appropriate or specific as the principles and conditions of learning. When we affirm the patient's capacity to learn we mean always 'provided the right conditions are set up'. Learning is not inevitable.

This attention to definition is central to the psychological method, and readers are begged not to dismiss these distinctions as 'academic nit-picking'. The demand for a more detailed definition of 'growth' demanded by Shoben (1949) and others was repeated throughout the 1960s to the point where Truax and Carkhuff (1967) explicitly included a chapter conceptualizing counselling as a learning experience: 'The implications of learning theory and behaviour therapy for effective therapeutic encounters'. This examines the reinforcement given by counsellors for various client behaviours which occur in therapy:

(1) reinforcement of approach responses to human relating,
(2) reinforcement of self-exploratory behaviour by the patient,
(3) elimination of specific anxieties or fears,
(4) reinforcement of positive self-concepts and self-valuations.

Once we are able to introduce the principles of learning theory into the way we think about therapy and counselling, we immediately have a much tighter and precise way of investigating what happens within therapy and we begin to be able even to think in terms of prediction. Thus what Rogers calls 'growth', other theorists call 'new learning'; both look at the same coin, but at different sides, but whereas the terminology of the Rogerians is misty, almost mystical, that of the learning theorists is relatively precise and exact.

If criticism of the universality of Rogers' claims has come from the academic theorists, I suggest that it comes too from the intensely difficult and frustrating world of social work; it seems extremely likely that certain types of difficulty (particularly, as Truax and Carkhuff (1967) suggest, those with a high component of 'felt' disturbance, such as some reactive depressions, and anxiety states) would yield readily to the 'therapeutic ingredients' but how many counsellors and social workers have found their clients with 'overt' disturbance, their truants, their alcoholics, and their violent clients as well as their young people on supervision orders 'growing' as a response to client-centred therapy alone, and 'growing' moreover into ways which keep them out of court and out of debt? Client-centred therapy appears to be admirably suited to the needs of people wishing to unburden themselves of a heavy weight of unhappiness or anxiety, or wishing to think their way through a difficult decision, such as whether to leave a cruel husband or whether to seek an abortion; it seems inadequate to affect significantly problems such as truancy, child abuse, alcoholism, classroom violence, sexual disorders or delinquency, and yet counselling programmes are set up using client-centred approaches alone, in the apparent belief that this form of therapy is a universal panacea; it is not. It may be a valuable, even indispensable, component of effective help, but it is simply not robust enough, either in theory or in practice, to resolve the scale of problems social workers and counsellors encounter.

To conclude this brief review of the ideas about counselling for which there is strong support, it is relevant to report that Robert Carkhuff and Bernard Berenson (1967), have gone on to suggest that a relationship characterized by certain conditions is often not adequate to meet a client's needs; they realize that the provision of these conditions is a key component of the helpful relationship, but that counselling may need to be translated eventually into action. This reflects a development from conceptualizing counselling or case-work as having primarily a self-exploratory focus, intended to promote self-understanding, to conceptualizing it as having its fulfilment in activity.

For myself, familiar with something of the day-to-day problems of social service departments and the intractability of the situations which social workers encounter, this move towards 'action' seems to be a step in the right direction. As I explained earlier the adoption of client-centred therapy as an adequate theory for practice has seemed to me to be misguided; what appears to be needed is an approach that takes the best from the client-centred approach, its respect for and commitment to the client, and marries these features to the best of other models, including those which involve activity and action. The model for this way of envisaging counselling is developed in the last chapter; its key feature is that it is eclectic.

Chapter 2

The personality of the counsellor or caseworker

If my selection of research findings in chapter 1 has any validity then it seems appropriate that social caseworkers, counsellors and their trainers should take them into account in their work. I am fully prepared for criticism of my selection, but such criticism should be founded upon empirical evidence. Moreover, it is appropriate for trainees in the helping professions to expect trainers to be familiar with key research findings and to take them into account when drawing up their training programmes. In my view it is time that social work trainers and educators familiarized themselves with the wealth of material which is available to them from the discipline of psychology, and used it to the benefit of their students and ultimately, their future clients.

The importance of the personality of the counsellor and of his way of relating to others

Since, as I have indicated in the previous chapter, the research evidence for ideas about effective counselling is of varying strength, so that some ideas are supported by 'a measure of' evidence, others by 'considerable' evidence and yet others by 'strong' evidence, I propose to select for further investigation only the ideas in the last category, since these are by now so well established by frequent replication that they have virtually become 'theoretical fragments'— from which it is possible to make predictions. Although they may be further amplified or refined, it seems extremely unlikely that they will be rejected outright, as ill-founded. I plan, therefore, to look in closer detail at the aspects of counsellor personality which have been detected as having key importance, to examine whether they can be described behaviourally (i.e. in terms of what the counsellor *does* rather than what he is) and to try to understand why these components are so effective. The implications for the trainee counsellor may then be clearer. I shall look at the other ideas supported by 'strong' evidence in Parts two and three of this book.

The therapeutic components, and how the counsellor demonstrates them

Genuineness, sincerity or self-congruence

This concept, which is difficult to describe, involves the counsellor's responding to the person in need of help not in terms of his status, his role or some professional stereotype, but naturally and spontaneously, as one might meet a good friend. For the person seeking help requires a helper who conveys the impression of personal security and of social ease. If the helping person is himself easily embarrassed, and finds it difficult to enter into relationships without subtly conveying the difference in status between the participants or resorts to criticizing his client if he himself feels attacked, then the person seeking help is obliged to take into consideration the anxieties and sensitivities of the counsellor when deciding what it is safe to say and how he may express himself. This characteristic has been described as transparency—a willingness to be seen for what one is, without resort to cover up devices or preoccupation with one's image. The person coming to such a 'transparent' counsellor then, comes to someone who gives the impression of consistency and of being at one with himself; he therefore represents (in psychological terms) a strong social model both of self-acceptance and of openness which can offer great reassurance to a person seeking help.

The person coming to a counsellor or social worker who does not convey this impression of genuineness and consistency comes to someone who immediately puts him upon his guard; rather than lessening some of the client's tensions the non-genuine person increases them. The message which the client receives in these circumstances is 'You must be careful how you deal with me: you're here on my terms, remember.' This is likely to be more than the client can cope with; he has come for help with his own problems, and to be confronted with the anxieties of the counsellor, his expectations of certain types of status treatment or his unwillingness to be challenged may soon amount to an unacceptable 'cost' to the client; in the terms of social-exchange theory, such costs may soon outweigh the benefits of counselling and the client may not keep his next appointment.

Some possible behavioural characteristics of the genuine person are:

(1) His verbal and non-verbal behaviours support, and are congruent with, each other.
(2) He is willing to be open about himself, where appropriate.
(3) He does not draw attention to his status or role.
(4) He is consistent in his behaviour within and without the counselling situation.
(5) If challenged, he can tolerate this and explain his position without enlisting his 'authority' to put the client in his place.

Readers may be able be able to suggest other characteristics.

Non-possessive warmth

This is a personal characteristic conveyed mainly by non-verbal means, where tones of voice, facial expression, eye-contact and the like seem to convey the predominant message within an interaction—where the 'music behind the words' conveys the feeling component of the relationship. It is not enough, therefore, for a social worker to be concerned for a client and to have a number of positive feelings towards him: he needs to be able to communicate these attitudes towards his client so clearly that there is no ambiguity. Non-possessive warmth then can be described as an attitude of active and positive caring by the counsellor, conveyed to the client both verbally and non-verbally, but which is directed towards encouraging independence rather than dependency.

Perhaps one of the best descriptions of the characteristic I am trying to convey is given by Cameron (1963):

> The patient must feel free to establish psychological closeness with the therapist, or to put psychological distance between himself and his therapist, without fear of arousing personal affection or personal offense. The therapist, for his part, remains always friendly, warm, firm and accepting, but he avoids anything that approaches a personal entanglement with his patient. The competent psychotherapist is not offended by a patient's coolness, criticism, hostility or provocation.

Within this field of close communication, it becomes necessary for the social worker or counsellor to retain as much control of his non-verbal cues as he can: this is such an important topic that I have devoted chapter 5 to it. Similarly, when embarrassing personal feelings are being acknowledged and the client scans the counsellor's face for signs of disgust or rejection and when even a narrowing of the counsellor's eyes can be interpreted by the client as 'It is not safe to say any more; this person can't take it', then awareness of one's own reactions so that one may control them, is essential. The counsellor needs to practise 'unshockability', so that there is absolutely nothing which cannot be discussed; this does not mean that the counsellor implicitly condones all that may have happened or be happening but rather that only when actions and feelings are out in the open can a clear-headed assessment be made of what should be done.

From the standpoint of social learning theory, which will be explained in chapter 6, the counsellor's tolerance within the counselling situation acts to counter-condition the assumptions which may have been made by the client that a certain topic or behaviour is not discussable; within the counselling situation the previous conditioning both by significant others in the client's world, and by himself (since we often tend to adopt the pattern of approval and disapproval of ourselves which originally stemmed from others) is, for the time being, not reinforced; it is lifted, and its inhibiting effects are set aside. The counsellor's warmth and acceptance are central in this process. Stack Sullivan (1954) describes the situation well:

> For instance, sometimes the interviewer may ask a question which leads the interviewee to make what he feels is a most damaging admission so that he then becomes intensely anxious —although he may cover the anxiety by equally intense feelings of anger or another emotion. The remedy lies in the interviewer's then asking a question about the 'damaging admission': for example he may ask, 'Well, am I supposed to think badly of you because of that?' Now this may seem like a strange kind of operation, but its value is that it puts into words the content of the interviewee's signs of anxiety. The answer is ordinarily 'Yes', and the next step is to ask, 'Well, how come?'

Many counsellors and social workers will have had the privilege of a person's saying to them, 'I never thought I could talk about that with anybody—but you have made it possible.' For all the sexual freedom which exists nowadays, this is an area still shrouded in ignorance, shame and fear for a large proportion of people and the worker in any setting is likely soon to find himself the focus of many difficulties and anxieties concerning sexual relationships. We cannot be all things to all men, but we can with compassion and openness provide a setting where the concealments and conflicts which people struggle to bear alone may be freely and unashamedly discussed. For instance despite the changes in the law regarding homosexual activity between consenting adults, here is an area still surrounded for many by the most intense embarrassment and guilt; I recall still the hesitant and tentative way in which one client, who had grown up in a succession of children's homes and who had become the object of homosexual advances by older boys, gradually grew confident enough to speak of the life-long guilt he carried because of his now established sexual attraction to men: 'To be able to talk about this, and to be able to talk about it to a *woman*. . . . It's unbelievable!' he said. These things happen—if we have the tolerance, and time, to let them happen. Sadly, we often do have the tolerance but not the time.

Some possible behavioural characteristics of the person showing non-possessive warmth are:

(1) He is at home in the world of feeling and emotion, and can talk about emotion easily.
(2) He shows his liking for people.
(3) He conveys to each individual by both verbal and non-verbal means his positive attitude and interest in him.
(4) He can give encouragement and appreciation readily.
(5) He is tolerant; although he may find certain aspects of his client's behaviour personally unacceptable, he can distinguish between his feelings towards the behaviour and towards the person.
(6) He has a well-developed sense of humour and can smile and laugh easily.

Accurate empathy

This concept implies an ability and willingness on the part of the counsellor or worker to enter into the subjective world of the person seeking help, to feel and think with him through his perceptions, his emotions and his values; this capacity, which some people are fortunate enough to acquire through their own childhood experiences but which can also be learned, then offers direct awareness of the 'reality' of the other person, and when expressed verbally offers to that person a sometimes intensely reassuring experience of not being alone, of being understood, and being accepted for what he is. This component appears to be a key element in the counselling relationship; in evolutionary, existential and anthropological terms it may well gain its central position because it offers to the individual a profound sense of being less isolated and alienated from other fellow creatures, while in psychodynamic terms it may be seen as a reconciliation between the 'child' who has feared the total loss of love and the warm and accepting parent.

The counsellor, for his part, may be enabled to enter into his client's world (as he is able where appropriate to enter into the world of his wife, or husband, child, friend or employer—in other words this is an ability which is not just related to the counselling situation) through his ability to concede that, as I suggested earlier, we live in a world of 'interpersonal subjectivities'. I myself, as a counsellor, need to recognize that my perceptions, the meanings I place upon my perceptions and the values I have learned or thought out, are my subjectivities, of intense and integral reality to me in my sense of identity, but subjectivities none the less. With this recognition it may then be possible to enter into the subjective and personal world of another, to affirm the reality of his world as it appears to him by attempting to describe it together—'It sounds as though you have come to the conclusion that men are not to be trusted?'—but without confirming his reality as accurate and absolute.

A most vivid experience of this kind took place with a very shy and inarticulate boy of about twelve, who could not even begin to describe the urgency and intensity of feeling which had brought him to see me. In the course of our meetings he could barely bring himself to speak at all—only to nod or shake his head. The only path open was for me to try to construct his world, with suggestions such as 'I guess today you are wishing you hadn't come?' and then by using his nods or shakes of the head as reply to amend or amplify my suggestions. Gradually, so gradually, we were able to share what he saw as reality, to draw out from the fastness in which he had learned to imprison his emotions, the fantasies and fears which had beset him for so long; he never was able to speak openly about them, but at least they were shared because I could speak of them and he could acknowledge them by nodding; some of their terror was lost as another person was allowed to enter his inner world and drain off the intensely inhibited feelings.

Some possible behavioural characteristics of the person showing accurate empathy are:

(1) He can tolerate the expression of any emotion in the counselling situation.
(2) He does not attempt to remonstrate with the client for experiencing powerful feelings.
(3) He is able by his receptivity to enter into and describe his client's inner subjective world, without losing hold of his own.
(4) He can do this not only for single individuals, but for the several participants within a contentious situation, so that he can distinguish the separate 'realities' of each one.
(5) He is aware of his own probable identifications, and of the dangers of over-identifying with one person at the expense of others.
(6) He is prepared to adjust his perceptions of another person's world, in order to attain increasingly accurate understanding.
(7) By becoming familiar with inconsistencies in the client, through the medium of his empathy, he detects the bogus and fake—when he is being 'conned'.

Towards understanding the theory of why these ingredients are so effective

Although Truax and Carkhuff (1967) adhered in their description of the therapeutic experience toward the Rogerian standpoint (i.e. the client-centred model) they are liberal and eclectic enough to take into account the possibility of formulating at least part of the experience in different terminology, that of learning theory. (This ability to show that one writer is saying virtually the same thing as another, but from a different standpoint and using different terminology, seems to me to be urgently required by teachers and exponents of ideas in psychology.) Thus in their chapter, 'The implications of learning theory and behaviour therapy for effective therapeutic encounters' they consider how the interactions which take place between a counsellor and a client may be conceptualized from that viewpoint:

It might be tentatively proposed that these three 'therapeutic conditions' have their direct and indirect effects upon patient change in the following four modalities:

(1) They serve to reinforce positive aspects of the patient's self-concept, modifying the existing self-concept and thus leading to changes in the patient's own self-reinforcement system.

(2) They serve to reinforce self-exploratory behaviour, thus eliciting self-concepts and anxiety-laden material which can potentially be modified.

(3) They serve to extinguish anxiety or fear responses associated with specific cues, both those elicited by the relationship with the therapist and those elicited by patient self-exploration.

(4) They serve to reinforce human relating, encountering or interacting, and to extinguish fear or avoidance learning associated with human relating.

From a different, psycho-dynamic, theoretical standpoint one might add the following:

(5) They allow an opportunity of liberating deeply personal or powerful feelings. (This is not quite the same as (2) above, for there is a different emphasis. This is an example of how theorists confuse each other and their students; a difference in emphasis may not be seen as such, but as a major and dividing cleavage.)

From a third, cognitive, theoretical viewpoint a further function of counselling can be added (of course there will be others):

(6) They allow inconsistencies of feeling, attitude and behaviour to be unravelled and a fuller integration to emerge.

How do we see these theoretical ideas in actual practice? Let us consider each in turn:

(1) *They serve to reinforce positive aspects of the patient's self-concept, modifying the existing self-concept and thus leading to changes in the patient's own self-reinforcement system.* Because I am persuaded that how we have learned to think of ourselves, i.e. our self-concept, has such profound effects upon our morale, our confidence and our willingness to try out new ideas and experiences, I have deliberately devoted chapter 8 to this topic. Suffice it here to draw attention to the last phrase, 'leading to changes in the patient's own self-reinforcement system'; for not only are we the object of reinforcements (i.e. rewards and criticisms) of others—just as we are the bestowers of reinforcement—but we applaud ourselves, 'I really think I made a good job of that', and disapprove of ourselves. 'What on earth was I doing? How could I have made such a mess of it?' by reference to a standard which we have internalized and against which we have learned to measure ourselves. Sometimes our self-criticism is very much harsher than that which might be brought against us by others.

The young school-leaver, unable to find a job, and depressed by the stigma this carried in his community and by his parents' disappointment, found the social worker's interest in the fact that he spent his spare time helping voluntarily in a community centre very restorative. To the teenager it was 'better than doing nothing', but to have it pointed out by the social worker that he was making a valuable contribution to several groups in the centre (as he was) enabled him to see his role in a much more positive light. This was a deliberate but completely genuine and honest response by the social worker; she did feel that what the boy was doing was extremely useful, but rather than just nodding in a neutral and non-committal way, she took this opportunity to say what she felt, and to contribute to a shift in the way in which the boy assessed his own worth. Some readers may object that this sort of response brings direct influence on a client; my reply to that is that in a sense we are all influencing each other all the time; unintentionally, and without any realization of what we are doing, we shape and mould each other's view of ourselves; we affect how others feel about themselves, their worth and their potential. It is one of the responsibilities of the professional to be aware of this power, partly because our very role intensifies the impact of our responses, and to use it to positive and constructive ends. There is nothing to gain by diminishing people, by embarrassing them or by treating them discourteously; there is a great deal to be gained by being tactful and considerate.

(2) *They serve to reinforce self-exploratory behaviour, thus eliciting self-concepts and anxiety-laden material which can potentially be modified.* If we describe self-exploration, as do Truax and Carkhuff (1967), in terms of the client's actively exploring his feelings, his values, his beliefs and his wishes while the counsellor attempts to facilitate the process, then the likelihood of emotionally charged subjects arising for discussion is apparent. This may of course occur in a group or individual situation, but the process is the same. A young mother, having difficulty in managing her very active and demanding child, was bitterly self-reproachful and fearful of her child's stability in the future, blaming the unsettled way of life which her child was experiencing upon her own 'inadequacy' and unsuitability to be a mother. The child was extremely lively, but with many endearing and attractive characteristics, which the poor mother in her anxiety could no longer see; when some of the anxiety had been taken out of the situation by the social worker's drawing attention to the child's many qualities, eventually the mother could speak of her fear that her own previous history of emotional disorder had been transmitted genetically to the child. The social worker could then reassure the mother that the particular disorder she had experienced seemed to have no genetic basis, (as was so) and this had a deeply calming effect upon the mother; from then on, relationships within the family improved: anxiety in the mother had caused a vicious circle of tension which was reflected by difficult behaviour in the child; the removal of the primary source of tension by the giving of accurate information brought a much more relaxed management of the child, who responded accordingly.

(3) *They serve to extinguish anxiety or fear response associated with specific cues, both those elicited by the relationship with the therapist and those elicited by patient self-exploration.* If, as will be explained more fully in chapter 6 we understand the 'extinguishing' of a response to mean the 'dying away because it is not reinforced' of a response, then in the counselling situation we can often see this phenomenon before our very eyes. As we learn to avoid acting or speaking critically to the person seeking help, and to avoid condemning his half-expressed attitudes, so we enable him to allow more and more of that emotion or attitude into free awareness and expression, and liberate him to explore both the emotion and its implications. Sometimes, over a series of meetings, we can actually see a person's anxiety dying away when he realizes that he may talk of some part of himself or his experience without calling forth from us the response which he fears: 'It is wrong/strange/mad/immoral to have such feelings.'

This situation arose in talking with a young man, the father of two small children, whose wife had, he believed, been devoted to himself and the family. He had brought to his home his former close friend, a man whom he had known all his life and whom he naturally wanted his wife to meet. Some months later his world had been torn apart by a message from his wife to say that she was leaving him and the children to make a new life with her husband's friend; they were apparently abroad. The deserted husband was distraught; not only had he to cope with the care of two tiny children as well as continue with his job, but he had to live with the turmoil of his feelings aroused by his wife's departure. Many people might have spoken immediately and with great intensity of their bitterness in such a situation, but not this young man; yet he was visited by moods of the blackest depression which effectively immobilized him; when we spoke of how he might be feeling towards his former friend he replied dully that his wife must live her own life and make her own decisions. Any suggestion that he might be experiencing more aggressive emotions than he displayed led to immediate anxiety and denial; but the intense depressions continued. Gradually it emerged that this young man had grown up in a home in which 'love your neighbour' had been lived out in principle and practice, an equable and happy home where the teachings of Christianity were accepted and lived out; feelings of hostility and anger were matters for prayer.

As a counsellor, I was in a dilemma. While respecting this young man's creed and having no wish to become involved in matters theological, my training in the psychodynamics of unexpressed anger led me to link his depressions with unrecognized emotion. All I could do therefore was to avoid reinforcing the view that anger should not be expressed, and within the limits of my relationship with him, to allow the anxiety linked with the expression of anger to extinguish or die away. (I do not mean that I solemnly thought about it in these terms at the time, but in retrospect this is a theoretical reconstruction of what happened.) Gradually, as in our meetings the spontaneity of his anger arose again, he would watch me, awaiting reprimand, but meeting none he was able slowly to allow into awareness the aggression and bitterness which had been struggling for expression. Soon there was a flooding forth of the pain, harshness and fantasied revenge which he had managed to conceal from himself, and of which his profound depressions had been the reflection. The intense moods lifted, and he was able to go on to distinguish between 'the honesty of acknowledging before God the reality of one's feelings' and 'acting vengefully on the strength of those feelings'. Acknowledging his bitterness and hatred did not lead him to blacken his rival's name in the community or to behave threateningly towards his wife; the emotional release of itself acted as a safety-valve and relieved the immobilizing depression; his religious principles remained valid for him and he was able to cope with the children and his job.

(4) *They serve to reinforce human relating, encountering or inter- acting, and to extinguish fear or avoidance learning associated with human relating.* The very experience of talking with an- other person in close relationship may be a new and difficult exercise for some of those we met. If we conduct our interviews so that they are rewarding to those who find it difficult to com- municate, then there is a possibility that this sense of satisfaction and confidence will generalize to other social situations as well.

The girl of twenty-two with a drinking problem who found herself in a psychiatric hospital and who would talk to no one except the doctor, first of all saw the social worker round the place, then saw her smile each time they encountered each other, next heard her greet her by name and then gradually, day by day, was drawn into exchanging a few words. Before long, the girl was looking out for her, wanting to talk to her, and was mentioning her to other patients as being easy to talk to. Little by little her reserve and fear gave way to trust and the tale of her parents' separation, her loss of contact with them, experiences in three foster homes and her gradual addiction to alcohol resulting in virtual withdrawal from social contacts al- together was pieced together. Her own self-esteem had been totally undermined by the situation in which she had arrived, and she found it less painful to avoid people than encounter the rejection and stigma she experienced so many times when it became apparent that she had a drinking problem. Gradually, by the kindness of the nursing staff and the co-operation of the whole psychiatric nursing team, the girl's mistrust of people gave place to a willingness to enter into simple, undemanding human relationships with others; when these were rewarding to her she was willing to entrust herself further. Finally it was possible to introduce her to a very supportive and sensitive Alcoholics Anonymous group, where her fears of rejection were fully allayed and she became more and more able to participate in the members' activities and discussions.

(5) *They allow the possibility of liberating deeply personal or pow- erful feelings.* It appears to be a physiological law that powerful feelings require expression, and that since strong emotional arousal is associated with hormonal secretion, particularly

adrenalin and nor-adrenalin, some minimal physiological discharge is necessary for the biochemical process to function smoothly. As is the case with so many other aspects of our lives, however, the way in which we cope with emotion is socially learned; we are both trained as children and copy parents as models in the ways in which we deal with feelings, and naturally these ways persist into adult life, for good or ill; moreover, they seem the 'natural and obvious' ways to deal with them, and alternative ways adopted by other people, however 'natural and obvious' to them, are likely to seem 'uncontrolled', 'inhibited', 'aggressive' or 'colourless' to us. There seems to be a wide range of 'tolerance' from a physiological point of view, but many of us and many of our clients struggle through life weighed down by memories of experiences or responses to situations which carry a powerful and unexpressed emotional charge.

There is, in the counselling situation, the time and the opportunity to allow expression to these undischarged emotions; the widows and the deserted husbands or wives can set aside 'brave fronts' and for a brief spell, need no longer 'put a good face on it'; strong men may cry and children grieve for unknown parents, while those who have struggled to love all men at all times may allow their hostility to flow unchecked. Usually the single telling of a tale of tragedy does not suffice; the traumas of bereavement, marriage breakdown, betrayal and intense loneliness are not dealt with by a single telling, but neighbours tend to weary of an oft-repeated tale of wretchedness and woe; the need for an audience does not fade with two or three tellings, however, and the physiological demand for discharge requires frequent release.

I am reminded of a widow whose husband died in hospital after a very sudden illness; she was of course distraught with shock and pain, and bitterly upbraided the hospital for what she claimed to be its neglect of her husband and its failure to recognize the severity of her husband's condition. She demanded interview after interview with the doctors, reproaching them and the nursing staff for incompetence, while they, who had done all in their power to save their patient, grew increasingly resentful under such criticism. I was asked to see her, and it took many meetings in which tears flowed freely before she could speak of her fear of loneliness as well as her resentment that someone upon whom she had come to depend so completely had left her poured forth; it was months before she reached composure and some measure of reconciliation to what had happened. She was shocked by the depth of her resentment, and it was this combination of sudden bereavement, grief, and anger with her husband which had been visited upon the doctors and nursing staff. To find that all this could be openly talked about, without reservation or embarrassment, and that the same topics could be raised again and again, seemed to enable her gradually to accept both her loss and the bitterness towards her husband which the loss provoked; a single telling of such powerful emotions would not have sufficed to restore the body chemistry to its normal quiescence.

(6) *They allow inconsistencies of feeling, attitude and behaviour to be unravelled, and a fuller integration to emerge.* In the counselling situation a person is offered a setting in which the conventions of day-to-day social encounters (that one should not appear too self-centred, that the conversation should be 'kept going', that certain topics are taboo and so on) can be set aside. In almost no ordinary relationship do we tolerate a person's dwelling entirely upon himself, his life and his private circumstances; there is usually a powerful expectation that one party in a conversation shall stop talking about himself and say, more or less willingly, 'And what about *you*?' In most forms of counselling (apart from co-counselling, where an attempt is made to reach a completely reciprocal relationship) this is not the convention, and the client is offered the opportunity to be as 'self-centred' as he wishes to be.

For example, a person is able to learn within the counselling situation, that although his childhood experience may have taught him that certain attitudes, emotions and anxieties must be kept controlled and hidden, the counsellor can, unlike those who brought such controls to bear, allow these attitudes and anxieties to be acknowledged and discussed so that aspects of his personality which a client has been trying to hold at a distance can be accepted and integrated. As suggested, one way of describing this process is to call it 'promoting growth': another is to call it 'bringing about new learning'; whatever one calls it the process seems to involve the counsellor's helping the client towards a greater flexibility of feeling and behaviour, so that he is enabled not only to become aware of and experience a wider range of emotion but may also behave increasingly constructively in his day-to-day life. For some this may mean that they become more spontaneous and less anxious about others; but for others it may mean that they become more aware of the needs of others, more aware of the necessity for venting emotion in activity rather than upon those around them and more able to control their behaviour in day-to-day situations.

This situation arose within one large family I came to know, in which a boy had begun to be difficult at school and was thought to be responsible for a number of petty thefts in the locality. The parents had, of course, been notified of the school's concern, and assured me that they had taken steps to discipline the boy physically; this appeared to have had no effect, however. We spent some time talking of father-son relationships and of the amount of physical punishment which this particular father had experienced, and of the resentment he had felt; over time he came to realize that because of the models of his own childhood, he knew of no other way of managing children than by firm discipline and physical punishment. When we spoke of parents taking an interest in their children's activities and actually spending time doing things with them he found this a difficult role to contemplate because it was so alien to his own experience. However, he agreed to try to give this particular boy more individual time and attention devoting an hour or so regularly each Saturday and Sunday to some shared activity, and found himself surprised both by the readiness of the boy's response and by his own pleasure in this new dimension of his role as a father. It seemed that he needed reassurance from me, and from the authority with which he invested me and my agency, that it was acceptable to feel and behave towards his son in a way which was so different from that in which he himself had been trained.

If these therapeutic ingredients are so important, are we seen as possessing them when we act in a counselling role?

Since there is abundant evidence that the characteristics which I have described above, genuineness, accurate empathy and non-possessive warmth, are of central importance in promoting beneficial results in those with whom we work then it surely is important to discover if, when we act in a counselling role, we are seen to possess them.

I deliberately make the proviso of 'when we act in a counselling role' because many people, social workers, youth leaders, community workers and others, do not find themselves called upon to function purely in the capacity of counsellors: this is often merely one of a range of roles which they need to be able to adopt as circumstances require it. Student and school counsellors, together with marriage counsellors, are perhaps more fortunate in that their title defines their role for the public at large and leaves them freer to concentrate upon developing that specific role: this is not so for the social worker, however, who, although he may wish he could operate purely as a counsellor, in practice finds himself required to act at different times in a variety of other ways: as representative of the court, as the official responsible for supporting a compulsory admission to a psychiatric hospital or even as the leader of a social action group in a community project. Yet the capacity to perceive when an individual or a family is seeking an opportunity to talk of personal matters in a confidential relationship, and to be able to respond to this, seems to be a central and necessary skill for anyone working in the helping professions. The extent to which counselling features in one's day-to-day activities will of course vary enormously.

How then do we find out if we possess these desired characteristics? Since those who seek our help are very unlikely, because of their client/seeker-of-help status, to tell us what they think of us (clients are expected to know their place) then it is probably to our friends, families and colleagues that we must look for this important information. When we pass beyond the formalized position of pupil, student or trainee, we pass in our culture and in our professions, into a world in which we do not learn except very indirectly about how others see us. Even during the supervision experiences which we undergo in training, it appears to be unusual for students to be given much help with, or even information about, how others perceive their 'manner', whether they seem to be able to communicate and put others at their ease, or whether they are seen as impersonal and uncaring. For these, of course, are highly delicate matters, and even within the training relationship they are often left undiscussed because feedback on such counts can seem so terribly damaging and destructive. Supervisor and student often tacitly agree to avoid such a potentially embarrassing topic, although it may be of great importance for a life-time of clients, and how that student is perceived in terms of his personality characteristics and his manner of relating to others may go unremarked.

For if such matters cannot be discussed within the supervisory relationship, where else may they be discussed? If we have already passed beyond that relationship then I suggest it may be very helpful for us to seek the views and impressions of someone whose work we respect upon how we measure up against the central characteristics described above. For the point seems to be that these characteristics are spontaneously socially rewarding; people who possess them offer a great many socially appreciated behaviours in their day-to-day life, and naturally they take this practice with them into their counselling.

How are these characteristics acquired? Can they be learned?

It seems improbable that these personality features, found to be so useful in counselling, are innate; it seems much more likely, though I do not know of any research upon this topic, that, as with many personality features, they are acquired via the socialization process, by imitation of, identification with and responsiveness to parents and other important people in the young child's world. It is true that Thomas, Chess and Birch (1970) found that certain features of personality, detectable in the very young child of only several months old, were also detectable in the same children many years later (for instance, length of the span of attention, responsiveness to change, and level of activity), but it is also true that learning continues throughout life, particularly if the learner is actively involved in and motivated towards learning.

Those who have been fortunate enough to have had in their early years experiences and models which have enabled them to acquire the characteristics of personal warmth, genuineness and empathy with others are undoubtedly fortunate (assuming that they wish to be counsellors) but there is ample evidence that it is also possible to train people in displaying these characteristics. There seem to be many indications that very disparate groups of people, provided they are motivated to enter upon training and are committed to it, can become as helpful as full-time professionals.

What seems a pity, however, is that despite the availability of the research data, and of training manuals and procedures, the practice of attempting to train counsellors and social workers (when working in a counselling capacity) in displaying these characteristics does not seem wide spread. A paper, 'Empathy training', by LaMonica and others published in a nursing weekly in 1977 focused on the particular role of empathy as the primary ingredient in any helping relationship; it also evaluated a training programme designed to increase the levels of empathy demonstrated by nurses towards their patients. If such a characteristic is now seen as a vital ingredient of the role of the nurse, perhaps its importance within the role of the counsellor and social worker should be given more recognition.

Part two

Some ways in which people interact

Chapter 3

Social exchange theory

An increasingly useful way of looking at social interactions, particularly those which take place between people who seek help and people who give it, is offered by exchange theory. This may appeal particularly to social workers and counsellors since the focus of the theory is on the relation between individuals rather than on the individuals themselves.

The suggestion is that in all encounters between people each person is continually assessing the likely benefits and losses to himself, according to his own particular expectations, values, needs and ambitions. (There is an obvious parallel between this idea and that of cost-benefit analysis in the field of economics.)

Consider any day-to-day situation: Mrs Smith, walking down the street to the post office, sees Mrs Jones, a former neighbour, on the opposite side of the road. Should she cross over and speak to her or not? Exchange theory suggests that Mrs Smith makes a swift assessment of the pros and cons of crossing the road, reaches a decision on the basis of this assessment, and acts upon it. Some of the considerations which may affect the decision are as follows:

Rewards To go and speak to her would show friendliness, and Mrs Smith wants to maintain her reputation as a friendly person.

Mrs Jones may have some recent news about the Ratepayers' Association plans.

Mrs Smith has heard that Mrs Jones is standing for the council: she might be a useful person to know.

Mrs Jones was always an interesting person and Mrs Smith enjoyed talking to her.

Costs   Mrs Smith is in a hurry; the post office closes in five minutes.

Once Mrs Jones starts talking, she never stops.

Mrs Jones might ask Mrs Smith to deliver leaflets like she did last time.

One can speculate that as Mrs Smith's paramount need at that time is to reach the post office before it closes, she will compromise with greeting Mrs Jones from this side of the road. In this way she meets the expectations which both her social group and she herself have concerning friendliness; she avoids possibly offending someone who, at a later date, might be the source of considerable advantage to her, but she maximizes her own benefit by giving Mrs Jones no chance to impose costs. So Mrs Smith waves and calls 'Hello, how are you? Haven't seen you for ages. Sorry I can't stop, but I must catch the post. Lovely to see you.' and passes on to her next social encounter, at the post office.

Psychological research on social exchange theory

Thibaut and Kelley (1959), who were among the first to explore this way of looking at human relationships, found that it provided them with a practical means of understanding much which had formerly not been elucidated. By envisaging each person as attempting to maximize his satisfactions, in his own terms, a way is made open both to establishing a general principle of human behaviour and to recognizing the vital importance of individual differences.

These writers, and others who took a similar view, realized that what they were suggesting was effectively a model of social exchange very similar to that of monetary exchange in economic theory, and this idea was developed to a sophisticated level by Homans (1961). He compared the role of money in economic theory with that of social approval in exchange theory: thus, for example, a person may conform to a norm of behaviour because at that time he hopes to obtain the reward of social approval by conforming; later, when that source of approval is no longer available or no longer important to him, he may cease to conform. A man may accompany his girlfriend to church when he visits her family in order to win her parents' approval: the practice is likely to lapse when he meets a new girlfriend whose parents are not church-goers.

Blau (1964) developed the theory, suggesting social exchange 'refers to voluntary actions of individuals that are motivated by the returns they are expected to bring and typically do in fact bring from others.' This means that one can see the probability of a given social behaviour as related to the 'profit' likely to be obtained—according to the individual's own assessment of it.

Fundamental concepts in social exchange theory

The theorists then see social interaction in terms of 'exchange processes', and suggest four fundamental concepts:

Rewards

These are understood as anything which contributes to an individual's sense of well-being or which gratifies his needs or wishes. Some of the obvious and less obvious rewards which one person may obtain through interaction with another person are:

Useful information relevant to one's own affairs.

Enhancement of one's self-concept.

Gratification, if the interacting person is of higher status.

Endorsement of one's own viewpoint.

An actual or promised offer of help in forwarding one's interests.

Costs

These are understood as the opposite of reward; anything which detracts from the individual's sense of well-being and which exacts from him effort or other contribution which he is reluctant to give. These may include:

Demands for help from others.

A sense of being criticized or looked down upon.

Disappointment of expected rewards.

Diminished self-esteem.

On-going anxiety, discomfort or stress.

Outcome

These are the overall rewards minus the overall costs. This may take a little while to calculate, since rewards and costs are seldom clear-cut; moreover the calculation is seldom performed on a conscious level. Thus a student who decides to attend the lecture of a visiting speaker may find the content of that lecture exceedingly boring and wish he had not come; he may comfort himself (since we do not like putting ourselves in positions where we experience costs) that it had been worth the effort after all since he was seen there by his tutor, who commented that he was glad to see him taking such an interest in the subject.

Comparison level

This is a minimum level of expected reward from that interaction by comparison with the levels which might be expected from other sources of reward. The implication is that unless the individual achieves at least a slight sense of gain from the interaction, he will be reluctant to invest much effort in that relationship on a future occasion.

Although the student obtained a slight gain, through his tutor's commendation, for attending the lecture, he might well judge that he could obtain no further benefit by going to hear the visiting lecturer next time he came, especially as the date clashed with an invitation to supper. The comparative rewards to be gained by staying away would seem greater than being bored a second time.

Using social exchange theory to understand human behaviour: an example

Consider for instance some of the factors which may make a person decide to change his general practitioner. Suppose we have a man whose original doctor, Dr Oldman, retires, so that he is automatically transferred to the list of a new general practitioner, Dr Newman. Mr Brown wakes up one morning with his old pain, and goes to visit Dr Newman who, although well qualified, is a shy and socially anxious young man, just out of medical school and new to the neighbourhood. He examines Mr Brown, makes arrangements for a lot of tests, and writes a prescription for the drug which Dr Oldman used to recommend; he also suggests Mr Brown should take more exercise as he is considerably over-weight. Mr Brown feels dissatisfied. Why should Mr Brown feel dissatisfied? He has had a thorough examination by a doctor who seems professionally competent, and tests have been arranged. His prescription has been renewed. What possible cause is there for dissatisfaction? Let us look at the situation in the light of exchange theory.

Rewards

To many outside observers it might appear that Mr Brown should have been well content with the attention he received, but this would fail to take into account that Mr Brown's contentment with Dr Oldman was made up of a great deal more than purely medical attention. It may well have been composed of:

A sense of being 'in with people who matter in the community', since Dr Oldman treated him more as a friend than a patient.
Twenty minutes of supportive talk about the difficulties which Mr Brown has in relating to his wife.
Information about the proposed siting of the new health centre.

Costs

By contrast, in his encounters with Dr Newman, Mr Brown not only foregoes all these former rewards, but he experiences the following costs:

The indignity of being examined by a mere boy.

A sense that socially the new doctor is his inferior.

The lack of an opportunity to voice his complaints about Mrs Brown.

Loss of self-esteem when it is indicated that he is over-weight.

Outcome

Mr Brown is now in a position to make a mental comparison between his satisfaction when he visited Dr Oldman and his satisfaction when visiting Dr Newman. He cannot anticipate that his rewards from Dr Newman will increase, and his cost-benefit analysis is therefore likely to emerge as predominantly negative.

Comparison level

Mr Brown has sadly to accept that Dr Oldman has retired, and that the rewards he formerly enjoyed from that relationship are no longer available. Might comparable rewards, however, be available from some other doctor than Dr Newman? Since his present satisfaction is so low Mr Brown may well survey the field of general practitioners in his neighbourhood, and if Dr Barrington-King appears likely to offer greater rewards of the kind which Mr Brown seeks, then he may well go to the trouble of withdrawing from Dr Newman's practice and entering that of Dr Barrington-King.

It seems highly probable that this kind of running balance is being kept by us all concerning our social interactions, though of course the calculation is not upon the conscious level which the above exposition suggests. Indeed, Thibaut and Kelley (1959) held the view that the subtlety of these calculations almost certainly occur at a level removed from consciousness, but that what the individual does become conscious of is the end product, in the case of Mr Brown, the feeling that 'Newman is really too young: better to go to a more experienced man'. Perhaps it is only at times when we are finding the costs of a relationship more than the rewards that we become aware of discomfort, and are motivated to seek greater satisfaction.

Further explorations in social exchange theory

Informal relationships

Secord and Backman (1974) have suggested that social exchange theory offers a way of understanding not only close relationships between friends or lovers, but also the enforced relationships of, say, a teacher and his pupils. It also seems possible to apply the theory to the different stages of a strengthening or weakening relationship. These writers put forward the view that at a first meeting between two people whom circumstances have thrown together, a form of 'sampling and estimation' occurs in which each person makes inferences from the appearance, apparent status, verbal and non-verbal behaviour of the other whether or not the relationship is likely to prove beneficial or costly to him. If both parties are free agents, and the situation is an informal one, as at a party, then the relationship will be pursued or not according to the assessment made by each; but if one person finds the relationship rewarding and the other does not, then the first may continue to look for rewards until the other makes it quite clear that he is incurring costs by staying where he is; he therefore attempts to increase his rewards by moving away and finding someone less costly to talk to.

Blau (1964), in particular, has noted the delicacy and subtlety of this balance in assessing costs and rewards within a relationship. He illustrates this by the example of two young people attracted to each other in a romantic relationship. If John, say, is very attracted to Tessa and would like to know her better, he is likely to try to spend as much of his time as he can with her in order to maximize his own rewards. If, however, Tessa is unimpressed by John, she will find his demands on her time costly. Her reluctance to meet John will soon be apparent to him, and this in itself will prove a cost to him both as a blow to his self-esteem and to his hopes. If these costs are very painful (i.e. if the 'outcome' at that time is clearly negative) then John may examine the 'comparison level' of an alternative relationship, and seek Stella's company. Tessa in turn may hear of this, and missing the reward of John's attention, may make a fresh appraisal of what John has to offer; but if she now approaches John, he may find it difficult and costly to extricate himself from Stella. John may therefore play 'hard to get', and so the game goes on, with each party attempting to maximize his own satisfactions at least cost to himself.

Formal relationships

If both parties are not free to maximize their satisfactions and to abandon the relationship if it proves non-rewarding, then that lack of freedom in itself constitutes a considerable extra cost. A teacher attempting to manage reluctant pupils, or a social worker trying to build up a 'good relationship' with young people on supervision orders, has an exceedingly difficult task, since he has virtually no rewards to offer and, moreover, by his mere presence he exacts a cost. Left to themselves, the teacher and his unwilling pupils would not meet, were it not for the even greater costs which might be incurred either from the head, parents or in the last resort, the law, if the lessons were not held.

In these situations, however, calculations of anticipated costs and benefits continue on both sides: the pupils are likely to see the teacher as potentially offering nothing but costs, but it is here that the sensitivity, training or wisdom of the skilled teacher, or the skilled social worker, is called for. If in any way he can offer rewards tangential to his formal role, say, in giving appreciation to individuals concerning things that are of personal importance to the pupils' out-of-school life, or in arranging weekend expeditions for those on supervision orders, then the assessment made of his potential rewardingness is likely to alter sharply, and predictably the pupils will then respond more rewardingly to him. For it is by deliberately increasing the personal and social benefits which are peripheral to the formal role that any person who is thrown into an authoritarian relationship with others may hope to emerge unresented and even appreciated.

It is when the teacher or social worker does not perceive the need to increase the personal and social benefits, or having perceived the need, is unwilling to respond to it, that formal relationships go to pieces. Both parties anticipate the future in terms of increasing costs; truancy builds up, petty offences increase and resignations from the teaching or social work profession reflect the conclusion that there are greater rewards to be found elsewhere.

How can social workers and counsellors make use of these findings?

Although the ideas set forth in the early part of this chapter may appear obvious, and although the teasing out of the operation of exchange processes may seem to yield more than an interesting, even amusing, idea, I believe that exchange theory is in fact a very important concept: it carries not only explanatory power but also predictive capacity. Below are three ways in which social workers and counsellors, and indeed anybody working with people, can test out and make use of the ideas implicit in the theory.

(1) Examining if we ourselves are conducting cost-benefit analyses, in an attempt to maximize our satisfactions.
(2) Using exchange theory to understand what is going on.
(3) If our client is assessing costs and benefits, then we should realize that our overall impact must be rewarding to him.

Examine if we are conducting cost-benefit analyses

I suggest that we are. Examine for a few moments the reasons why you are in your present job. If you are settled and content there, then it is likely that the satisfaction of your work, the fact that your husband or wife likes your present house and the fact that your children are settled in school together outweigh the attractions of applying for a more senior post elsewhere; this would involve your having to move, disappointing your wife, upsetting your children, and the additional salary might very well not compensate you for the expenses of moving and the additional driving time. So it goes on.

I believe that we also conduct similar analyses in relation to our clients. I am quite clear that in my own work those whom I am most ready to visit are those I find most rewarding: those who apparently like me and who tell me that I have helped them. The visits I enjoy least are those where I feel I can do little, where things have become so bad that there is virtually nothing positive left to reinforce and build on, or where there are practical difficulties of travelling or access which I personally shirk. Who are the clients whom we delay visiting? Those whom, I suggest, we know will make more demands upon us than we are able to meet, and who will remind us of the ineffectiveness of our contribution. Is this not why we feel such mixed emotions towards the client who does not keep his appointment? Relief that a difficult interview has been avoided for the short term, but anxiety because of the implication that he has found our attempted contribution profitless?

There are, no doubt, some whom, were it not for legislation, we should not visit at all: those who resent our visits, and those who clearly would choose to be out were it not that certain legal powers are vested in us which carry greater costs than those of 'seeing the woman from the welfare' every month or so. We in turn would be elsewhere were it not that we should expose ourselves to crippling costs if we neglected to visit a statutory case.

Use social exchange theory to understand what is going on

So many times it happens that a certain type of behaviour is almost impossible to understand: why for instance does a child persist in disruptive behaviour in a classroom despite repeated punishment? why does a wife, constantly beaten by an alcoholic husband, stay with him? The answers may well not be found in deep intra-psychic conflict, but in the assessment by the persons in question of the advantages and disadvantages to them of particular courses of action. The disruptive child may well be found to receive attention (a very rewarding event to most of us) only when he is rude and aggressive, and since he sees himself as having no alternative sources of reward, he may well find the satisfaction given by notoriety vastly outweighs the temporary inconvenience of the punishment given. His very capacity to take a rise out of the teachers may well be his best claim to a relatively high position in the pecking order of his class, as time after time they react to his provocations by giving him maximal attention. To give the boy the absolute minimum of attention necessary for curbing his activities is likely to be a much more effective response on the part of the teacher—particularly if this is coupled with careful and on-going attention offered to the boy in some other aspect of his school life. In terms of social exchange theory, the rewards available to the boy should be minimized when he is disruptive, but maximized when he is constructive.

Similarly, the wife who stays with an alcoholic husband may not necessarily be re-enacting an infantile tie to her father: it may just be that the advantages of staying where she is do still, from her vantage point, outweigh the advantages of leaving. Her own personal cost-benefit analysis may be so very individual that we are unable to grasp its intricacies; this does not mean that we have the right to postulate some unconscious tie from which the woman cannot break. The following letter by a reader of the *Guardian,* 26 October 1978, illustrates the point.

Why will a woman live with kicks?

I AM ONE of 'these women', as Erin Pizzey calls them (October 16), who has been battered. On the way out of my first marriage I had a relationship for two years with someone from a socially impeccable background who threatened to kill me the first time I tried to end it. After that he was violent to me more than a dozen times over a year — he broke my nose once when my sister was staying, tried to strangle me in another sister's house, and once, when I escaped from my flat at 6 am (leaving my two children in bed) chased me down the street, hit me around and dragged me back to the house. Sex was something I had to provide to prevent violence, even when I was deathly tired.

Eventually it ended when it no longer suited *his* needs to have a relationship with *me* — though the last thing he did before walking out was to hit me on the head three times.

I was not brought up in a violent household — I liked him at the beginning and (less and less) in between acts of violence — I knew perfectly well he was capable of carrying out the threat to kill me. He was charming to members of my family so that it felt as if *I* were mad.

The reasons women stay with violent men are legion, connected with fear, economic dependence, the culture which makes women invest their energy in relationships and feel optimistic about male promises to 'reform'. The only 'kicks' women get out of violence are the real, physical kicks. In spite of Erin

Pizzey's assertions, the women involved in the hundred plus refuges of the National Womens Aid Federation know that there are *no* 'these' women — with kinky violent backgrounds — it *could* be you, it *was* me, for a time.—Yours, A. B., Tyne and Wear.

It is because of the very individuality of such analyses that the principle of client self-determination, so important to social workers, still holds good; only the client can know the detail of what goes into his own personal account, so to speak, and while it may well be appropriate for us to explore with him, as in traditional counselling, the implicatons, costs and benefits of various courses of action, we have no right to impose our assessment of what would be good for him.

Exchange theory also offers the best explanation yet of the 'I've done nothing, but she keeps on thanking me for being so helpful' phenomenon experienced by many counsellors. A woman going through enormous personal stress because of a broken marriage, or acute anxiety concerning children may make a counsellor or social worker feel useless and ineffective, because there is so little which can be done: to his surprise the counselling relationship may prove enormously helpful to the client, and she may say so. Wherein lies the discrepancy? It may well be that, without being conscious of it, the counsellor is exhibiting many non-verbal indications of concern, empathy and warmth to the client and these in themselves are enormously rewarding, quite apart from anything the counsellor may be able to do, or even say. These rewards, added to those of being able to speak freely of highly emotive subjects to a non-involved and non-critical person, are not small ones.

A further way in which exchange theory may help us to understand what is going on is the light that it throws on the subtlety of the factors which count when people make decisions; in other words, the highly individual way in which we assess costs and benefits.

Consider briefly just one of these factors: social status. The relatively low status of the social work profession is constantly being demonstrated by the attitudes of our clients; we are not a set with whom people are usually glad to be associated. We do not confer reward merely by calling, and indeed there are indications that merely to have a social worker calling at your house carries something of a stigma. This is not surprising: much of our work is linked with people in trouble, people in unpopular social situations and people with poor reputations, and although this very association may be one of the primary satisfactions to social workers personally, we should not marvel that it does not commend us to all men. In other words, mere association with a social worker or a counsellor may well be seen as a cost. There are occasions, of course, when we provide the only route to some desired benefit, and then we confer a reward.

If our client is assessing costs and benefits, then we should ensure that our contribution rewards him

This is the chief message of exchange theory for social workers. Somehow, the overall impact of what is offered to a client must add up to more than the costs which our involvement exacts from him. Some of the ways in which we can try to bring this about are:

By communicating clearly

So often people come into contact with social workers with very little understanding of how this came about, what their role is and what the implications of the involement are. One way of rewarding people, is by clarifying with them how they came to be referred (unless they referred themselves, and even then there are confusions) what their expectations of the relationship may be (cf., chapter 3) and what the main features of our work with them may be, e.g. how often it seems appropriate to meet and for how long. Thus, before saying goodbye to a person who has been referred we should see that he has details of:

(1) Our name, and the name of our job.
(2) The organization from which we have come, social services department, hospital, probation office, etc.
(3) The address and phone number thereof.
(4) The hours when we are usually available there.
(5) A clear understanding of anything which has been agreed shall be done; e.g. telephone call by worker or letter to be written by client.
(6) Whether and when we shall be seeing the client again.

Much of this information can be printed upon a simple visiting card which can be used by several people based at the same office, but if no such cards are available then the above information seems to be the absolute minimum which we should offer to a client—unless of course we are happy about the statement frequently made to the next caller, 'Someone did call, but I don't know who she was. I think she said she was from the welfare.'

To be informed is to be rewarded, and for people to know where they stand is also rewarding. It is therefore often helpful to invite questions, but if people find it difficult to formulate these for the worker to explain what his powers are, what he can and cannot offer, and what are his relations with other people in authority. In this way fears and fantasies can be exploded ('They told me you were coming to put me away') and anxiety and muddle reduced.

By appreciating how rewarding empathic attention can be

The finest example I can recall of this occurred in connection with a youth leader who was charged with indecent assault and after pleading Guilty felt humiliated and ashamed by being placed on probation. He felt that his life, his reputation and his dedication to youth work were undermined beyond repair, while his self-respect was shattered. When I saw him a few days after the court hearing he was deeply depressed, very bitter and utterly opposed to the idea of being on probation.

I saw him again, two or three days later, with a letter in his hand. 'Read that', he said, thrusting the letter at me, 'that letter has done me more good than anything since this nightmare began.' The letter came from the probation officer to whom the case had been allocated, and it was along the following lines:

Dear Mr Collins,

I am writing to introduce myself to you before we meet, as I am the probation officer to whom your case has been assigned. My name is David Lomax, and I am sorry that I was unable to be in court on the day of the hearing, because of illness. I should have liked to meet you then, and offer you my encouragement in what must have been very difficult circumstances for you.

As you will know, reports were submitted by several people on your behalf, and I must tell you how impressed I was with the sincerity with which they spoke of your excellent record and the many, many years of unflagging effort you have put in helping the young people of this city. I have come to feel the highest respect for you in view of the excellent testimonials which were submitted to the court, and I shall do all in my power to help you. This is probably a bad time for you, but I should like to assure you of my deep regard; I look forward with pleasure to our meeting as arranged.

Those few lines, written by a perceptive and empathic probation officer, had the profoundest effect on this man; his eyes shone, his sense of self-respect revived and hope for the future dawned afresh. To me this was a splendid demonstration of the power of accurate empathy and personal warmth or, to formulate it differently, it showed the effectiveness of offering rewarding and sensitive attention to a person's withered self-esteem.

By displaying warmth openly in our relationships

It may well not be appropriate to show affection to our clients (although I am not sure of this); I am, however, sure that it is appropriate to show appreciation, to give praise, to enjoy fun and laughter with those we are trying to help, and to strengthen them with our encouragement. Much traditional counselling seems to have its roots in psychoanalytic theory and practice, with the result that some present-day counsellors, as well as some social workers, often learn to display detachment, non-involvement and impassivity while deliberately restraining their own spontaneity and warmth. This stance is the exact opposite of what Truax and Carkhuff (1967) found to be a vital component of successful counselling—namely, conveying a sense of authenticity, of genuineness, rather than playing a role.

This giving of appreciation and warmth seems to be one of the most valuable responses which a social worker or counsellor should have in his repertoire. It comes very easily to some (usually those who have themselves received a great deal of open, easy affection in their childhood), but others can learn to commend, encourage and praise. The effectiveness of this response (since it is so rewarding to those who have few other sources of commendation) is likely to make it all the easier to learn. Consider the situation in a case of child abuse in which, following a court appearance, a care order has been made and a social worker has been assigned to visit the family at home. In the light of exchange theory, there are very few rewards for anybody in such a situation. In some areas the near impossibility of one worker dealing with such a situation has been recognized and at least two workers (one social worker and another from a different agency) visit the family; in this way one may act in a more formal way, and be prepared to receive something of the brunt of the anxiety of the family, while the other has more of a rehabilitative role.

Where such an arrangement is not in force, however, the social worker has to fall back on her own skill and the resources of her own personality. She has somehow to inject enough reward into the situation for the parents to see her visits as offering a tiny benefit in their cost-benefit analysis. Probably she will have to fall back on her own ability to give warmth and approval in those areas of the family's life where they have had success—to find something, in short, where she can offer unstinted appreciation. In this way, by withholding any further criticism, at least initially, the family may come to see her as a source of support and help and while she must clearly continue to supervise the child's progress within the family, to see him and to talk to him, her success in the management of the case may well turn upon her readiness to find aspects of the life of the family which she can commend, or to provide practical help.

Many such parents, involved in court appearances and in the ensuing publicity are extremely frightened and on the defensive; often our best way of helping them is to convey in all the ways we can that we are alongside the family against the difficulties confronting them. We can do this only by showing ourselves to be more of a benefit than a cost, and one of the easiest ways of achieving this is to recognize and respond to opportunities of offering reward.

Exchange theory has, in my view, this valuable predictive capacity: unless our clients can feel that our meetings with them offer more hope of reward than of cost then they will not keep their appointments. It is therefore vital that we attempt to review each interview, however briefly, from the clients' point of view: was there enough in it for them? If we have any doubt then this is a sign that our next meeting must be clearly rewarding to them, and if circumstances do not support such an outcome then the reward must come from our skill, our sensitivity and the resources of our personality.

Chapter 4

Perception and points of view

The saying, beauty lies in the eye of the beholder, reflects our awareness that we do not all 'see' alike, and that to the process of perception is brought individual values, judgments and personal predispositions. It appears likely that although we all possess broadly the same physiological equipment, in terms of the way in which the eye, the optic tracts and the occipital cortex of the brain operate when they are functioning well, the individual variations of long or short sight, of colour blindness or normal vision give some indication of the subjectivity of perception merely on the basis of our visual equipment. But our perceptions are not influenced merely by physiological irregularities; they are influenced by our prejudices, our state of mind when we encounter a person, the information we already have concerning that person, our expectations of him and the state of mind we perceive him to be in. One is, of course, not conscious of such factors in operation, but they do operate none the less and in both directions, i.e. when two people meet, how the counsellor perceives himself and how the client perceives him may have little in common: equally how the client perceives himself and how the counsellor perceives him may have very little in common.

So a newly qualified social worker, seeing herself as genuinely committed to helping others and prepared to give generously of her time and energy, may be perceived and received by the families she visits as lacking in credibility solely because of her youth. This perception, with its implications of inexperience, and the network of inferences and assumptions which the family members understandably bring to their perceptions, is likely so to arouse disbelief in the capacity of such a person to be of use that the relationship may not be viable from the start. Social service departments and area teams should perhaps bear such considerations in mind when attempting to match worker and client.

A great deal of psychological research has been devoted to the attempt to understand some of the proccesses which occur in the perception both of ordinary phenomena such as objects, and of the infinitely more complex phenomena, people. Consider just a few of the findings which have emerged.

Psychological research on perception

Perception is one of the processes whereby we attempt to make sense of the stimuli and situations we encounter: as I sit and type here by the fire I find that every so often I become aware of visual, and auditory perceptions and occasionally I smell something as well— usually a smell coming from the meal in the oven. Although I am concentrating primarily on what I am going to write and typing it, my perceptual organs monitor the outside world for me, noting the passing of cars outside, the flickering of the fire beside me, the sound of someone strumming on a guitar upstairs. While the perceptions make sense in terms of what I expect of a Sunday morning's activities I can attend to them momentarily and then let them slip into insignificance again. When an outburst of shouting occurs, as it does from time to time, the monitoring senses which are scanning my perceptual world immediately focus this as a possible indication of trouble and I withdraw my attention from my typing and listen acutely for a moment to decide whether the trouble requires my intervention or whether it is a storm in a tea-cup between our two boys which will settle itself without me.

This simple, but real, situation highlights the selectivity of our attention: we cannot possibly attend to all the stimuli which are available in our environment at any one time. Instead we learn to focus on those we consider important, or which we have been taught to consider important. Similarly training in counselling and social work attempts to help students focus on certain aspects of people or of their behaviour which seem to be of particular importance in understanding and helping them.

Perception, whether visual, auditory or in any other form, is rooted in psychological processes, and it appears to be a meaning-seeking process, i.e. perceptual processors scan the available stimuli in terms of what has been found to have meaning for us as individuals in the past. We selectively attend to those stimuli which activate chains of associations, sometimes called cell assemblies, which we have come to consider as subjectively important. I emphasize 'subjectively' in order to highlight the highly personal nature of perception: as I said earlier, beauty lies in the eye of the beholder.

Among the many, many absorbing findings which psychologists have gathered in the course of their investigations into perceptual processes it is possible only to consider a few: I have selected those which seem to me to have particular importance for those who work with people, particularly people in distress. It has also been necessary to group them together under various headings.

(1) Perception as a subjective, individual and selective process.
(2) Factors found to be crucial in how a person is perceived.
(3) Factors found to be crucial in how a situation is perceived.

Perception as a subjective, individual and selective process

The near impossibility of perceiving with the 'innocent eye'

The expression, the innocent eye, draws attention to the tendency which we have to perceive in terms of how we have perceived in the past. 'Innocence' conveys a sense of freshness, of lack of bias and of prejudice (pre-judgment) which is doubtless desirable and to be sought, but which may be almost unattainable, particularly in matters in which our own interests are involved. For it appears that while the capacity to perceive and respond to visual stimuli is innate, and while we both perceive and organize our perceptions in terms of constant factors such as shape, colour, position and size, the meanings and values which we as individuals ascribe to our perceptions are both varied and highly individual. Bruner and Goodman (1947), for example, asked children from poverty-stricken and well-to-do homes to estimate the size of certain coins, and found that the poor children consistently over-estimated the size of the coins; the authors interpret this an an indication of the value attached by the poorer children to money as reflected by their greater need.

What appears to happen is that there is in our perception, both of objects and of people, an interaction between our innate capacities to respond to certain types of cue or stimulus and the learned significance which we attach to those perceptions. Thus two people at a jumble sale may perceive the same cracked cup and saucer, but one will not give it a second glance while the other will swoop on it as he recognizes the mark underneath. Similarly, an artist and a meteorologist will perceive the same sky through different eyes, as we say, while the houseproud woman will immediately detect the cobweb which is unnoticed by her more casual neighbour. We learn, then, habits of perceiving and to attend to cues in the environment which have personal significance for us. The expression, mental set, which psychologists have devised, indicates how we either consciously and with intent, or unconsciously, often 'set' our perceptions to respond to specific stimuli—as when a woman in need of a new pair of shoes finding herself looking at the feet of other women in the bus in order to gain some idea of what she wants and what is available. Most professional trainings guide their practitioners towards particular sets of perceptions: dentists notice teeth, beauticians notice complexions and, hopefully, social workers notice people.

To summarize, since it is impossible because of the richness and complexity of the environment to attend to more than a tiny fraction of the stimuli available, we tend, when encountering a new situation, such as entering a room or meeting a new person, to scan the visual scene and register briefly key cues in what psychologists have come to call the 'pre-attentive' stage; the information which we have gathered in this stage is then brought together and synthesized into forms which have meaning for us personally. Thus, when entering a room for a meeting, we may scan those present for a familiar face during the extremely short pre-attentive stage, which may last only a second or two; then while we are finding a chair that information may be synthesized into 'That's the social worker from Area 3 whom I was talking to last month' and we look up and meet her smile of recognition with one of our own. What has happened in this brief incident, however, has been not only the rapid scanning, registering of cues and synthesis of these into a familiar pattern, but the comparison of that pattern with the stored information within our brain and our memory and the finding that the two fit. Most of the time we make incredibly accurate comparisons between fresh incoming information about a person, and what we have stored about them in our memory; it is surprising how seldom we recognize people erroneously when one considers the wide variety and large numbers of people we meet; occasionally, though, we recognize on the basis of what we judge is a good enough fit only to be proved wrong and to be left with a tricky situation to negotiate. I was once greeted effusively in the street by a strange man whom I am certain I had never seen before, but because I couldn't be certain at the instant when unexpectedly he approached me (and I could almost feel the physical sensation of my brain feverishly sorting through memories in order to place this man), and because he must have perceived the hesitation in my response, his own manner faltered and we were both in danger of acutely embarrassing the other. In that fraction of time my old habits, acquired in childhood, took over: 'Always try to avoid making other people look foolish, dear', and I greeted him with a friendly smile, said 'hello' warmly and we both grinned and passed on. The incident was over in perhaps twenty seconds.

Perception as a process of information sifting and categorization

This relating of information to stored information (memory) and the search for a match is not of course usually a conscious process; as you read this page the patterns formed by the black marks of the printer's ink are so familiar that you are unaware of the matching process which is going on all the time. It is not even necessary for you to code the marks into categories of individual words—let alone individual letters: it is possible, instead, to code it into categories of meaning, to make sense of the information in terms of the message it is trying to convey rather than in terms of individual words. Moreover, the associations we bring to words are sometimes strong; one of my children, for example, revels in the word 'regardless' but cannot tell us why. It probably is a word with particular pleasant associations for her but the point is that even something as abstract as a word has the capacity to arouse emotional response.

A similar but more elaborate sequence occurs when we perceive people. The sight of a friend, whom we have been looking forward to meeting, or someone whose presence is rewarding to us stimulates memories and anticipations associated with enjoyment and pleasure; the sight of a critic or an enemy stimulates chains of self-protective reactions, causing tension and anxiety. The categories to which we assign people—teachers, army officers, Italians, women libera-tionists—revive not only simple associations of meaning but often also of emotion. This occurs sometimes on the basis of individuals one has known and sometimes on the basis of what has been conveyed by others, by the media and by stereotyping. For the latter, stereotyping, despite its unpleasant connotations, appears to be an inevitable product of the design of the human brain; we are so designed that we allocate isolated items, people as well as objects, to categories; this is a means of bringing some order to what would otherwise be a confused rag-bag of sensory impressions.

If I can look at a mass of visual stimuli and 'say' 'That's a tree, that's a flower and that's a bush', I am thereby enabled, by dint of drawing upon learned categories, to find order and meaning in the otherwise overwhelming mass of stimuli. Similarly, when we go to a meeting of the newly formed action group, we 'say' 'That's Bill, from our tenants' association—we can count on him; that's Mike from the welfare rights group; who are those two women—where do they stand? There's Jane—that's good; and that must be the new community worker they've just appointed; he looks as though he might be useful . . . and there's the chap from the local paper, hoping for trouble.'

This sequence of scanning, drawing on memory, and allocating to categories, many of which have emotional connotations, occurs within moments of an encounter; it is going on throughout our day-to-day lives, and it also occurs reciprocally: other people are categorizing us as we are categorizing them. We find 'sense' and 'meaning' in our interactions by relating fresh, incoming, sensory data to categories we already have, although our perception on a given occasion may be influenced by our physical or emotional condition. Warr and Knapper (1968) conceptualize the process as one in which information from the past and the present concerning the person perceived interacts with the perceiver's 'habits of perceiving' as well as with how he is feeling at that moment. For example, a counsellor may find himself struggling to make sense of his perceptions when he actually meets the spouse of his client. On one occasion an unhappy woman told me of the tyrant to whom she was married and, having pictured him vividly in my mind's eye before meeting him, I just did not believe that the nervous and shy schoolteacher who came in could be my client's husband. I had noticed him in the waiting room and had seen how frightened he looked. And yet here he was, the brute himself. I spent the first fifteen minutes of that interview in a very confused state of mind, attempting to reconcile my client's perception of her husband, my imagined perception of him and my new perception of him. In the end I could not do it, but I found that by drawing upon empathic perception I could see him as my client saw him, and her reality was as valid as mine. It became another instance of what I had had to do on other occasions: move round within people's perceptions of each other.

The bringing of emotions, assumptions and expectancies to perceptions

Warr and Knapper (1968) go on to suggest as shown in Figure 2 that a perceiver, in addition to his habits of perceiving, will bring to his perceptions an almost inevitable emotional 'colouring' or response, a tendency to make assumptions on the basis of his perception and to generate expectancies based both on the perception and on the assumptions. The very act of perception is likely to initiate a long sequence of associations, visual and experiential, which may very well colour, consciously or unconsciously, the attitude and response of the perceiver to the perceived. A student said to me recently, 'I've always found it difficult to come and talk to you; you have the misfortune to remind me very much of my mother; she looks just like you' which I felt was rough on me, but provided a perfect illustration of the point I am making. This sort of thing is, of course, happening all the time; we are all unwittingly triggering off attitudes towards us, for example by our very appearance or the sounds of our voices, of which we are unaware; perhaps counsellors need consciously to think whether clients remind them of anyone else, by, say, appearance or by name, and to invite their clients to do the same, so that those old associations do not get in the way of the new

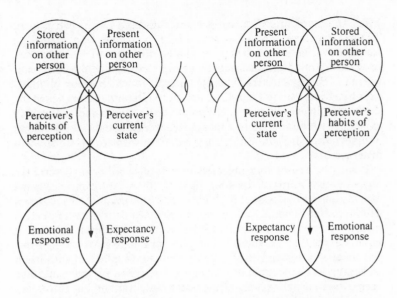

Figure 2 *Schematic representation of aspects of perception (after Warr and Knapper (1968))*

relationship. It looks as if this type of perceptual process linked closely with past learning, predisposes us to make certain assumptions and to conceive certain expectations both about the characteristics, personality and probable patterns of behaviour of the person we are perceiving. As Warr and Knapper (1968) suggest, it is almost impossible to describe 'person perception' in terms of what is: the nearest is to describe some of the events which happen; 'truth' appears once again to be a matter of negotiation rather than of fact. And, of course, they are happening within each of those persons who perceive me, as well as within me, as I perceive each of them.

Important factors in how a person is perceived

The importance of first impressions

A considerable amount of research has been devoted to what is known as the primacy effect, namely, the greater impact of our first impressions of a person than those which he makes on us later. An early experiment by Asch (1946) asked subjects to report impressions of a person whom he described to them using a number of adjectives, both favourable and unfavourable; however, the order in which the list of adjectives was presented differed for the two groups. To the experimental group the favourable adjectives were read first, followed by the unfavourable; to the control group the order was reversed. Asch found that each group reported their impressions of the person being described mainly in terms of which group of adjectives had been read to them first, i.e. although both groups heard the same adjectives, albeit in a different order, it was the ones which came first which contributed most to what was thought of the person in question. These findings have been confirmed by subsequent investigators.

It may be reasonably objected that to give a list of descriptive terms to a group of people, inviting them to come to some conclusions on the basis of such inadequate information is an unreal situation, but I should have to point out that this is the very process which is occurring when social workers submit case histories or court reports, and that we should therefore take particular care in our choice of words, and the order in which we place them, when compiling such documents. Moreover, Asch's original work has been repeated and extended several times, and in his continued inquiries he found that many people organized and simplified the list of descriptive traits into a core or central feature under which the other traits were subsumed; thus a list containing the words 'generous', 'wise', 'happy', 'good-natured', 'humorous' and so on tended to be clustered round the core concept 'warm', while another list containing such words as 'stubborn', 'critical', 'withdrawn', tended to be clustered round the core concept 'cold'.

Kelley (1950) was able to reproduce the essence of Asch's original inquiry using a person as distinct from a list of descriptive terms. He introduced a guest speaker, who was party to the investigation, describing him before he came in with the stimulus words from Asch's experiment, using 'warm' or 'cold' to describe the central trait to different groups of subjects. Both in this experiment, and in a further one by Veness and Brierly (1963) in which a speaker, a speech expert, conveyed the characteristics 'warm' and 'cold' in the tonal features of his voice, Asch's original hypothesis was confirmed: first impressions do appear to be lasting ones. Moreover, the dimensions 'warm' and 'cold' seem to be primary ones in our assessment of others, whether this is perceived by manner, expression or voice. Such factors will of course, also be operative in how *we* are perceived.

Other important variables in person perception

It is perhaps disturbing to discover, according to a great deal of evidence, though admittedly gathered mainly in the USA, that a central criterion upon which we base our perceptions and subsequent liking of others is that of personal appearance. This phenomenon was found to occur across the age range, and Dion and Berscheid (1972) found that physically attractive boys and girls aged as young as five and six were more popular with their peers than less attractive ones. The awareness of physical appearance as a central feature of interpersonal interaction appears to be borne out by the finding of Douvan and Adelson (1966) who asked large numbers of adolescents which aspect of themselves they would most like to alter: 59 per cent placed physical appearance first; only 4 per cent mentioned ability and school achievement. It can certainly be objected that physical appearance is a culturally related value, but the increased emphasis placed in the Western world on vital statistics, hair-style, complexion and fashion sense by commercial interests make it likely that this will become a more rather than less important variable in our interpersonal perceptions.

Another variable which has been found to be of key importance is that of similarity between ourselves and those with whom we interact; this was found by Newcomb (1961) and Byrne (1971) to refer not so much to appearance as to perception of shared attitudes and values; seen from another point of view, we perceive favourably those whom we perceive as like ourselves and as confirming our self-concept. Who has not breathed a sigh of relief when a difficult client is found, like ourselves, to be interested in canal preservation, jazz, or the fortunes of Nottingham Forest; a shared interest of this kind and its development can contribute much to the professional relationship.

Highly pertinent to this finding is that by Aronson and Linder (1965) who investigated liking of one person by another; they found that a main determinant of liking, i.e. of favourable perception, was the level of esteem which subjects felt was accorded to them by the other person. Assuming that counsellors and social workers do feel it appropriate to be favourably perceived by their clients then it seems fitting that they should be sure that they are perceived by their clients as treating them with respect and esteem, and that both verbal and non-verbal behaviour carries this message.

Assumptions made on the basis of perception

The technical name for the study of this process, which occurs in us all, is implicit personality theory. It refers to our inherent tendency to come to firm conclusions concerning those whom we encounter, although we have very limited data on which to base such assumptions. This is, of course, the process which lies at the heart of stereotyping, and it is important that this should not be seen as intrinsically wrong; because of the impossibility of registering specific data concerning every single individual whom we meet we of necessity come to some general conclusions on the basis of our experience of, for example, smiling people, frowning people, soldiers, policemen, and so on; some of these generalizations we are specifically taught within our culture, others are rules of thumb which we build up for ourselves.

The essence of the process is that on the basis of a very small amount of learning, we make extended assumptions concerning the personality, character and probable behaviour of the individuals we encounter; as I have mentioned lengthy chains of associations linked with past names, words, or situations, rich in emotional attitudes, are readily triggered by chance occurrences. In the same way we assume that clusters of personality attributes are assembled round a core characteristic: few of us for example find it easy to conceptualize a 'hippy civil servant' or a 'timid general'—so powerful are the popular stereotypes.

Our implicit personality theories also lead us to see people as much more consistent than they actually are. In an early study Newcomb (1931) kept daily records of the behaviour of a group of boys at a summer camp and found that there was little consistently 'introvert' and 'extrovert' behaviour, i.e. most boys displayed both types of behaviour. Camp leaders, however, perceived regularity of behaviour in a way which was just not consistent with the records; they imposed a framework or pattern which made sense of their observations because they expected consistency. Steiner and Johnson (1963) pursued this interesting topic further, and found a general unwillingness among all their subjects to tolerate the possibility that 'highly desirable' and 'highly undesirable' traits co-exist within the same person; it appears that we so organize our perceptions as to impose consistency on people. How then do we do this? It seems that another element in organizing our perceptions is to attribute to people characteristics which we believe are associated with other characteristics; our evaluation of others (for there always seems to be an evaluative component in perception) is not only against certain dimensions, but involves drawing on our own internal and highly individual assumptions about others. Secord (1958) found that he had only to show photographs of unknown people to his subjects to find that they were prepared to make judgments not only about these people's emotional states, but also about their personality. It is encouraging to read in the following extract from the *Guardian,* 8 February 1978, that although at the magistrates' court the young mother in question suffered the penalty of presenting herself untidily, in that a number of assumptions were made about her behaviour, this process was resisted by the High Court Judges.

'Untidy' mother wins appeal

A teenage mother's appearance weighed against her when she
went to court to fight for custody of her 21-month-old
daughter.

The magistrates felt that the untidy young woman, with
buttons missing from her coat and an apparent lack of interest
in the outcome of the case, showed lack of competence and
care over her little girl. They ordered her to hand over the baby
to her estranged husband so that his mother could care for her.

But yesterday the young mother won her baby back because
two High Court judges felt the magistrates were wrong in their
opinion of her.

'It is a bold deduction that an untidy mother is likely to be
a bad mother,' said Mr Justice Arnold, sitting with Sir George
Baker, president of the Family Division. 'She was only a young
girl, with the background of a failed marriage, and the court
hearing was an unpleasant experience.'

The judge said the magistrates had contrasted her record
with the 'warm interest' showed by her husband and the
'loving care' of his mother.

It was true that the inexperienced girl had been forced to
seek her mother-in-law's advice about caring for the baby—for
instance, when it developed nappy rash. But she was not the
first 18-year-old to seek such help over a troublesome baby,
said the judge. It showed responsibility rather than lack of
care.

It was also true that she had not been frank with the
magistrates about her friendship with a neighbour—but that
again did not make her a bad mother.

The judge said there was nothing to disqualify her from
having custody of her own little girl.

Further studies have indicated that we allow traits which are
important to us, as evaluators, to carry great weight when we judge
others; thus if I pride myself on my efficiency or aesthetic sense,
these dimensions will carry particular weight in my evaluations of
others. Rommetveit (1960) showed that observers had a greater
liking for persons who possessed traits which were important to
those observers. All these studies are, of course, borne out by the
data yielded by Kelly's 'personal construct theory', to which reference
is made on the chapter on the self-concept, and which essentially
draws attention to the personal and highly individual way in which
we perceive and evaluate others.

Some ways in which people interact

Important factors in how a situation is perceived

It is implicit in what has been said above that person perception is a reciprocal, two-way process, and that those who are perceiving and evaluating must take into account how they are perceived and evaluated. Moreover, perception is not an isolated event, separate in time and circumstances from all that has gone before and all that may follow. It occurs within a context, and to that context is brought an understanding of the meaning of that context for each of the individuals involved. Here we enter the world of 'phenomenology', the study of the personal and idiosyncratic meanings which individuals attach to the events and circumstances in which they are involved. How then can one hope to arrive at a shared view of a situation? David Hargreaves (1972) writes convincingly of this predicament:

> Each participant in an interaction is trying to establish a definition of the situation. If then the interaction is to proceed smoothly, there must be some agreement between the participants in the definitions of the situations they are trying to project. Such consensus about the definition of the situation involves a recognition and acceptance by each of the roles and goals of the other, an agreement about how each will treat the other, and the formulation of rules that will regulate conduct. For the consensus to be high, the definitions of situation projected and intended by each participant must be similar or compatible.

In simple situations, such as buying a stamp or asking the way, there is likely to be a shared interpretation of events—though there may well be differences of perception concerning the tone of the interaction: person A may report 'I didn't know where I was, so I inquired the way of someone passing by', while person B's view of events may be 'This strange man pulled up and shouted at me from the other side of the road; I had to put down my shopping bags and cross over to him, through the traffic. And when I'd given him directions, he just nodded—never even said "Thank you"—and drove off.' How much more room there is for different perceptions and interpretations when, for example, one visits the doctor or consults a marriage-guidance counsellor.

This situation is complicated even further by the fact that situations are not merely static and once and for all: they are usually interactions, continuing over time. Thus while it may be obvious that the behaviour of a person towards us, as we perceive it, may affect our evaluation of him, it is perhaps less apparent that his behaviour towards us may well be strongly coloured by his perception of us, or of our role; in other words, we ourselves may have induced the very perception of him which we obtain. Secord and Backman (1974) point out that in studies of games which can be played either competitively or co-operatively,

the co-operator's view of other persons is that they may be either co-operative or competitive. But the competitive type thinks that all persons are competitive, because his own competitive behaviour elicits competitive behaviour from his opponent.

They draw the parallel that

behaviour is partly a function of the observer's own behaviour toward the other person. Each observer elicits certain behaviours from those around him. For example, a hostile observer is apt to believe other persons are more hostile than they are, simply because his own aggressive behaviour draws hostility in return.

How a situation is perceived then is likely to be related to whether both, or all, the participants arrive at that situation with shared expectations, and with shared attitudes towards the event; it will be related to the way they interpret the actual happenings which occur, and to the way in which they themselves behave towards those happenings and interpretations. And the more people present, the more sets of perceptions there are to complicate the issue.

How can social workers and counsellors make use of these findings?

In view of the subjectivity and individuality of our perceptions, how are counsellors and social workers to use this awareness to the benefit of their clients? Several areas seem to lend themselves to consideration.

Be aware of the criteria on which we assess other people

It is very difficult to step outside the individuality of our own perceptions—unless possibly under unusual conditions such as during meditation, high fever, the influence of drugs or some other deliberate practice. Yet I believe we can attempt to discover what are the implicit scales against which we are measuring other people when we encounter them. One of these dimensions is almost certain to be appearance (see p. 87); however much we may like to think of ourselves as being uninfluenced by physical endowment, the evidence is to the contrary. The individuality of our response may well vary according to sub-cultural factors, whether we like or dislike certain hair colours or styles of dress, and whether we react protectively or with embarrassment to physical irregularities, but whatever the individual pattern of our response, it is surely important to be aware that we are almost certainly being markedly influenced by the physical appearance of the person whom we are encountering. It is also appropriate to be aware, since we are involved in reciprocal relationships, that our appearance will be likely to colour markedly the response of others to us. This theme will be elaborated in chapter 5.

Other factors are undoubtedly operating, however: earlier in this chapter I reported the considerable evidence that we tend to prefer people who share our beliefs, attitudes and values, since these are in one sense 'confirmations' of ourselves. It seems fitting, therefore, that we should attempt to discover what are the particular values and attitudes which are dearest to us, so that we can·at least be on our guard against premature decisions: how easy it is for counsellors, themselves often from middle-class backgrounds, to assess the personalities and potentials of their clients against their own values and patterns of behaviour. A beautiful example of this, quoted by Gordon Cree in a personal communication occurred when he was working with a family in which the children were at risk of non-accidental injury, and had reached the end of a contracted period of a behaviour modification programme aimed at improving family relationships. Discussing whether work should end there, or to carry on with a new contract, for example to learn to sort out difficulties by talking to each other, one of the teenage girls said, 'That's what posh people do!'

The point then is that the main attitudes and beliefs which we hold ourselves are likely to provide the criteria against which we assess others, and on which we make implicit judgments about them. Let us at least find out, probably from others since we are unlikely to be able to discover them by introspection, what our main values and yardsticks are seen to be, so that we can be on our guard against evaluating negatively those whose strengths lie on different dimensions from our own.

Deliberately attempt to revise our impressions of others

Since we now know something of the powerful effect of first impressions, and of the distorting effect of physical appearance upon those impressions—so that people who are conventionally 'attractive' within our culture are seen as possessing characteristics and qualities merely by being 'attractive'—it is important to bear this phenomenon known as the 'halo effect' in mind and consciously to revise our impressions of others from time to time. I personally find this exceedingly difficult to do, so powerfully does the primacy effect operate in my own case, so I have therefore adopted the practice of asking a colleague who also has met Mr X or Mrs Y how he perceives these clients; often the discrepancy is very great. If I find that not only are my impressions very different from that of my colleague, but that I am also making a number of negative evaluations on the basis of my impressions, then the time has probably come for that client to have a change of counsellor.

Be able to 'move round' within the perceptions made by others

It seems that this capacity is desirable in all those who work with people, i.e. the ability to perceive through the eyes of others. Readers will have encountered the same concept dealt with in more detail in chapter 3; in that context it is described as 'empathy', and it has emerged as a central characteristic of effective counsellors.

To recapitulate, it is the capacity, which can be learned, to put oneself into the position of another person, or a series of other persons, and to perceive a set of circumstances in a way approaching their perception of it. It is highly unlikely that we shall ever perceive a situation in exactly the same way as another person does, but we need to be able to perceive it in sufficient detail and with sufficient fluidity to see that from his standpoint his behaviour or his opinion makes sense. This seems to be the crucial test; can we lend ourselves to how another person perceives an event or a situation to such an extent that his behaviour makes sense to us? If so, we can often then understand why he does what he does and says what he says—even though we may subsequently have to distance ourselves from his viewpoint and decline to confirm his perceptions.

Moreover, we need to be able to extend this capacity, so that we can enter into the perceptions not just of one individual whose appearance appeals to us, or with whom we sympathize personally but into the perceptions of several individuals—even if those individuals are disputing with one another, and particularly if one wins our sympathy more than another. For if we are unable to do this, and to do it with a fair degree of accuracy, so that we can detect the spurious from the genuine, then we shall be perceived as 'on the other's side'; we need rather to say explicitly that we realize from X's point of view the situation looks such and such, while from Y's it looks such and such; this recognizes the perceptions of both parties, but confirms neither. A counsellor can use this device to demonstrate his willingness to enter into the viewpoint of, say, both husband and wife, or both parent and child; both thereby feel rewarded by the recognition afforded to their viewpoint but the way is left open to negotiate a more integrated viewpoint acceptable to all. It is again as though in matters of perception there is no 'truth'; only different points of view.

This ability to move round within perceptions, but without losing hold of one's own broader perception seems to me to be one which is both valuable and which may be attained by practice and experience. So many of my perceptions of mothers changed when my own children were born; I am dismayed to remember the total inadequacy of the perceptions I made of family life before I experienced it myself. Yet one can also gain experience in this capacity by deliberately selecting someone for whom one can feel no sympathy and understanding and attempting for several minutes to put oneself in his shoes or to see the world through his eyes. Such an exercise takes several minutes at least; but perhaps it needs to be undertaken in respect of those clients for whom we feel the least concern and sympathy. Role-play can also be of great value here.

This willingness to enter into the perceptions of a variety of others offers opportunities for creating very supportive relationships to entire families, as distinct from relationships seen as focused on a particular individual. In one family I came to know the wife had associated herself with a particular religious sect at least partly out of sheer loneliness; her husband mistrusted the members of the sect and the wife's attendance at its meetings became the subject of bitter and violent disputes between them. After talking at some length with each of them separately and gaining, as I think, some perception of the situation as seen through the eyes of each (and finding myself in genuine sympathy with both partners) we spent a few sessions together in which no attempt was made to come down on one side or the other but the focus of our discussion was how, in the circumstances of all that had gone before (and both had had difficult lives) each had arrived at a different perception of the wife's joining the sect. Neither was 'right', neither was 'wrong'; both partners' reactions made sense in terms of how they perceived the situation; this was an area of difficulty in a marriage which in other respects had been very successful and happy. To have the validity of both points of view accepted in this way brought visible relaxation. It was possible to move on from here to make with both partners *together* the closer relationship which seemed essential in order to localize this area of difficulty and prevent its spilling over into the many other areas of strength and happiness in their marriage. When meeting with them it was important, on each occasion, to remind them of the many positive aspects of their relationship and to avoid spending all our time focusing on the area of disagreement; had we given this topic all our attention it would have had the effect of reinforcing that component. It would have allowed no opportunity to remind them of and to hear the achievements and many areas of great satisfaction they had arrived at together.

In summary, the key points appear to be three: first, a counsellor or social worker needs to be able to move round within the perceptions of others or to empathize with others to such an extent that he can genuinely say to an individual 'Yes, I understand that you see the situation as one in which . . .'; second, that he can say this genuinely to each individual locked in conflict with another; and third, that while he really does know how the situation must appear to each of them, he can nevertheless avoid identifying himself with one viewpoint or the other; if he can do this he may be able to act as an interpreter of perceptions, one to another. For example 'I wonder if you can see, Jane, that to your mum it looks as if you don't care about her and your dad at all?' and 'If you were in your husband's shoes, Mrs Jackson, seeing all that's happened but wanting still to make a go of it, how would you be feeling now?'

Be sure that our definition of a situation is shared by our clients

Let us recall Hargreaves' (1972) suggestion that 'Each participant in an interaction is trying to establish a definition of the situation. If then the interaction is to proceed smoothly, there must be some agreement between the participants in the definitions of the situation they are trying to project'. As several writers have pointed out this agreement cannot come about unless there is an interlocking of roles: one cannot play the customer unless someone else is prepared to play the shop assistant: one cannot play the author unless someone else is prepared to play the publisher; nor the social worker unless someone else is prepared to play the client. As was pointed out in chapter 3, people are not often ready and willing to play client to the social worker unless on their own terms. 'Why on earth don't you alter the name?' I was asked when I went to see a family having difficulty with their youngster, having signed myself 'psychiatric social worker' in my letter to them. At that instant I became aware of what an unnecessary load of anxiety I was heaping on that family merely by my insensitivity to how they perceived the implications of my role. Their understanding of the situation which, with its implications of stigma in having a 'difficult' child, had already been hard for them to arrive at, had been threatened by my unthinking definition of the situation conveyed in those three words, 'psychiatric social worker' — implying mental disorder and illness. I had added to their anxiety, not diminished it.

Moreover, since we set such store by treating people as individuals, we are thereby presumably attempting to be aware of the definitions of the situation of all the participants involved—including our own. I cannot help wondering sometimes when I hear social workers speak of their intention to offer family therapy to a family which is having difficulties; the implication is that this is a unitary concept, with a body of established theory, whose principles have been tested and replicated. Much of that which I have attempted to do in this book is to show that in any interaction between people there are countless variables operating, and that even in the simplest of situations the same set of stimuli give rise to a different set of perceptions to each of the participants. Can one really be sure that what is blithely offered to the family as 'therapy' is going to be perceived as such, and that each practitioner of family therapy is drawing on a tried and tested body of theoretical understanding?

Finally, when working in cross-cultural settings, how difficult it is for us to perceive a situation through the eyes of, say, an immigrant family to whom the notion of mental illness is even more alarming than it is to ourselves. It is probably impossible for us, however empathic we may be, to approach any situation concerning or involving immigrant families with adequate understanding of the cultural practices and attitudes of people towards, say, child care, mental handicap or mental illness unless we have received specific teaching on such topics. Our own perceptual sweep, however broad, is unlikely to accommodate the perceptions of people from other cultures of such emotive issues; in other words, it is highly likely that we shall define such situations differently, and fail to see the implications of such situations in the same way, unless we make deliberate attempts to familiarize ourselves with the traditional views of such cultures.

One therefore hears with pleasure of efforts being made in some cities at the present time to provide a special mental health service for immigrant groups: attempts are being made to provide out-patient treatment for Asian patients, since to be hospitalized is a severe social stigma, and there is seen to be a risk of breaking dietary rules; moreover one team deliberately elects to work with all Asian patients in order to build up a fund of awareness of how the various immigrant groups perceive and respond to the intense threat posed by mental illness. Since it would be quite impossible for a generic worker to acquire such a specific and detailed knowledge of how such situations are perceived by a range of immigrants we appear to have here yet another indication of the vital necessity to encourage individualized areas of work and knowledge within generic teams.

Chapter 5

Communication:
verbal and non-verbal

Next time you get involved in a discussion, or next time you are listening to a speaker on television, try to notice something of all that is going on as well as the mere production of words. Pitch and intonation will vary, some words or phrases will be emphasized or carefully articulated, pauses or deliberate silences may be incorporated into the flow of speech, while the speaker may well frown, smile or hammer on the table to drive home particular points. We *expect* this varied presentation, and indeed often complain of the monotonous (single-toned) speaker who puts us to sleep by the dullness of his delivery. It seems that style of presentation is at least as important as content. The conveying of information, often unintentionally, by means other than the spoken word is known as 'non-verbal communication'.

Consider first what a central role non-verbal social behaviour plays in our day-to-day lives; the implications of the following expressions will be familiar to everyone:

'He won't look me in the eye.'

'She will stand too close to you when she's speaking.'

'I don't like his familiar tone.'

'It's not what he says, but how he says it.'

'I didn't know where to look.'

'I smiled at her, but she cut me dead.'

'It's rude to stare.'

'Don't point.'

Implicit in all these remarks is an appeal to what the speaker considers to be an understood and accepted medium of communication familiar to, or in the case of the last two examples, to be learned by, his listener. This medium appears to have a very much greater impact than has hitherto been recognized, and we are only just beginning to accord it its due position in our attempts to understand what goes on between people—any people—when they encounter each other. A sensitivity to non-verbal communication is clearly of acute importance to anyone whose work is based on interaction with people, and is clearly particularly necessary for counsellors or social workers who aspire to close relationships with those who seek their help. The area of non-verbal communication has been the focus of a great deal of detailed research by psychologists over the past few years.

Psychological research on non-verbal communication

I propose first to devote some attention to specific channels of non-verbal communication which have been found to be important, and thereafter to consider some of the functions which such communication fulfils.

Some channels of non-verbal communication

The eyes, and face gaze

As Michael Argyle, whose book *The Psychology of Interpersonal Behaviour* (1972) is a rich and absorbing source of detailed information, reminds us, very tiny babies only a few weeks old will increasingly direct their gaze to the eyes of any person bending over them, or indeed to 'eyes' drawn on a cardboard mask which is presented to them. This response is universal and appears to be innate. As we grow older we do not lose our interest in eyes: rather, most of us learn to conform to the conventions of the Western world whereby we look at each other intermittently as we speak with them. A speaker tends to look at his listener only about half the time that the listener looks at him, so that the eyes of the two respondents actually meet, typically, between 15 per cent and 50 per cent of the time, for periods of one to three seconds.

The meeting of eyes conveys heightened communication of one form or another. It is emotionally arousing, and Argyle writes that 'While short periods of Looking may simply be part of the signalling and information-gathering process, longer periods signify a heightened interest in the other person—either in an affiliative, sexual, or aggressive-competitive sense'. Presumably social workers would wish to avoid most if not all these innuendoes.

There are several reports of research which yield information useful to those working with people: Argyle, Lalljee and Cook (1968) found people felt ill at ease when speaking to others wearing dark glasses; Exline (1963) found that the tendency shown by women to look at people more than men reflects their greater concern with affiliation rather than domination; several researchers have found that although people enjoy being looked at (watched) for short periods, long periods produce discomfort and anxiety. This suggests that counsellors should only allow long periods of silence to occur if they can be certain that their effect will be beneficial. It also suggests that a non-participant leader or member in, say, a formal T-group, may give rise to acute and perhaps destructive anxieties among the members. Clearly this effect is sometimes intended: it should not be allowed to arise unintended through the leader's ignorance of, or insensitivity to, non-verbal communication.

Facial expression

A key experiment in this field was conducted by Rosenfeld (1967) who investigated the effects of different interviewing styles; interviewers were trained to conduct their interviews in either a 'positive' or 'negative' style—the former characterized by much smiling, head-nodding and agreeing with the opinions of the person being interviewed, and the latter by frowning, looking bored or even looking away. (It might be possible to conceptualize these as 'rewarding' or 'non-rewarding' styles of interviewing.) Rosenfeld's findings were that not only did the person being interviewed in the positive style himself respond with much smiling and many nods of the head, but he also talked more and for longer sequences than did the person who was interviewed in the negative style.

Smiling is (usually) an outward sign of an attitude held by the smiler towards the other person; it conveys a positive and friendly feeling, and in biological terms conveys a non-threatening and benign attitude towards someone who might feel that the other person was menacing their territory, their food, their mate, or perhaps their self-concept. It appears to convey absence of threat in all cultures, and the regularity with which the smiling response appears in babies at about four to six weeks seems to indicate an innate predisposition to smiling. It is not long, of course, before environmental influences begin to have an impact and Brackbill (1958) was both able to elicit and to extinguish the smiling response in babies by reinforcing or not reinforcing it with her own smiles.

For smiling is in itself a powerful social reinforcer; it implies acceptance of or approval of what has gone before, be this an action, a facial expression or a statement; in other words, we retain our sensitivity to the smiles of others almost as acutely as when we were infants, although, sadly, our own readiness to smile may have faded because of unsmiling models round us, or the extinguishing effect of bitter life experiences. To be smiled at is to be rewarded, and we all need experiences of being rewarded. Yet in our culture we make no deliberate effort to teach children this simple but immensely valuable social skill; it is a matter of pure chance whether a person retains his original endowment or not.

Bodily posture and orientation

As Argyle (1972) points out, posture is another signal which is largely involuntary but which can convey, or can be interpreted as conveying, superior or inferior positions or attitudes. Sommer (1965) found that sitting alongside, immediately opposite and at right angles to another person sitting at a table carried respectively, connotations of co-operation, competition and equality of status, while Lott *et al.* (1969) found marked cross-cultural differences in the physical distance which people from different races like to maintain between each other: Arabs and Latin-Americans stand very close, while Swedes and Scots are the most distant.

Clearly such findings should be borne in mind by those working with people, and indeed many counsellors do position their furniture so that client and counsellor sit at an angle to each other, on equal levels. Yet there are still social workers who conduct interviews across a desk, sometimes even with the client's chair a good deal lower than their own. If they are not aware of the implications of such an arrangement, their clients will be.

Style of social behaviour: affiliative, dominant, etc.

The work of Truax and Carkhuff (1967), described in chapters 1 and 2 indicates that one characteristic of successful counsellors is 'non-possessive warmth'. This corresponds very broadly to what psychologists call 'an affiliative style' which in our culture is conveyed by smiling, physical proximity, above-average eye contact and a friendly tone of voice. Some people are endowed with these attributes naturally, or rather circumstances so combine that they arise from innate tendencies shaped by environmental influences; this becomes their spontaneous way of relating to others, and of course they take this with them into the counselling situation. Other people less fortunately endowed (for their choice of profession) have to practise the relevant social skills, but many researchers have found that such skills *can* be acquired if appropriate training is given.

People with a dominant style of relating may have trouble in keeping people motivated to continue to meet them. People may put up with a dominant doctor or a dominant teacher, either because they have no alternative or because he offers other rewards of knowledge or skill. Dominant counsellors or social workers, however, are likely to be in a more difficult position: as it is by no means generally accepted that these professions can provide a reliable and distinctive skill, the rewards they provide therefore have to be all the clearer. Such potential rewards are readily obscured by a manner which conveys superiority, lack of interest or a critical attitude.

This is not to suggest that at all times 'dominance is bad; affiliation is good.' There may very well be many situations where behaviour which is characteristically dominant (e.g. advising, directing and guiding) may be desperately needed and asked for by clients, only to have advice denied them because counsellors have been trained to be non-directive at all costs. Rather the implication is that flexibility is needed: either predominantly affiliative counsellors should learn to give a lead where appropriate (it was found by Phillips (1960), for instance, that excellent results were achieved by giving parents simple advice on the management of their children in contrast to in-depth interviews) or predominantly dominant counsellors should look to the effect of their non-verbal style.

Functions of non-verbal communication

It appears increasingly that the role of the spoken component in communication is primarily concerned with information-giving, but that the non-verbal component is 'the music behind the words', conveying emotion and attitude, and is also the monitor of the encounter, obtaining feedback on the responses of the listener to what is said by scanning his appearance and expression and synchronizing their two contributions.

Conveying interpersonal attitudes and emotions

We are taught from early childhood to recognize the signs of parental emotion, and even though the extent to which such perception is innate is still unclear children do learn very early when to approach and when to avoid parents. 'I don't like you making that cross face!' screamed a three-year-old at her mother. 'Take that cross face away!' The anxiety felt by this little girl is echoed by most of us to a greater or lesser extent when we perceive signs of disapproval or anger on the faces of those about us, especially when it occurs on the faces of those with power over us. Some people feel such acute anxiety when they are disapproved of that they go to great lengths to avoid the slightest hostility: a few people enjoy rows; but almost all of us look for signs of acceptance and reassurance when we go as patients or clients to seek help.

One particularly arresting study of Michael Argyle *et al.* (1970) attempted to examine which 'language', the verbal or the non-verbal, carried most weight in an encounter. A speaker presented a message by video-tape to an audience in a manner conveying dominance, equality or submissiveness; the dominant style, for instance, was characterized by an unsmiling expression, a loud voice and with the head held high, the submissive style by a subdued and placatory manner. The impact of these messages conveyed under different conditions was studied, and it was found that 'the non-verbal style had more effect than the verbal contents, in fact about five times as much; when the verbal and non-verbal messages were in conflict, *the verbal contents were virtually disregarded*' [my italics]. The message for counsellors and social workers appears to be clear: look to your non-verbal communication.

Sadly, social work does not seem to be a high-status profession. Clearly this makes our work more difficult, for all the obvious reasons, and because we are expected to behave in a low-status way. A psychiatrist, a doctor and possibly even the vicar may be able to get away with the haughty manner and the flying visit; a social worker, however, is expected to fulfil a certain role if he is to avoid the unspoken charge, 'Who does he think he is to behave like that?'

The subtlety of these interactions is conveyed by the comment of a medical social worker who went to visit the home of a professional man in hospital. Notice the differential status implied by who visits whom.

I knocked on the door fairly firmly and waited; then, as there was no sound, I knocked again. Mrs Harrington opened the door with raised eye-brows, and in that instant I *knew* that the interview was going to go badly. Knocking twice had sounded peremptory; who was I to knock like that at her door?

Maintaining the communication

We are all familiar with the flurry of confusion which occurs when two people begin to speak at the same moment. Unless there is a clear indication of precedence it often takes several seconds before the social tension resulting from these muddled cues is dissipated by one speaker's insistence upon deferring to the other, and before the smoothly timed exchange of speech is re-established. (Needless to say, I refer to the convention prevailing among adults: children have to be taught not to interrupt.) This mild discomfort points up the social skill in which we have been trained of reading intention to speak, reluctance to speak, or frustrated desire to speak in those about us. 'I think Mr Smith will burst if we don't hear what he has to say,' says the chairman at a public meeting. Kendon (1972) was able to show moreover that not only do gestures complement speech in a general way, but that the two are linked down to the level of the word, with more expansive gestures corresponding to larger verbal units like paragraphs, and more discreet ones corresponding to sentences.

A great deal of speech exchange has of course a purely social value: 'How are you?'; 'Fine, thanks; how are you?'; 'That's a pretty dress/nice sweater'; 'It looks like rain'; 'It's all go, isn't it?'. These and similar phrases do the useful job of oiling social wheels, and their very neutral quality serves to maintain communication without fuss. A similar function, with even less fuss, is served by non-verbal communication: the smile of recognition, the raised hand, the nod are all accepted within our culture if used appropriately. But the language of non-verbal communication has its own rules and woe betide the person who waves, or winks at the director.

The conveying of reinforcement

Whether we are aware of it or not, and whether we conceptualize our behaviour in these terms or not, we are in our meetings with clients giving or withholding reinforcement for opinions, statements and behaviours. This is best explained by quoting a passage from Argyle (1969).

If some act by A is followed by a reinforcement or reward from B, A will produce that kind of act more often. This process has been demonstrated in social situations by experiments on 'operant verbal conditioning'. A subject is interviewed by the experimenter; first there are ten minutes of relaxed, non-directive questioning on the part of the interviewer; for the next ten minutes the interviewer systematically rewards certain types of behaviour on the part of the client. For example, every time the client offers an opinion, the interviewer smiles, nods his head, agrees, looks him in the eye, and makes approving noises. For the third ten minutes the interviewer responds negatively to opinions—by disagreeing, looking away, looking at at his watch, or by making disapproving noises. The subject increases the frequency of giving opinions in the second period, and decreases it in the third period; this response is extremely rapid, and happens with a variety of types of social behaviour; the reinforcement may be any of the agreeable and agreeing social responses listed above. Some laboratory experiments have found that this process works only if the subject becomes aware of what the experimenter wants him to do; however, experiments conducted under more natural conditions have found that the effect occurs without awareness. Other experiments suggest that the person who delivers the rewards and punishments is also not aware of what he is doing—he is merely reacting spontaneously to behaviour that pleases or displeases him. During social interaction each person is constantly reinforcing others and being reinforced himself, without either being aware of it.

It is to be hoped that the implications of this evidence will not be lost on readers.

Some pitfalls in verbal communication

The main theme of this chapter is non-verbal communication, since this medium carries so much 'information'. A great deal of work, however, has been devoted to researching communication in general, and Parry (1967) has produced an account of what he considers to be the seven main barriers to good communication, which is particularly relevant to the work of social workers and counsellors.

Limitation of the receiver's capacity

This describes the process of the giving of information beyond that which the listener can 'take in'. Within the social work setting the concept applies to such situations as when the worker has to convey details of legal matters, or to try to unravel National Insurance claims which, he perceives, his client does not understand. If there were unlimited time one could go over the information again and again, but sometimes the most helpful course may be to write down the essentials of the information one is trying to convey and leave these with one's client, so that with more time and perhaps with the help of a neighbour or relative, he may be able to absorb the key points at his leisure.

Distraction

This refers to the extraneous factors which compete for our attention when we are trying to talk with someone. People with a formal counselling role are usually lucky enough to have a room set aside where interruptions are minimal, but social workers and others, such as youth leaders and health visitors, who become involved in counselling in a variety of settings often have to contend with interruptions from other young people, from the telephone and from the television. I have always found it particularly difficult to conduct a delicate interview with the television on only a few feet away, but here is a situation where one has to assess, in each individual case, whether and when it is appropriate to ask for it to be turned off. It is important to remember that if we make such a request, this conveys the message 'I am the one who is defining this situation, and whether it is all right to have the television on or not'; this message may be very much at odds with how our client understands the situation—particularly during the early stages of a relationship when we have yet to prove that we have anything to offer.

The unstated assumption

Countless misunderstandings arise because two parties in an interaction assume that they both mean the same thing when they use a word or concept, but they do not. A typical message on a telephone pad may read 'Mrs Harvey rang about her mother in hospital; will you please go and see her; it is urgent.' To whom does 'her' refer? Mrs Harvey, or her mother? Mrs Harvey lives ten miles away, and is not on the phone, and the hospital cannot give further information. One makes the best guess one can in such situations, but frequently one is wrong and hours are wasted. It is better to be meticulous and explicit about detail than to make assumptions that people understand each other.

Incompatibility of schemas

This refers to the predisposition which we all have to perceive and interpret events and information from our own individual standpoint. A strike by social workers is likely to be seen very differently by management in County Hall and by the strikers themselves; similarly, a family who places high value on sporting and athletic achievement may find themselves at a loss to understand their son's preference for music and meditation. As I have said in chapter 4, by moving round within different people's perceptions it is sometimes possible to translate these one to another, and to 'negotiate' a definition of the situation which accepts the perceptions of both but endorses neither.

The influence of unconscious and partly conscious mechanisms

This refers not so much to psychoanalytic notions of the 'unconscious' as to expectations and prejudices regarding the other person at various levels of conscious control. If one has been taught explicitly, or has acquired from one's sub-culture, the belief that immigrants or Catholics or people with red hair are not to be trusted, then that sequence of associations is likely to be reactivated each time we encounter a person with that characteristic: the stimulus 'man with red hair' may be associated with the response 'beware—he can't be trusted', and we may accordingly avoid dealings with him. What may have slipped out of consciousness or memory, however, is the intervening association, i.e. that when mother expressed her mistrust of men with red hair she was generalizing on the basis of having been jilted by such a man.

Confused presentation

In the social work and counselling fields a major pitfall is that of our choice of words to express ourselves. Training in social work, and probably in counselling too, is strewn with jargon and technical terms; at the beginning of one's training these are often very alarming but by the end of the course most of them are beginning to have some meaning for us—so much so that many of them have become part of our vocabulary. This book may be an example of this concept; although I have tried to make the ideas clear, readers will no doubt be able to point to passages which are extremely obscure. Similarly, our clients must be regarded as though they were just beginning on a course, and our talks with them should contain the minimum of technical terms; most of the things we will want to say can be said simply; there is nothing to be gained by mystifying our clients.

Absence of communication channels

Within social work, the channels of communication tend to be downwards from County Hall to social workers, and from social workers to clients. While there is some machinery for feeding information back up to County Hall from the social work level, there is relatively little machinery for feeding back information from client level to social workers. *The Client Speaks* (Mayer and Timms, 1970), is one of the earlier direct sources of information on the way in which we do our job as seen by the recipients. We should do well to become familiar with the review of studies of clients as consumers of social work (Shaw, 1975).

How can social workers and counsellors make use of these findings?

Several ways in which counsellors and social workers can try to take into account some of the ideas implicit in the findings about non-verbal communication are:

(1) Carefully watching for, and becoming sensitive to the meanings of, a wide range of non-verbal communication, and of our own

responses to this: for example, when we have lost a person's attention, do we nevertheless still go on talking?
(2) Becoming aware of the implications of one's appearance, age, behaviour, etc. on a variety of other people.
(3) Becoming aware of one's own non-verbal style.
(4) Modifying one's behaviour or practising new social skills, in the light of the discoveries made about oneself.
(5) Helping others by teaching social skills.

Watch for a wide range of non-verbal communication

Within any culture there is likely to be a whole range of behaviours, many of them non-verbal, which convey feelings and attitudes within that culture, but which may be a mystery to people beyond it. As our

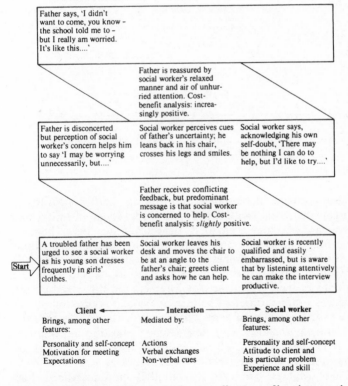

Figure 3 *The upward spiral of mutually rewarding interactions*

Some ways in which people interact

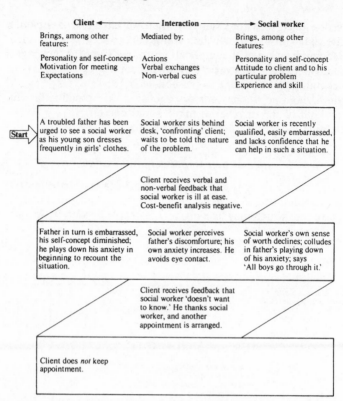

Figure 4 *The downward spiral of unsatisfying interactions*

community grows increasingly multi-racial, and hopefully increasingly integrated, so the mix of non-verbal styles and what they communicate becomes even more dense. We can never hope to become fully conversant with them all, but before we attribute 'aggressiveness', 'defensiveness', 'hostility' or any other label to those with whom we attempt to work, let us be sure that our perceptions of these characteristics in others are not based on our experiences within a different culture, religious background, ethnic group or social class; even more pertinently, let us be sure that our clients are not reacting with defensiveness, hostility or whatever because of their perception of the non-verbal messages which we are sending, and yet of which we are not even aware.

We can heighten our sensitivity to the communication which occurs between people by watching any pair or group of people interacting, whether on the bus, at a meal, in the classroom or in a shop. What happens in terms of eye contact, tone of voice, orientation one to another, gesture and facial expression? Figure 5 is a simple way of highlighting the discrepancies which often occur between the signals conveyed verbally and those conveyed non-verbally.

Verbal message	Non-verbal message	Are the two messages congruent?

Figure 5 *Congruence (or agreement) of verbal and non-verbal communication*

Within the counselling situation we can gradually increase our perceptions of discrepancies between what people communicate verbally and non-verbally and, if appropriate, gently convey that our client's unhappy expression does not match his claim to be 'All right'. As we have read in the earlier part of this chapter it is likely to be the non-verbal channel which conveys a person's true feeling.

Become aware of one's impact on a wide range of other people

Some readers may already have found that as one grows older one is able to help a wider range of people more effectively. This does not seem to stem solely from increasing experience, although that is clearly a key variable, but it is linked also with the greater credibility lent by advancing years and by the experience and understanding which people therefore attribute to us. 'Don't send us a dolly bird!' was the plea of one father having difficulties with his young children, 'Send us someone who's brought up six of her own!' If there is little I can do about my age, how important is it that I should dress for the job? The answer seems to be that unless we do dress for the job we are making our task that much more difficult because, whether we like it or not, people's perceptions will be influenced by appearance.

One major consideration therefore should be with whom we are planning to work. There is no point in making life more difficult for ourselves and our clients by, say, turning up in court tousled and late; the non-verbal messages which that sort of behaviour sends do not merely undermine the confidence which the magistrates and the police may have in us personally; they undermine confidence in the whole profession. By contrast, the probation officer who goes to court in collar, tie and nicely pressed suit, may be unable to win the confidence of the young men he would like to help: the detached youth worker in plimsolls and dirty jeans may do an infinitely better job, because he is perceived differently.

May I emphasize that this matter of how we are perceived is so important because impressions are formed the instant people set eyes on us, and their effects are long lasting. First impressions do count, and it takes a tremendous amount of work to dispel an initially unfavourable impression. We may barely have an opportunity to practise our counselling or social work skills if people don't 'take to us' at the start, so it is worth spending time examining what impressions we do convey in a variety of situations to a variety of people. If readers complain that I am implying that we should perpetuate well-worn stereotypes of social workers, my answer is 'By no means', but let us at least be aware that the non-verbal messages we convey by our appearance and manner are at least as important as what we say.

Become aware of one's own non-verbal style

Earlier in this chapter I mentioned Argyle's (Argyle *et al.*, 1970) finding in his experiment that 'the non-verbal style had more effect than the verbal contents; when the verbal and non-verbal messages were in conflict, the verbal contents were virtually disregarded.' It appears that one's non-verbal style is of enormous importance, and that intending counsellors and social workers need help and practice if they cannot, for instance, smile at others, or seem domineering, bored or off-hand in social situations. It might, therefore (and as I have already suggested in chapter 2), be a valuable experience for us to seek the opinion of someone whose work we respect on how we measure up against the characteristics of warmth, empathy and genuineness which have been found to be so central and which are so often conveyed non-verbally. Simple but fundamental questions which might be discussed concerning our non-verbal style include the following:

(1) Am I punctual?

(2) Do I smile at clients as we meet each other?

(3) Do I make sure that he is not kept waiting or if he is, do I apologize?

(4) Are our chairs positioned to indicate equality?

(5) If time is limited, do I make it clear how long we have?

(6) Do I give him my full attention—or allow my gaze to wander?

(7) Do I make sure I am not interrupted?

(8) Do I sit in a relaxed, but not over-casual, position?

(9) Does my facial expression usually convey friendliness, tension, anxiety, aloofness, warmth? What *does* it convey?

(10) Is my 'manner' confident, over-confident, tentative, condescending, cold, aggressive, distant, anxious? What 'manner' have I?

(11) Do I avoid making notes as a client speaks, apart from absolute essentials, e.g. amounts of debts, ages of children, schools attended, etc. as when a social history is required? (Generally, people do not seem to mind our writing down factual information, but do not like notes being made on their emotional condition or on personal matters.)

One could go on adding to this list, but these queries do highlight some of the important ways in which we are communicating non-verbally with those whom we seek to help all the time. It is worth reflecting on what messages we are sending.

Modify one's behaviour or practise new social skills

Suppose, regretfully, you come to the conclusion that life has not blessed you with an easy, relaxed manner, a smiling expression and a spontaneously friendly personality. Is there anything to be done about it? Happily, assuming you think it's worth it, there is. A student, guided by a supervisor, is in an excellent position to gain an understanding of his weaknesses in this area. If the supervisor notices, for instance, that the student never looks at him, or looks at him so seldom as to make him feel uncomfortable, this information can be gently fed back to the student and he can then attempt to practise 'looking at the person you are talking to'. Similarly, 'keeping a pleasant expression on your face' can be practised, as well as 'sitting back comfortably in your chair'. A daily record of one or two behaviourally defined skills can be kept by the student, and his progress in acquiring these skills discussed with and reinforced by the supervisor.

Once the qualification has been awarded, however, things become very different; the 'bit of paper' is naturally seen as an endorsement not only of one's knowledge but of oneself as a person with all one's individualities and characteristics. While there are no doubt senior social workers or advisers on counselling who feel it appropriate to comment on a junior's general management of a case, there must be very few bold enough to make what may well be seen as 'personal remarks'. Hence virtually no feedback on these issues is given and we continue to help our clients less than we might by sending them, against our best intentions, the wrong messages.

If, then, one is on one's own, without a supervisor, and yet realizes there are social skills which would be useful, what is one to do? The answer is, practise. It is quite possible to select a specific piece of behaviour, such as smiling, and quite deliberately to practise it. This does not have to be confined to working situations: on the contrary, smiling is appreciated and responded to in almost all social circumstances, and is therefore a particularly rewarding art to practise. The beneficial effects which a smiling approach bestows on the difficult task of conducting a first interview are considerable (although of course there are situations where smiling would be highly inappropriate). Such skills, however, and other similar ones such as looking at people when speaking, are not acquired without practice, but when they are practised they soon begin to bring their own rewards.

Help others by teaching social skills

If we were lucky enough to have learned social skills easily in childhood, or to have acquired them with difficulty later, then we are in a position to help those of our clients who may never have realized that they are important. Many young people concerned primarily with behaving in a way acceptable to the peer group, may have an inappropriate scorn for 'fancy manners', perhaps equating them with middle-class or capitalist values. Yet we may well be doing these youngsters a service if we explain to them the innate basis of much non-verbal communication, relating the messages it sends not so much to a class or politico-economic system as to indications of friendliness developed by our animal forebears.

In this way young people can be helped, by role-play or similar methods, to practise coping with interview panels or with difficult social situations like visiting a solicitor. Just as all manner of salons and parlours have sprung up to remedy the deficiencies of our appearance, and to teach us skills in grooming, so perhaps there is a need (for the schools do not yet fulfil it) for centres to remedy the deficiencies of our interpersonal behaviour, and to teach us skills in social interaction.

This may seem very far from the role of a counsellor, but clinical psychologists are already beginning to offer this sort of help to those who seek it; I submit that anyone who works with people should not only be aware, for their own sake, of the importance of non-verbal communication, but should be prepared where appropriate to discuss and perhaps teach such knowledge to those who seek help. Understanding the effect of early impressions and actually practising social skills may well lead to a much happier outcome for a client than hours of examining his emotions.

Part three

Some ways in which people learn and change

Chapter 6

Social learning theory

One of the areas in which a few fragments of fairly reliable theory to which I referred in the first chapter are emerging is that of learning. This is not surprising, since the area is one to which an enormous amount of research has been directed, and is still being directed. In view of the key role of learning in education, whether in nursery, primary or secondary school or at higher levels, in training for skills, crafts and management and in the abilities which we acquire as individuals, parents and professionals as we grow older, this focus upon learning seems entirely appropriate.

Learning can be defined as a relatively permanent change in behaviour which occurs as a result of prior experience, although the change may not be apparent until a situation arises in which the new learning can be demonstrated. Thus the baby crawling on the floor who sees his mother press down the door handle to open the door, may have learned that this action is necessary to open the door but we cannot claim that he has learned this until we can see him in due course heave himself up, and pull down the handle himself on several occasions. A single event of this kind would not demonstrate learning, for we could not be sure that it had not occurred purely by chance—a 'fluke', in other words; it is the repeated evidence of ability to play an instrument, to score goals or to produce a perfectly risen soufflé which convinces us that learning has taken place, and on the basis of which we are prepared to make predictions.

Psychological research on social learning theory

It is customary in psychology text-books to set out theories of learning under several main headings, representing the main branches of investigation into learning as they developed historically.

Thus one might find headings such as
  (1) Classical conditioning
  (2) Operant conditioning
  (3) Observational or vicarious learning
  (4) Cognitive learning.
Each of these headings would be followed by an exposition of the main findings within each branch of inquiry and in view of my wish to adhere fairly closely to 'tight' psychological theory in this book, that format might have been a suitable one to copy. Such an approach is somewhat academic, however, and since I wish to clarify the relevance of theoretical material to counselling and social work I have rejected that in favour of a more general description of a specific branch of learning theory which seems both to incorporate many empirically derived principles and to lend itself particularly readily to the everyday world in which the helping professions have to work; this branch is called social learning theory.

Social learning theory focuses on patterns of behaviour which the individual learns in coping with the environment, and the emphasis is on the interaction between behaviour and environment. Some of the features of social learning theory which need further clarification, but which I have attempted to reduce to essentials, are as follows:
  (1) Principles of reinforcement—sometimes called 'conditioning'.
  (2) Cognitive, or thinking, processes.
  (3) Learning by observation of others.
  (4) Self-evaluative processes.
  (5) Perceptual processes; the understanding of what constitutes 'meaning' for different individuals.
Each of these features needs elaboration.

Principles of reinforcement as part of social learning theory

The concept of 'reinforcement' is closely associated with that of 'conditioning' and it is important that these concepts should be understood by anyone working in the fields of human interaction and behaviour. The ideas are happily fairly simple. A conditioned or conditional response or behaviour merely means the learning of a behaviour because it is associated in time with some other event which immediately followed it, i.e. that a bit of behaviour is learned 'conditionally', or 'on condition that' it is followed by some other event. The principle therefore is this: if behaviour by an individual is followed quickly in time (for this has also been found to be very important) by a happening which is agreeable to that individual, it is likely to be repeated: if it is followed by a happening which is disagreeable to that individual, it is not likely to be repeated. Thus, if Susy is shopping with her mum in the supermarket and sees a toffee bar, she may well set up a yell; her mother can silence her either by giving in immediately or after much to-do (in which case Susy has learned to go on shouting whenever she wants anything); or she can clearly and consistently say 'No', and march straight past the sweets (in which case Susy has learned that shouting achieves nothing).

The technical term used by psychologists for giving a specific response to a certain behaviour is 'reinforcing': a rewarding response is a 'positive reinforcement' and a penalizing response is a 'punishment'. Below are some definitions which may serve to clarify the principles involved.

What is meant by reinforcement

Positive reinforcement (*reward*) This is any event which has the effect, when presented, of increasing the probability of the behaviour which preceded it occurring again. Positive reinforcements are personal to each individual but often take the form of tangible items, such as money, sweets and so on, or of social recognition, such as thanks, praise, appreciation, and attention and promotion.

Negative reinforcement This is technically any happening which, because it is unpleasant (such as loud noise) has the same effect as positive reinforcement when it stops. In popular usage, however, negative reinforcement is often equated with penalty.

Penalty (*punishment*) This is any event which has the effect, when presented, of decreasing the probability of the behaviour which preceded it occurring again. This is often social, in the form of criticism, blame or withdrawal of one person from another. (Thus a person who summons up his courage in a discussion group to put forward an opinion, and is snubbed by another member, is unlikely to venture an opinion again in a hurry.)

Characteristic ways in which principles of reinforcement operate

Acquisition of a behaviour Although there are many ways in which people acquire new behaviours, one of the clearest-cut ways in which this occurs is as a result of their being positively reinforced for doing so. The giving of reward very soon after a certain behaviour has the effect of eliciting that behaviour again. This principle appears to operate whether it occurs in a planned way, with deliberate forethought, or whether it occurs accidentally. Thus a parent who is trying to teach a child to use a spoon when eating should give some thought to the extent to which she is rewarding the child for his attempts to eat using an awkward tool rather than his fingers. If one looks at the situation through the child's eyes, what possible incentive is there for using a spoon rather than his fingers—unless he receives something else out of it—namely his mother's attention and praise?

The principle is that when one is trying to teach someone a new skill or behaviour, any demonstration of that skill should be immediately rewarded; this is called *continuous reinforcement*. The same principle is valid whether one is trying to encourage a child to keep her room tidy, to increase the language range of a mentally handicapped child or to help an alcoholic to stop drinking. Any small steps in the desired direction should be continuously reinforced.

In bringing up children, or in trying to get on with husband or wife or colleague at work, we know how we want them to behave and to treat us and, particularly in the case of children, we often tell them how we want them to behave. Sometimes in response to instruction children do attempt to do as we ask: to stop interrupting, to stop fighting, to wash themselves or to get in on time. This is the cue to give immediate positive reinforcement, to say something along the lines of 'You've come in on time tonight; thank you very much', with pleasure in one's voice. In this way the other person gains something immediately for his efforts; both verbal and non-verbal recognition. In practice, what often seems to happen is that the parent or wife says something like 'Well well; so you've actually managed to get in on time for once', in a voice heavy with sarcasm; this has the immediate effect of acting as a punishment, and the attempt to get in on time has been discouraged rather than encouraged.

Providing that consistent and positive reinforcement is offered, and providing that the task of 'staying out of trouble' or 'treating me better' is broken down into small component behaviours by whoever is trying to bring about a change, rather than approached in a global and therefore unspecified way, then small 'bits of behaviour' can be reinforced regularly and frequently, and progress becomes visible. Alcoholics Anonymous arrived at the same principle when they established the practice of encouraging their members to stop drinking 'a day at a time' rather than exhorting them to sign the pledge or to recognize the evil of their ways. The satisfaction and accumulation of rewards after short-term effort provide the incentive and motivation to repeat the rewarded behaviour, and this principle seems to be rooted within our physiological or psychological make-up. Once a behaviour has become established through regular reinforcement, such as the acquisition by a child of the habit of bathing or washing himself at the end of the day, and when the parent feels that to wash himself regularly really has become part of the child's 'habit behaviour' then the need for continuous reinforcement diminishes; for the behaviour to be maintained, however, some form of on-going reward is still needful.

This occasional recognition of effort which is already fairly well established is called *intermittent reinforcement*. In the example of a child's nightly bath or wash, a weekly check, on a different evening each week, is called for. This occasional reinforcement is central in maintaining a behaviour in existence.

Readers may feel that to write of such psychological principles in a book for counsellors and social workers is inviting them to become party to a process in which people manipulate each other. My reply is that readers should indeed consider the ethical implications of these principles, for the key issue seems to be that they are operating whether we like it or not, and often outside our awareness. They are an intrinsic feature of human interaction, so it is important for people who find themselves working with and intervening in other people's lives to be aware of how these principles operate. They are, moreover, extremely powerful principles and to turn away from them because they are alien to the way in which we like to think of ourselves working, as promoters of 'growth' or as 'facilitators', seems to me both unprofessional and dishonest. They are not, of course, the whole story, but to look at a situation in terms of exactly what is being reinforced, how regularly, and whether that is what is wanted by the people concerned, can both throw great light on interactions, as well as giving indications of how future progress, in a direction desired by the client, may be achieved. For example, one can see these principles operating in a tight way when a father trains his son in his own skills as a footballer, musician or do-it-yourself man, although identification and imitation are of course also in operation: things go wrong when the son does not receive enough encouragement or make progress which he finds to be rewarding; when that happens the costs of learning how to control the ball or the trumpet exceed the benefits, and father and son abandon the undertaking in disgust with each other.

One can detect them operating in a loose way when a mother, with the best of intentions, nags her children to do their homework; her object is to get them to complete the exercises set, but instead of rewarding and commending their efforts whenever they do settle down to work, she may well be in fact offering considerable punishment, saying, 'You haven't done very much' or 'Your teacher's not going to think much of that'; in other words, once again the costs exceed the benefits, so that in terms of social exchange theory, the young person has no incentive to remain engaged in the undertaking. While the mother might well claim that she gave her children a lot of encouragement with their homework, this encouragement is often not perceived by her children as such: rather it is perceived as nagging, a punishment rather than a reward.

It is also useful to distinguish the concept of *shaping*. This is the same principle as occurs in good coaching or training, the rewarding by the teacher, parent or coach of 'successive approximations' towards the desired behaviour. It occurs from early childhood onward, as children are taught to use spoons, to hold the beaker themselves, to become toilet-trained and to dress and undress themselves. The effective teacher, sports coach or parent rewards with his approval and encouragement each move in the desired direction, using only enough criticism or negative 'feedback' to keep the pupil, trainee or child on the right lines. The same principle has been found to be central in helping physically handicapped children to become mobile, in enabling mentally handicapped children to speak and to participate more fully in the social world, and it is at the heart, too, of the developing field of social skills training.

To summarize: one way in which a new behaviour or skill may be acquired or taught is by the rewarding at first continuously but subsequently intermittently, of any activity which is in the desired direction. Since in the ordinary course of day-to-day interaction we are participating in the operation of this principle whether we like it or not, and whether we realize it or not, it is important to try to be aware of it so that we may not only detect it in operation but may also employ it constructively to help bring about the changes desired by our clients or those we are trying to help. Such an approach is not imposed on a client: often the principles can be explained and demonstrated simply and the changes desired can be then planned and implemented together. We can then both work towards common, ethically agreed, objectives.

Generalization of a behaviour   This is the tendency of a behaviour, once learned, to reappear in situations similar to that in which the behaviour was learned. It appears that, physiologically, much of our learning occurs by a process of association, so that, for example, experiencing a very frightening event seems to cause the 'firing' of certain brain cells in conjunction with other physiological experiences interpreted as 'fear'. The subsequent encountering of similar situations or situations which are perceived as similar, is likely to reactivate the association with 'fear'. At its simplest, a burned child dreads the fire.

How can we see this principle in operation in the more complex situations of human development and behaviour? Perhaps the most obvious example of this is the way the behaviours which as children and young people we have learned as 'normal' and 'natural' in our own families generalize into the new relationships we form when we become adults or parents in our turn. From infancy we are taught the ways of our family and assimilate these as part of our very identity and being, and although we may reject some of the more overt features and practices we tend to absorb without reflection and as completely 'natural and obvious' such patterns of family living as who does the washing up, whether you save or spend and what to do on Sundays. When, some years later, we find ourselves as marriage partners and parents we may consciously reject some of the practices to which we objected as children, but the little customs and ways of doing things are so well learned, so habitual, that we seldom question them, indeed we may not even be aware of them. Our earlier childhood learning has generalized to new situations and new relationships.

Who, then, is not familiar with the violent rows which can arise out of such disagreements as whether meals should be formal or eaten on the move? whether the husband or wife should get up first in the morning? how money which the wife saves from the housekeeping should be spent? whether children should be smacked or not? whether mother-in-law can drop in at any time? how to make a bed? and whose job it is to take the dog out? When two people have each come with a wide repertoire of ways of coping with life which seems to them to be 'obvious' but which is really early learning generalizing into a new situation, then I suggest social workers and counsellors do less than service to their clients if they see such disagreements merely as symptomatic of deeply disturbed marital relationships. Sometimes it may be much more practical and helpful to acknowledge the importance to us as individuals of these intimate details of domestic life, how central they appear to our identity, how they arise and how some compromise between different sets of learning can be arrived at.

Extinction of a behaviour   The dying away of a behaviour because it is not positively reinforced or because it is negatively reinforced is known as extinction. This principle also is in constant operation in day-to-day living. The husband who, in an effort to improve relationships, takes a hand with the housework and who is met with 'It's about time you did your share!' is unlikely to help again in a hurry; the teenager who clears up her room for once and is told 'Just you make sure you keep it like that!' will probably not comply; and the child who gives his mum a hug out of sheer affection and is put aside with, 'Enough of that, young man: you're only after something!' may never risk his love for her again. All these behaviours have been extinguished—often without the awareness of, and indeed often contrary to the wishes of, the persons who did the extinguishing. Surely we ought to be aware of the central importance of how we respond to others so that we can see that we do not snuff out their tentative gestures towards kindness, and warmer relationships, by our own lack of perceptiveness or sensitivity?

Sometimes, of course, it is appropriate for behaviour to be extinguished, and a clear signal that certain activities are unacceptable should be consistently sent, as by the parent to the small child who bites others. He or she needs to be watched closely in playgroup or at home for a few days so that on every occasion when he approaches another child with the apparent intent of biting, the parent can offer continuous and consistent restraint and say, 'No! you must not do that: that hurts people.' If such restraining statements are accompanied by clear non-verbal indications of the mother's mood—sharp voice, frowning face and flashing eyes, the incidence of biting is likely to drop sharply.

Awareness of these principles is now being taught to many student teachers, so that they may be conscious of what types of behaviour they are reinforcing in the classroom, for here too these principles are central. A teacher may for instance complain that a certain boy is uncontrollable, when in fact the teacher may well have been treating him with extreme inconsistency, rounding on him fiercely at one moment and then allowing his amusement to show the next. Such a boy is being offered the exact conditions required for maintaining an item of behaviour in existence: intermittent reinforcement.

Much attention-seeking behaviour can be readily extinguished by ignoring it; attention is usually a powerful social reward in many situations, and behaviour such as teasing, pestering and whining by young children is maintained by the rewards it brings: the child who is teased cries, the mother who is pestered for sweets reaches for the tin, and the child who whines for attention usually wins it. All these behaviours will extinguish if they are ignored or, if particularly objectionable, if they are consistently penalized. One needs to be sure, however, that the child's seeking attention is inappropriate and that he is not genuinely unhappy. Clearly, he needs regular attention and stimulation at other times, as well as praise and encouragement for desired behaviour.

Other principles Several other principles have been established. One is that the *timing* of a reward or penalty is of great importance. Thus a reward or a penalty should follow as soon after a behaviour as is possible, so that a clear association may occur between the two. 'You wait until your dad gets home' is therefore clearly misguided as a means of dealing with difficult young children. The parent needs to give immediate reinforcement to a behaviour, and the promise of a bicycle for doing well at school is, from what we know of learning theory, likely to be of almost no effect by comparison with regular, day-by-day encouragement for trying hard and for small achievements.

Another principle is that the *amount* of a reward is of importance. I found during my own experience that while parents claimed that they gave their children a good deal of encouragement, they were often in fact extremely sparing in their commendation and praise. One mother said to me 'I think the world of our Tom—but I'd never let him know it.' This attitude, that it is in some way shameful to acknowledge, let alone demonstrate, strong positive feelings towards others, even children, seems surprisingly widespread and is indeed part of the popular stereotype of the English: reserved, controlled and unemotional. No doubt such characteristics, if true, confer some advantages but they also deny us the easiness and warmth of relationships which can arise where children are openly and unequivocally assured of love by the regular demonstration of affection. Glenn Doman *et al.* (1965), when conducting the experiments which led them to formulate their ideas on teaching young children, noticed how the children of the 'dizzy blondes' who praised their offspring in what might have been thought an immoderate way, progressed much faster than the children of the more reserved mothers. Indeed two well-loved teachers have each independently told me recently, when reflecting on a lifetime of instruction of the young, 'I have always taught by praise'.

A third principle is that one can often bring about a considerable change in behaviour by a dual or two-pronged approach: by penalizing or negatively reinforcing some aspect of unacceptable behaviour but rewarding or positively reinforcing its opposite. The technical term for this is *differential reinforcement of other behaviour.* Consider, for example, the common practice of stealing or nicking in primary or indeed secondary school children. Parents who discover that their child steals things may become very distressed and anxious; they may either ignore the matter completely or treat it with great severity. In terms of learning theory neither approach seems ideal: the child will be obtaining some satisfaction from the acquisition of small articles at no charge, so the behaviour is unlikely to extinguish spontaneously, while to punish the child very fiercely may well increase attention-seeking behaviour. What appears to be needed instead is a response by the parent which clearly conveys the message 'We do not like stealing: we do like honesty.' In other words clear social disapproval should follow discovered instances of dishonesty, but much more social approval should follow instances of honesty; the parent is in a position to give the child opportunities of being honest and to commend him for them. Thus a child who has been caught with sweets in his pockets which have clearly not been paid for should be unmistakably reprimanded, but soon afterwards that child can be deliberately entrusted with a small sum of money to do some shopping and asked to bring the change, no more than a few pence. If that goes well he should be told that he has done well and praised for his honesty. If that does not go well then the child should have to make up the difference from his pocket-money, but another opportunity should be presented soon in which the child perceives that he is being regarded as honest, not dishonest. The only area in which a child is honest may initially be in handing in his dinner money, but that is at least a start; the parent needs to point this out, and make something of it so that the child has some positive reinforcement as a foundation for behaviour change. (I can anticipate social workers saying that many of the children who steal things are on free school dinners anyway, but there is always some aspect of a child's management of money which can be praised—even if it's only lending mother 2p for a phone call.)

This principle of discouraging one behaviour and encouraging its opposite is a powerful technique of behaviour change; it may sound a highly manipulative tool also, but the point I repeatedly wish to make is that we are operating in this way towards each other all the time; every teacher who says 'Don't hold the pencil like that, hold it like this' and every mother who says 'Don't throw your coat on the floor when you come in, hang it on the peg' is in the very heart of the business of behaviour management. As people who claim to be competent to intervene in other people's lives, we should at least be aware of how these principles operate so that we may take them into account.

One further principle is a restatement of a theory introduced earlier (p. 63): social exchange theory. For it can perhaps now be seen that social exchange theory both derives from the same principles as social learning theory and is a logical extension thereof; that is, both theories deal in terms of perceptions and assessments of rewards and penalties, as they appear to the recipient. If we see people as attempting to maximize their satisfactions, as they perceive them, which is the essence of social exchange theory, then the laws of learning theory offer substantial underpinning to this notion. If the principles of rewards and penalties as we perceive them have such powerful effects in inducing us to repeat, or to abstain from repeating, certain behaviours, then it appears that these principles rank high among the criteria which determine our actions. Are we not constantly assessing pros and cons, weighing the advantages and disadvantages, deciding what would be the best thing to do? Is not 'making up our minds' basically the same event as deciding that one course of action offers more gratification than the other? There is of course a cognitive, or thinking, component, but the assessments of anticipated costs and benefits is apparently the fundamental calculation.

This is not the same as saying that people are inherently selfish: to a person who has been taught as a child that one should always help others, it may be very rewarding indeed to spend a great deal of time helping others; the costs of rejecting a request for help may be very considerable because of the self-reproach which he feels. Another person, who has learned that 'people should stand on their own feet' may feel a sense of genuine satisfaction when he refuses a request for help; he may see himself as contributing to that person's independence in the long run, and this is rewarding to him—as he perceives the situation. It seems that we behave in ways which, as we perceive and assess the probabilities, offer us the greatest satisfaction.

Thinking or cognitive processes as part of social learning theory

The principles of learning theory to which I have referred above are to be found in any standard psychology text-book, but the social learning theorists, for example Bandura (1973) and Mischel (1973), have enriched the bald principles by drawing attention to the contribution made by cognitive or intellectual processes which occur within individuals. Thus, for example, one could not expect a child moved from one foster home to another, and then to another, to begin to respond to warmth and encouragement quickly, as simple learning theory might predict, for this child has learned the intellectual and experiential lesson that people are not to be trusted; the greater lesson contains the smaller.

Further, because we can think about situations we can anticipate consequences, and this can motivate behaviour in much the same way as actual consequences. When I discussed with children ways in which they could demonstrate the affection which they often felt for their parents but which they had learned to hide, I found that most of them *knew* intellectually which particular actions on their part would please; my role was just that of mobilizing their willingness to try once again to improve relationships after so many disappointments. My own experience of the value of learning theory and the general predictions it can generate made me able to speak with confidence of what consistent and sincere positive reinforcement of behaviour can achieve, but my confidence was rooted both in my cognitive learning and in my experience.

Learning by observation of others as part of social learning theory: modelling

Social learning theory also stresses the importance of learning by watching others. This field is expanded in more detail in chapter 6 where the roles of the two processes of 'imitation' and 'identification' are considered further. As Hilgard *et al.* (1975) write:

Many patterns of behaviour are learned by watching the behaviour of others and observing its consequences for them. Emotions can also be learned vicariously by watching the emotional responses of others as they undergo painful or pleasant experiences. A young boy who observes the pained expressions of his older brother in the dentist's chair will probably be fearful when the time comes for his first dental appointment. Social learning theorists emphasise the role of models in transmitting both specific behaviours and emotional responses. And they have exerted much of their research efforts toward discovering how modeled behaviour is transmitted— what types of model are most effective, and what factors determine whether the modeled behaviour that is learned will actually be performed.

This extract gives some idea of the progress which has been made within social learning theory as a way of understanding behaviour and how it is acquired. Kevin Wheldall's, *Social Behaviour* (1975), has a useful section on modelling as it operates within groups in general and within encounter groups in particular.

Self-evaluative processes as part of social learning theory

According to social learning theorists people respond to their own behaviour in self-satisfied or self-critical ways, and thus reinforcement has two sources: external and self-evaluative. Only recently a student told me bluntly that my approval of his essay meant nothing to him: he knew it was third rate. I genuinely disagreed with him, and had thought it was extremely good, but my honest rewarding of his efforts had no effect at all by comparison with his own evaluation.

It would therefore be inaccurate to suggest that there is any general and universal 'reinforcement' which is felt to be rewarding by everyone. Most of us value social approval, but some care little for the opinion of others; many of us seek goods or wealth, but some spurn these; even life-sustaining food and water are shunned by those on hunger strike who have set themselves what they see as a higher value than their own life; the self-evaluative processes would at such times condemn what are ordinarily felt to be innate drives.

Social learning theorists have developed a number of techniques whereby people can first determine what behaviour they would like to learn, for example giving up smoking, control of eating or drinking habits and even the control of violent and destructive temper, and using the principles of self-evaluation and self-reinforcement have had considerable success with these. Readers who would like to know more are recommended to read *Self-directed Behaviour* by Watson and Tharp (1972).

Perceptual processes, and the understanding of what constitutes 'meaning' for different individuals as part of social learning theory

I have suggested above that what is felt to be rewarding is a highly individual matter—although most of us are responsive to social approval and some of us are responsive to financial or material goods. The social learning theorists have found in their analyses that the way a person *perceives* a situation is a most important factor in determining behaviour, and that thus the major determinant of behaviour may lie in the particular 'meaning' that a given social situation has for a particular individual.

Thus a curt 'That wasn't too bad' thrown out by a normally highly critical sports coach to an aspiring trainee may be savoured for days as a source of intense reward by comparison with the near rejection of the 'gush' of the other coach whose standards are low; the former carries far more 'meaning' than the latter for the recipients. In a different vein a child who has been much beaten, may shrink back in fear from an arm up-lifted merely to throw a ball: the action is contingent upon the meaning which the child has learned to set on a raised arm. In one paper by Beck and Rush (1975) it is suggested that some painfully shy and socially anxious people had been taught to perceive the world as hostile and likely to be critical by parents who used comments such as 'What will people think?' as a disciplinary measure.

How can social workers and counsellors make use of these findings?

These principles, while fairly simple when set forth on paper, are sometimes found difficult to detect in practice. This is because such a perspective is unfamiliar to many of us, particularly those trained in other ways of conceptualizing difficulties. They are, however, in operation all the time, within the classroom, the youth club and the family, and I therefore invite readers to experiment for yourselves: you will not need to wait to find yourselves in a professional role in order to test out these ideas—you can begin with members of your family and assistants in your local shops. Simply try out the different effects of saying something critical in response to some behaviour (negative reinforcement or penalty) and of saying something appreciative (positive reinforcement or reward). You may need to be alert to the non-verbal indications of these effects.

The more professional implications of these theories, however, require further clarification and I refer you to *Learning Theory and Social Work* by Jehu (1967); I propose to devote the next two chapters to a more detailed examination of how these principles are reflected in everyday life. The first of these will consider the processes of socialization to which we are all subject, both as children and as adults, and the second will take up a number of case studies in order to highlight the ways in which principles of learning theory can be applied.

Chapter 7

Social learning theory: its contribution to socialization

Since the 1960s one of the most noticeable developments in our attempts to understand people's behaviour has been the move away from considering psychodynamic influences as primary towards accepting a range of socializing influences as all contributing to this understanding. This has arisen, at least in part, from the upsurge in the study of sociology and many consider this a desirable counter-weight to the inappropriate emphasis formerly laid upon purely emotional and intrapsychic interpersonal origins of such phenomena as premarital pregnancy, truancy and juvenile delinquency.

The concept which has emerged as offering a broader under-standing of some of the influences which affect us is that of socialization—the on-going process of response and adjustment to the emotional, behavioural and cultural influences which impinge upon the individual, and particularly the individual child. The process can be seen as both passive and active: passive inasmuch as the baby is malleable and learns, as he grows, to respond to the socially accepted language, sex roles and behaviours of his sur-roundings; active inasmuch as he seems to bring with him into the world a temperament, a predisposition, for instance to activity or passivity, a capacity to interact effectively with his mother and a preparedness to bring his own requirements to bear upon his world as he passes through the successive stages of maturation and development.

The process of socialization does not of course stop in childhood—as we adapt to the expectations first of the family, then of the school and the community and later of the wider world we are, in a loose sense, still being socialized, but since the learning of the earliest years does seem to be particularly readily acquired (perhaps through the brain being, in evolutionary terms, very receptive to the first lessons, or perhaps because they are reinforced throughout life by one's culture) this area has attracted a good deal of research. A very small part of this is reported below.

Psychological research on socialization

Before it be thought that I am suggesting that socializing influences are applied in an almost calculated way by parents to their young child, as though they were moulding a piece of Plasticine, let me emphasize at the outset that the process of bringing influence to bear is a reciprocal one; just as the behaviour and personality of the mother and father has profound effects on the child, so the behaviour and developing personality of the child has marked effects on the parents. And in our culture both parties are unable to withdraw from the relationship; they are bound to each other.

Some of the research on socializing processes can be classified under several headings:

(1) Conditioning and shaping of the young child's behaviour through positive and negative reinforcements by parents and others: this is seldom a conscious and deliberate process, but occurs none the less.

(2) Imitation by the young child of the behaviour of others.

(3) Identification by the young child of himself with significant others, particularly parents.

(4) Role learning, within a particular culture.

(5) The part played by the child's thinking about his own behaviour and that of his parents and taking action thereon; this applies to older children.

I propose to consider each of these in turn.

The conditioning and shaping of the young child's behaviour through the giving of rewards and penalties by parents and others

Parents begin to employ the principles of conditioning, of rewarding certain responses in their babies and discouraging others, extremely early in life. Manifestly, they do not do this deliberately, or with stimulus-response concepts in mind, but it is clearly possible and sometimes very helpful to young parents to conceptualize their management of the child in terms of 'what is being reinforced'.

Several investigators have examined the intricate details of the social interaction between the developing infant and the person caring for him. Brackbill (1958) investigated the extent to which the smiling response of four-month-old babies was under environmental control, and found that it could be conditioned. A pre-test rate for smiling (called a base-line rate) was obtained while the experimenter stood motionless and expressionless over each of the babies; then in the test period for each baby his smile was socially rewarded by the experimenter's smiling back at the baby, talking to him and briefly picking him up. Some babies were regularly reinforced; others intermittently. In this way, Brackbill was able successfully to increase the rate of smiling during conditioning and also to show that the intermittent reinforcement resulted in a slower rate of extinction than was found among babies who were continuously reinforced. The amount of smiling was found to be thus related to the particular manner in which the baby's caretakers responded to him.

Brossard and Decarie (1968) attempted to refine this conclusion by examining which rewards most effectively elicited smiling; they compared several types of reinforcement, visual, auditory, tactile and kinaesthetic (rocking), used alone or in pairs. Picking up the infant was found to be the most effective reinforcer, merely touching him the least.

Such academic investigations may seem to add little to our understanding of human behaviour in general and of reinforcement systems in particular; they probably seem either obvious, or else unrelated to everyday life. Yet many mothers will remember their unhappy and anxious attempts to cope with fretful and demanding babies who seemed unwilling or unable to settle down either to play or to sleep readily, and who sought not only the presence of the mother, but her picking them up and rocking them or walking about with them for hours on end. In our culture mothers are very busy people who cannot spend hours of their time amusing their young babies, particularly if they have other children to attend to, and the strain placed on them by demanding babies, especially if they cry at night, can be unbearable. I remember my own frustration and anxiety at this stage, when all my efforts to comfort and calm my first child were unsuccessful; whenever I picked her up she stopped crying, but as soon as I put her back in her cot she started to cry again. I was completely at a loss what to do, and so terribly tired. It was with such relief that I found and read Dr Spock's *Baby and Child Care* (1962), particularly the section 'Spoiling', from which the extracts below are taken:

> If a mother is too ready to pick a baby up and carry him around whenever he fusses, she may find after a couple of months that he is fretting and holding out his arms to be carried almost all the time he is awake . . . . **How do you**

unspoil? . . . Make out a schedule for yourself, on paper if necessary, that requires you to be busy with housework or anything else for most of the time the baby is awake. Go at it with a great bustle—to impress the baby and to impress yourself. When he frets and raises his arms, explain to him in a friendly but very firm tone that this job and that job must get done this afternoon. Though he doesn't understand the words he does understand the tone of voice. Stick to your busy work. The first hour of the first day is the hardest.

Though Dr Spock chose to use the natural language of everyday life, it is quite possible to see his advice in terms of social learning theory. He is saying, in effect, that the spoiled baby is one who has become used to continual social reinforcement and who has come to expect it and demand it. The mother unintentionally strengthens this by giving intermittent reinforcement, i.e. sometimes she resists the demands for attention and at other times she gives way. If things have become completely out of hand, she has to manage the baby in such a way that the demand for attention is extinguished and allowed to die away by refraining from giving attention. (By implication there will be regular times of the day when she does give the baby her full attention.)

Dr Spock also suggests how to deal with a child who has difficulty in sleeping:

If the parents don't know how to put a stop to it, a baby may learn to wake not once but several times, to stay awake longer and longer each time, to demand not just company but walking, and to resist being put back to bed by furious crying. I've heard of cases in which it amounted eventually to 3 or 4 hours of walking each night. . . . Most cases can be cured easily. The baby has to learn that there is nothing to be gained by waking and crying. This can usually be accomplished in 2 or 3 nights by letting him cry and not going to him at all. It is apt to be 20-30 minutes the first night (it may seem much longer), 10 minutes the second night, none the third.

Whether Dr Spock realized it or not, he is recommending the application of strict ideas of conditioning. As before, he advises the extinguishing of inappropriate demand for attention by the total withdrawal of social reward by the parents, and he urges that this withdrawal must be both consistent and maintained by them. I doubted his advice when I first read it, but followed it out of desperation. It was incredibly effective, and I shall be forever grateful to Dr Spock for restoring both my sleep and my enjoyment of my baby. It is only now, when I know more than I did then about learning theory, that I no longer marvel about the effectiveness of his advice.

The above passage highlights the rewarding effects on many of us of social attention from 'significant others'. To 'be in the limelight', to 'have the spotlight on you' is often, though not always, as rewarding for children as it is for public performers and politicians, and it is often extremely useful to conceptualize problems which arise in families in terms of social learning theory, with attention and the distribution of attention examined as key factors.

This view is borne out by experimental evidence and by the increasing number of workers who use social learning theory as a key to understanding and helping. Allen *et al.* (1964) demonstrated in an impressive manner the way in which nursery school teachers were unintentionally reinforcing the isolation of Ann, a four-year-old. As she played frequently by herself, well-meaning teachers would attempt to draw her into the group of other children; but Ann apparently found this adult attention very rewarding, and this in fact maintained her isolation. To break this cycle the teachers gave Ann attention only when she played with other children; at first even approximations to social play, such as standing near other children, were rewarded by prompt attention from a teacher, and whenever Ann tried to gain individual attention from a teacher, this was withheld. Within ten days Ann had changed from spending less than 20 per cent of her time with other children to spending 70 per cent of her time with them. In order to test out whether conceptualizing Ann's behaviour in this way was valid, the teachers then reversed their reinforcements, and Ann was rewarded with attention from a teacher only when she sought individual play with them, and by the seventeenth day she was again spending about 25 per cent of her time away from the group. Finally reward and reinforcement for play with the group was again established, and once again Ann increased contact with the group at the previous level, round 65 per cent. With intermittent reinforcement from the teachers it remained at this level.

Although I know of no specific research on the topic, many social workers, particularly those who have attempted to carry out supervision orders, are likely to be able to translate the essential features of this model of social or behavioural learning to a great many of the families they visit where children are difficult to manage. I seem to have been involved in trying to help a number of families where the fundamental pattern was the same: of several children one in particular seemed to have become difficult to control, and a great deal of emotion and attention was focused on him as a result. Sometimes he was also causing difficulties at school, but sometimes the problems were still confined to the home. (I call him 'he' because the majority were boys, but there was also a considerable number of difficult girls.) Usually, it was possible to conceptualize the problem in either psychodynamic or social learning/behavioural terms, but because of my own discontent with the usefulness of the psycho-dynamic model in terms of bringing about lasting change I had come to the conclusion that 'insight' was not the goal I should be seeking. For even if I was able to bring about some measure of emotional ventilation and of understanding of some of the reasons or feelings which predisposed people to behave unconstructively, this insight or understanding did not of itself seem to bring about the desired 'growth'—at least not in terms of greater happiness of the individual or improved relationships within the family.

The social learning model, however, seemed to have more to offer; when I was able to consider a family, or a relationship, in terms of looking at what types of behaviour, or what attitudes were being reinforced and what rewards were being given either directly or indirectly, an infinitely clearer picture often emerged. Moreover, a clearer view emerged of how one could help. Thus in a family where a vicious circle of deteriorating relationships has come about, it is often apparent that the destructive and hostile behaviour on the part of the chief participants is reinforced by the attention given to it. A difficult child or abusive teenager is (naturally) often the object of much criticism from angry parents. This has the effect both of arousing reciprocal criticism and of focusing intense attention on the undesirable behaviour—thereby reinforcing it. *Seldom, in my experience, do parents give as much attention, or even any attention at all to behaviour which has pleased them; that, sadly, is often taken for granted and goes unnoticed and unremarked.* It seems almost as if we expect our close relatives to behave agreeably towards us most of the time, without recognition of their efforts, but to be open to criticism whenever their behaviour does not please us. Emerging understanding of some of the principles of human behaviour do not support this view; it seems rather that we thrive on appreciation and prickle under criticism.

Imitation by the child of the behaviour of others: modelling

The circumstances under which learning takes place have been areas of major research by psychologists, and investigators are now beginning to disentangle not only the principles which seem to govern learning by conditioning but are also teasing out the principles of learning by imitation. Questions currently being researched include the choice by children of adult models to imitate, and the features of models which influence this choice, as well as changes occurring in the choice of models as time passes.

Piaget (1951) was among the first to point out that children of less than a year regularly imitate activities of other people. He saw this as a simple development of the infant's tendency to repeat his own activities as he assimilates experience, so that the actions of others, clapping hands, playing pat-a-cake, covering the eyes and so on, are imitated because they are readily perceptible and the baby is ready, maturationally, to assimilate simple experience. Later investigators have gone on to inquire into other aspects of imitative behaviour: as Danziger (1976) points out,

> Children do not imitate everyone indiscriminately. Only certain persons are honoured by being taken as models and even then they are given this status only on certain occasions. A child may readily learn a skill from one person and resist strongly the attempts of others to teach him. What is the magic that makes one adult an admired hero and another a hateful nuisance?

One hypothesis about the source of this 'magic' has been that imitation occurs most readily where there is a high level of warmth, affection or nurturance shown by the adult towards the child, and certainly in the experimental situation studied by Mischel and Grusec (1966) it was found that a friendly adult is more likely to be imitated than an unfriendly one. Field studies, however, do not fully support this and Aronfreed's (1969) review of the current research literature relevant to this area suggests there is no direct proportional link between the 'warmth' of a model and the tendency to imitate. Warmth, however, has not been eliminated as an important component in imitation; the subtleties of its contribution are not yet understood.

Another hypothesis is that children imitate others who are perceived by them to have some kind of personal power—either over the child himself or over desirable resources. This marries with the evidence that rather than warmth itself being crucial in imitation, it is the fear of the withdrawal of warmth or love which is central in inducing the child to follow the lead of the model. This view, that imitation is most likely to occur when it is found rewarding to imitate, tends to be supported by the study of Bandura (1965) indicating that models whose behaviour is seen by children to be rewarded are imitated, and further that children, if rewarded for following a model's behaviour, will imitate it enthusiastically. In other words, the implications of social learning theory and of looking at events in terms of what is being reinforced or rewarded, are very far-reaching.

A third hypothesis is that children imitate others whom they perceive to have power or status in the social system of which both the model and the child are parts. This notion is invoked to explain the powerful imitative behaviour of young people towards sporting heroes and pop stars who are themselves no direct bestowers of reward but who are perceived by their followers as commanding great social power, and thus as enjoying rewards already.

Whatever the relative importance of each of these three possible views of the underlying reasons why children imitate models, it is now accepted in most theories of child development that the models available to children are of central importance. Since the models usually available to children are almost always the mother and father, or equivalent caretakers, it is important for those who seek to understand or predict child behaviour to look at the modelling and imitative processes occurring in a family or peer-group situation.

Identification of the young child of himself with significant others

Readers may be confused between 'imitation' and 'identification'. Some writers use the terms interchangeably but many psychologists are now tending to use the term 'imitation' when referring to direct copying of perceptible behaviour of one person by another, and 'identification' when referring to the apparent process which occurs when one person associates himself closely with another and thereby comes to behave and feel as the model does. It appears to be a process which occurs readily in childhood and adolescence, but it is also a phenomenon of adult life as well; it seems to have a valuable role in the socialization experience, and as such has received considerable research attention.

Whereas Freud used the term 'identification' to indicate a process which occurred, as he thought, when the young child, unable to gratify his sexual desires with the parent of the opposite sex, associated himself with the values and attitudes of the parent of the same sex in an ego-defensive way, this explanation does not seem adequate or necessary to account for all the data which the research oriented theorists have uncovered. Mussen and Distler (1959), for example, found in their study of thirty-eight five-year-old boys that the strongest evidence of identification occurred when the boys perceived their fathers to be not only warmer but also to be taking more interest in them and to be more rewarding to them. Thus it seems that there are more subtle factors at work than Freud could have possibly suspected, and these subtleties are only just beginning to emerge with repeated investigation.

Mussen, Conger and Kagan (1969), point out that parents are likely to be perceived by children as having great power—not only over the child himself in terms of their capacity to control his environment, but also in terms of their power over him himself; they can give or withhold the major rewards of the child's life, food, affection and security. They suggest, in accord with the ideas of the previous section, that it is this power to reward in crucial ways which brings about the child's identification with the parents, rather than a sense of vicarious sexual satisfaction. Second, they point out that when a child is told of, or perceives, his similarity to the model ('You've got lovely hair just like your mummy') this is an experience which intensifies the process of identification—just as the process can be confused if one parent produces conflict in the child 'You're turning out a no-good—just like your father.'

Several studies, including those of Becker (1964) and Hoffman and Saltzstein (1967) draw attention to the development of conscience as part of the process of identification; these studies indicated that a child's tendency to feel guilty about 'doing something wrong' was linked proportionately with the use of withdrawal of affection as a means of control (as distinct from physical punishment) and with an emphasis by the parents on the way in which the child's behaviour had 'disappointed' or 'hurt' them, as distinct from having angered them. The greater the 'hurt', the stronger the conscience.

Role learning within a particular culture

The concept of role implies a set of expectations to behave in specific ways in certain settings, and one person in the course of one day may find himself playing a strangely varied sequence of roles, each with its own set of loosely prescribed norms: in the morning he may begin the day as 'husband and parent', to be followed by a short period as 'customer' when he calls at his local garage; he may then go on to be 'teacher' at the school where he works, but briefly become 'patient' when he has to go for a dental appointment; after school he will revert to 'husband and parent' for a while, but in the evening may well become 'marriage guidance counsellor' or perhaps 'student' if he goes to evening classes.

We all have our own understandings of what these different roles involve; it will be noticed that they are all reciprocal roles, i.e. we cannot play our role as 'teacher', if other people refuse to play as 'pupils', and we cannot play as 'parent' if our children refuse to accept our interpretation of their 'children's' role. Much indignation is spent upon people who refuse to conform to popular expectations of 'the doctor', 'the vicar', 'the professional' and so on. It will be clear, however, that these distinctive roles have not the all-pervading quality which the role of 'child', 'girl' or 'boy' possess, and that the earliest training in roles is likely to be particularly important. The earliest learning tends to be the most enduring, possibly because the child is particularly malleable in its earliest years, and possibly because this learning is reinforced so consistently and repeatedly as the child develops.

Psychologists have found this a rich field for investigation, and the role learning and role teaching both of different cultures and of different families has yielded much absorbing material. Of particular interest are the cross-cultural studies: Caudill and Weinstein (1966) studied thirty Japanese and thirty American mothers and their three-to-four-month-old first babies, and noted several marked differences of response between the two cultures. First, the Japanese child usually lives and sleeps in the same room as his parents, and his mother responds to him by soothing or feeding whenever he begins to cry; in contrast the American baby usually sleeps alone and the mother often delays going to him when he cries. Second, the Japanese mother seems inclined to soothe and quieten her baby, while the American mother seems to enjoy active interaction with the child, encouraging him to smile or exchange baby talk. The authors of the study consider that the differences in maternal behaviour seem to derive from different philosophies about the baby; the American mother seems to believe that her baby is basically passive and that it is her job to mould him into an active and independent child: the Japanese mother seems to believe that her baby is basically independent and that it is her job to soothe him and make him dependent upon her and the family. If Caudill and Weinstein are correct, and impressionistically the differences between the stereotypes of the American and Japanese adult suggest that they may be, then such practices of social learning seem to provide us with much material for understanding some aspects of adult personality.

Another major way in which parents consciously or unconsciously influence their child's development in their efforts to socialize him, is in their encouragement of behaviour considered appropriate to the child's sex: from infancy boys and girls are given clothing and toys considered masculine or feminine, often of a specific colour; by the age of a year parents are often beginning to expect more out-going and assertive behaviour from boys and more docile behaviour from girls. Several studies, including Brown (1956), Hartup and Zook (1960), indicate that by age five most children are very aware of sex-appropriate interests and behaviour, and DeLucia (1963) found that between the ages of six and eight boys were so consistent in their choice of play materials (guns and lorries, as opposed to dolls and tea-sets) that he was able to use this as the measure of sex-role identification. There are, so far as I am aware, no studies yet published which reflect the efforts being made by some parents to blur the distinction between sex roles; it will be very interesting to see how far parents and children can tolerate this blurring before it is felt that there is a danger of genuine confusion of roles.

The part played by the child's reflecting on his behaviour and taking action accordingly

Several psychologists point out that the child cannot be conceived of as merely a passive recipient of adult influences, but stress rather the active participation of the child in his own socializing experience. They draw attention, for instance, to the way in which babies *initiate* interactions with their mothers rather than responding solely to stimuli from the outside world, and suggest that this capacity to initiate must mirror some reflective process occurring within young children who then 'decide' to take action partly on the basis of past experience. Further, they point out that if a child's imitation of or identification with a model is influenced by the perceived power of that model, as was hypothesized earlier in this chapter, then a complex process of perception, interpretation of events and calculation of outcome is occurring which intervenes between the simplistic stimulus-response notions of earlier investigators.

The older child, too, is manifestly participating in his own development, often in a fairly calculating way; the well-known phenomenon of playing one parent off against another is an indication of a sophisticated capacity to anticipate future behaviour and responses from two people and to weigh one against another. Within the broad framework of social learning theory Mischel (1973), for instance, has suggested that some of the variables which impinge upon what a person does in a given situation include (paraphrased from Hilgard *et al.* (1975))

(1) Competencies: intellectual abilities, social skills and so on.
(2) Cognitive strategies: habitual ways of attending selectively to information, and organizing it into meaningful units.
(3) Outcome expectancies: anticipations about the consequences of different types of behaviour.
(4) Subjective value to individuals of such outcome expectancies.
(5) Individual differences in rules guiding one's own behaviour; 'conscience'.

At this point social learning theory and social exchange theory come together, since what Mischel has done is to ennumerate some of the factors which we take into account in thinking out our cost-benefit analysis.

How can social workers and counsellors make use of these findings?

There seem to me to be several useful ways in which a knowledge of the powerful influence of early learning and socialization can enable a counsellor or social worker to help an individual or family more effectively. For the sake of clarity I have attempted to apply these ideas first to how they can help us to understand individuals, and then to how they can help us to understand interpersonal relationships.

Increase understanding of individuals

As I have suggested above, it appears likely that the effect of earliest learning is profound, and that although new ways of behaving and feeling *can* be acquired in later life the influence of this is likely to be much weaker and much more likely to give way, under strain, to earlier patterns of learning. (In psychodynamic terms, there is likely to be regression under stress to childish modes of action and attitude.) People do try, frequently, to behave in new ways; the equivalent of New Year resolutions are made by all of us—to eat less, to be more considerate, to get up earlier, to grumble less, to work harder and so on—but the powerful conditioning experiences of our lives defeat us, and the intellectual decision is often powerless against the weight of early learning.

It seems that the Jesuits' claim, broadly, 'Give us a child for the first seven years and we will give you the man' contains a powerful message; they realized, as we now do, that the psychological conditioning of a child programmes him to a considerable extent, for life. This appears to be rooted in biological and physiological processes which, evolving in thousands of years of evolutionary time, no doubt conferred survival value on the individual; this would endow him with some fundamental and immediate responses which would make him acceptable to the members of his community. In the telescoped time of the twentieth century, however, when change is detectable in terms of months rather than millennia, such profound and deep-rooted learning seems inappropriate to the intense need for flexibility which modern living requires of us.

When trying to work with individuals, as opposed to couples or families, therefore, it has always seemed very important to me to have, at the back of my mind, questions such as 'What did this person learn when he was young?', 'What was he taught about how he should behave?', 'How was the world interpreted to him?' 'What are the norms which he has accepted?' 'What were the models available to him?' Sometimes, just by talking and without a great deal of history taking, it is possible to become aware of the limitations of a person's behavioural repertoire and to see how his early learning has moulded or constrained him; how one person was trained to avoid close relationships (through identifying with the model set by his parents); how another was explicitly told 'You're on your own in this life; men are only after one thing, so steer clear of them'; how a third was taught that physical fitness and strength were the ultimate criteria by which people were to be judged; and how a fourth learned that the only rewards worth having were material ones.

The conditioning is often a good deal more specific, however, through the child's having quietly absorbed the norms of the family without anyone having explicitly taught them—'black people are not to be trusted', 'life is over at forty', 'kids are a nuisance', 'it is shameful to cry', and so on. These intensely powerful lessons, being learned so early and therefore appearing so natural to individuals, are often for those very reasons not accessible to awareness as having been learned; sometimes the counsellor, however, is able to conceptualize the difficulty of the person he is trying to help as possibly one of early learning which is no longer helpful in the changed circumstances of adult life, and then the possibility of questioning old conditioning and trying out more appropriate attitudes or behaviours becomes a logical focus for counselling.

I am reminded of the man whose wife had died without any warning at all leaving him at the age of thirty-eight with four small children to bring up and a mortgage to cope with. His early learning had forbidden sadness and tears, and from the very day following his wife's death, this man had put the past behind him and had set about forgetting his wife in the task of bringing up the children. He had 'succeeded' for a surprising three years, but then began to experience physical symptoms which he could not account for, and which led ultimately to my coming to know him. I soon heard about the death of his wife, of course, but he assured me that he 'was over this now' which at first I took at face value; it was only when I explicitly asked him to reflect on some of the unspoken lessons he had learned as a child that he commented 'Well, in our family, we weren't ever allowed to mope or sulk; we had to put a good face on things.' Gradually, with this early training as the focus for our discussions he saw how completely he had accepted 'putting a good face on things' as a primary guideline both for his own life and for the training he was giving his own children; slowly he was able to talk of his wife, to bring photographs of her, to think of their holidays and their good times together. My role in psychodynamic terms was to help him get in touch with suppressed emotion; in learning theory terms it was to avoid reinforcing the lessons he had learned so profoundly in the past; by 'loosening' the assumptions which he had drawn from that learning it was possible to allow the natural process of grieving to occur. He frequently looked for scorn or disapproval in my expression as he came nearer and nearer to tears and, happily finding none, was eventually able one day to give way to unrestrained weeping. His physical symptoms improved and he began to allow his children to talk of their mother and to have her photograph present in the house.

This is no unusual case; on the contrary, unresolved grief is probably a common source of difficulties in the experience of counsellors. I am drawing on it, however, to illustrate how the question held at the back of one's mind 'What did this person *learn* as a child which is no longer appropriate?' can lead rapidly to our understanding a difficulty in terms which are easily apprehended by both participants as well as to perceiving how to resolve the difficulty.

On other occasions, the question at the back of the counsellor's mind may be 'What did this person *not learn* as a child which might have been useful in adult life?' Such lessons as managing one's money, controlling one's temper or showing affection to one's children can then perhaps be pinpointed in discussion with the client, and the counsellor can act as teacher of the new skill.

Increase understanding of situations (i.e. involving more than one person)

Two areas in which social workers and counsellors frequently become involved are in the management of the young people of a family, be they pre-school or adolescent or at some stage in between, and in the interpersonal relationships of adults, often marriage partners. Some understanding of the process of socialization can be of considerable use in each of these fields.

The management of children and young people

In terms of learning theory, and its relevance to the process of socialization there are several key questions which anyone attempting to help a family might bear in mind.

Are parents actively encouraging and reinforcing behaviour in the desired direction while allowing undesirable behaviour to be extinguished? In attempting to socialize their child (though of course they do not think of their parental role in these terms), many young parents have some ideal of how they would like their child to behave and attempt to 'train' him accordingly. They tend to seek clean and inconspicuous eating habits, quiet sleep, social activity, either independent or dependent, in accordance with the cultural norms, and in due course dressing, washing and toileting by the child himself. Most of these activities can be attained by the child providing the parents are consistent in managing him and make sure that the rewards he receives, usually praise and attention, are directed at his achievements in the desired direction and not at his shortcomings or failures.

Any readers who know of families having difficulties in these directions, or know of health visitors who are asked to advise families on such matters, are recommended to read *Children and Parents: Everyday Problems of Behaviour* by Peine and Howarth

(1976). Another, more comprehensive and detailed manual which is based on principles of social learning theory, is *Behavioural Treatment of Problem Children*, by Martin Herbert (1981).

In the course of my own work I was frequently asked to help parents faced with regular and increasing tantrums by three-and four-year-olds. It almost always became apparent that these infant terrorists had learned that they could manipulate their parents into submission by throwing a tantrum whenever their wishes were frustrated; they would throw themselves on the floor and yell and shout until the mothers gave way; they would bite other children who were playing with toys they wanted, and would throw food, plates and cutlery if the meal did not suit them. My role was to explain to and to teach the exhausted parents how to resist such relentless exploitation, and by drawing upon learning theory, to support them in practising some control of their child.

The parents would be asked to keep a daily record of the frequency of the particular behaviour complained of, and the settings in which it occurred; this was to gain some base-line information against which future progress could be measured. Thus between my first and second visits, the parents typically recorded up to seven or eight tantrums daily. My job then was to show them how to penalize, rather than reward, such behaviour. In simple terms I asked them to show their anger with the child for this behaviour both verbally and non-verbally by saying 'No!' to him in a sharp tone and with a fierce expression, and to do this consistently on each occasion that he threw a tantrum. If he still persisted, I encouraged them to make sure that he gained no reward from such behaviour, either in material or social terms; in other words he should briefly be isolated in a separate room, such as a bedroom or bathroom, to complete his tantrum. At the same time I encouraged the parents to give much praise for the opposite and acceptable behaviours. As the theory is such an impressive one in its predictive capacity and as, moreover, it was supported by my enthusiasm for it, it was possible to help a considerable number of families in this way. The record of tantrums per day showed a steep decline.

The principle to bear in mind when trying to manage a difficult child is that it is the *desirable* behaviour which should receive recognition and attention.

Are parents offering young people an appropriate model of the behaviour they are seeking from their child?   'Do as I say, and not as I do' is a wry recognition of the powerful influence set by such models as parents, teachers and youth leaders. The socialization of young children is by no means always a programme of formal instruction; as many people have noticed, it is the unspoken norms of a family which often carry the great weight of influence. If mother is untidy, her daughters are likely to be untidy also; if dad smokes and drinks heavily, why should not his sons?

In searching, then, to help parents in the management of their children, one question which might always be in the forefront of a social worker's mind is, to what model of behaviour is the youngster, be he toddler or teenager, being exposed? To take a simple example, swearing by children is not generally approved of in our culture, but not only do parents, while complaining of this, frequently provide a model of this behaviour for their children but they reinforce swearing in their toddlers by laughing delightedly when the three year old starts 'effing and blinding'. Therefore, questions which might be tactfully discussed between social worker and parents who are complaining of their child include: If he bawls, do the other members of the family bawl at each other; if so, is it surprising that he does? If he's cheeky and his parents think he 'brings it home from school', do these same parents make clear that imitating such models at home is not acceptable, and demonstrate this attitude consistently? If he's starting to drink very young, does dad take him with him to the pub now and again and, while avoiding moralizing, provide a model of sensible drinking behaviour?

The consistent demonstration of the behaviour which parents wish children to imitate is a powerful inducement to that imitation.

Interpersonal, e.g. marital situations

Similarly, when trying to be of help first in understanding and then in trying to improve interpersonal relationships, it can be useful for the counsellor to bear in mind a number of questions. Sometimes these will be of direct relevance to the immediate subjects at dispute; at others the answers may merely provide a setting against which other arguments are set. Following are a few questions, there are doubtless others.

What is the nature of the early learning or socialization which each partner has brought to the marriage? Are the two patterns harmonious or not? The simplest example of this is the cultural clash which often occurs when an Easterner marries a Westerner, or even a Scot marries a Londoner. What we have learned as children seems so natural, so obvious and so sensible that to find one's partner has learned other, perhaps contradictory, lessons can be disruptive to an extent quite out of proportion to its apparent cause. In my experience family rows involving great bitterness have arisen not only out of major and well-publicized topics such as who is the bread-winner, and whether wives should go out to work, but over such apparent trivia as how to spend Christmas (quietly, with the family, or having a slap-up do in a hotel), the management of washing and ironing (it should all be finished on the same day, or can be done as time becomes available during the week) and where to keep the biscuits (alongside the cake in the same tin, or in their own box with a closely fitting lid to preserve crispness.) As the arguments rage, each partner defends his or her position as 'natural', 'obvious' and 'what all sensible people do', and not only does one's very identity and worth seem to be under attack, but that of one's entire family, nay one's ancestors, too.

Such cultural and mini-cultural clashes are, however, both bitter and entirely understandable in view of what we now know of early learning and the emotional investment which often seems to accompany it. The counsellor will probably do well to be able to view such conflict in terms of early socialization rather than looking for symbolic reasons why one husband insists that the bed be made in a certain way (as he was accustomed to, as a child) and why another fights with his wife because she manages the housekeeping money differently from his mother. Both partners need recognition of the validity of their own childhood experiences, and the counsellor should avoid endorsing any one cultural norm as 'natural', thus conveying that the other, by implication, must be 'wrong'. Once these early lessons are acknowledged as both 'right' (even if not always useful in the changed circumstances of married life) then both partners can emerge without loss of face, their individual identities affirmed, and just possibly with a readiness to meet each other halfway.

One such example is that of an English girl who, when she married an Indian, anticipated a close relationship with many activities and interests shared between herself and her husband, as she had seen them shared by her own parents. Her husband happened to come from a part of India where to consort with one's wife on social occasions and in the evenings was simply not the cultural norm, and her requests for his company seemed to him strange and unfitting, as well as potentially undermining of his role in the community. To have seen such misunderstandings in terms of dependency conflicts seems to me entirely inappropriate; simple discussion of socialization customs and the interpreting of the cultural expectations of one partner to the other so that greater knowledge and understanding could lead to greater compromise in responding to each other, seems a much more appropriate response.

Are both partners clear about how each would like the other to behave in small, 'discreet' ways? Just as it is appropriate to encourage parents to pinpoint areas of difficulty which they are

147

having with their youngsters so it can be very supportive if the counsellor can, after due discussion, arrive with those who seek his help at a shared understanding of ways in which each partner wants the other to behave differently. It is then possible to set very simple, short-term goals. Such goals should not be over-inclusive, as in 'I want him to be a better lover' or 'She must be a better mother to the kids', but should be broken down into small, attainable objectives which, because the situation has been openly discussed and the difficulties experienced by each partner have been accepted by the counsellor, now seem within the grasp and hopefully the commitment of the people concerned. It is not that the larger goals are not to be sought in the long run, but that they should be reached in small, agreed stages with the support of everyone concerned.

Thus in the case of the wife who wanted her husband to be a better lover, it might be possible to clarify first of all exactly what the wife meant by this; in one case this proved to mean not that she wanted him to be more skilful sexually, but that she wanted him to be more demonstrative and more affectionate.

Once this semantic difficulty had been sorted out, it was a relatively simple matter to help this couple see that the husband had come from an undemonstrative family where overt indications of affection were discouraged, but that he himself actually felt deep affection for his wife, though he could not express it openly. Once his wife was reassured of this, things became easier, and then it became possible, with encouragement from the counsellor who also by chance acted as a model of outgoingness in this instance, for the husband to do regular small things which delighted his wife: to bring her a cup of tea in bed now and again, to have flowers delivered on her birthday, to arrange an outing on their anniversary and so on. The counsellor *taught* the husband to behave more appropriately to his wife not because such things are 'right', but because these partners came from backgrounds whose social customs jarred upon each other.

Does each partner reward or reinforce positively the efforts of the other to behave more adaptively? Reaching an understanding of an interpersonal difficulty in terms of differing patterns of learning or socialization can be helpful but attempting to implement a plan in order to reach simple objectives will not succeed unless both parties obtain enough reward from the efforts of the other, and from the counsellor, to keep them engaged in the exercise. This is why it is very important to set simple goals initially, so as to be sure that they can be achieved, and why many counsellors now ask partners to make some commitment to the effort they are all undertaking, and even to enter into some understanding or 'contract' to keep trying for so many weeks. Contracts in this form are a practical expression of social learning and social exchange theory, since each party undertakes to reward the other. Thus in the case of the husband who complained that the wife should 'be a better mother to the kids' it was possible first, to drain off a great deal of the bottled-up resentment of both partners in separate interviews, and then to explore gently with the couple how the husband expected his wife to be at home most of the day, just as his mother had always prided herself on doing, while the wife felt she should fulfill her family's insistence that women should make the most of every opportunity to develop and educate themselves. Both partners had a deep sense of knowing 'what was right' based on the attitudes of their families as they grew up; both considered the other contravened 'what was right' and so felt morally indignant. When this impasse was looked at in the light of what each partner in the marriage had actually learned in his or her youth, rather than in the light of the rightness or wrongness of the actual principle, it was possible to gain something of a sense of perspective on the problem, and indeed to reflect on other implicit assumptions which each was making because of how they had been socialized.

This understanding, however, was not of itself enough; although the couple conceded that each member had learned his or her attitude this did not prevent each from still feeling 'more in the right' than the other; it was therefore necessary to use the flexibility given by this new understanding to devise a scheme of planned behaviour change which carried inherent rewards for both parties. Thus, rather than the husband's insisting that his wife give up her job in order to be at home after school and in the holidays, as he had previously demanded, he agreed that if his worry about the children's being on their own at four o'clock could be allayed by his wife's going part-time in school hours, he would try to adjust his work programme to spend more time at home in the holidays. This his wife gladly agreed to, for she had thought she would be persuaded by the counsellor to give up her job completely, and was quite satisfied with the 'reward' of part-time working.

Starting from this base, the counsellor helped this couple see the necessity for each partner to recognize the concession that the other had made and to behave appreciatively as a response. He helped them negotiate an arrangement in which by setting and working towards small goals, e.g. that the wife should have the husband's family to stay twice a year in return for the husband's looking after the children for a week while she went to a summer school, a considerably greater degree of flexibility and adjustment to each other came into the marriage. In all this, however, it was essential for the counsellor to act very supportively to this couple, working with them on the details of their 'contract', offering encouragement and positive reinforcement to them, as a couple, when things went well, and commiserating with them, without allocating blame, when they went badly. In this way the couple moved towards offering each other a much higher level of reward than formerly, increasing the benefits of staying together and making a divorce a much more 'costly' affair.

Chapter 8

Social learning theory: its contribution to the self-concept

The principles of social learning theory provide a particularly rich source of guidance when trying to understand how people have come to feel about themselves: to understand their self-concept or level of self-respect. The principles are not adequate alone to account for the exceedingly broad range of emotions and attitudes which people have towards themselves, but they make a particularly clear and discernible contribution.

The psychological notion of the self-concept is a well-defined and explicit one, and has been the focus of careful investigation and research; it can be defined as the set of attitudes which a person has about himself, some of which may be purely descriptive—I have brown eyes—but most of which contain an implicit or explicit evaluation—I have brown eyes, but I wish they were blue. More loosely, the self-concept represents a person's sense of worth or value in his own sight.

Psychological research on the self-concept

Although the popularity of different areas of inquiry with psychology has waxed and waned, interest in the nature of the 'self' has never entirely faded, even at the height of the psychoanalytic and, subsequently, behaviourist periods of popularity. Indeed the origins of the 'self' is now a subject which attracts a great deal of research. Many absorbing findings have emerged, some of which may be loosely grouped as follows.

Attitudes and feelings towards the 'self' are learned

It was Cooley (1902) who first suggested that the main source of the view of the self is the reaction of other people, and this idea is readily comprehensible in terms of social learning theory. In other words, not only do we teach children how to behave and adopt emotions towards others, we also teach them how to behave and adopt emotions towards themselves. The well-beloved child, wanted by its parents and welcomed into the world, is told from infancy by his mother's and father's actions and words that he is 'a beautiful baby', 'a lovely child', 'a wonderful boy'; his parents' attention is and remains directed towards him and the effect of their love and care is to establish his worth in his own eyes. He feels and hears evidence of their prizing him, mixed, albeit, with injunctions about how they want him to behave, every day of his young life. To be told and to have it demonstrated day by day that 'you are a happy little chap' or 'you're a smashing little boy' teaches the child quite directly what he is. If, as he grows older, his parents tell him what they like about him, 'Your dad was really pleased with you when you mended that gate without being asked' and 'Your teacher said you find school work difficult sometimes but you always try really hard; that's what we like' then the child learns not only specific information about what his parents want from him and how they like him to behave, but also an attitude towards himself: that he is 'the sort of person who does things for other people without being asked' and 'a trier'.

By contrast the child born fifth in line to a harassed mother, coping perhaps on her own or in terrible housing conditions, may receive only a minimum of time and attention because of so many other pressing demands on the mother. If there is a grandparent or neighbour with time to tell him, as he needs to hear, that he is a 'beautiful boy' all may be well, but harassed parents have little time and many other preoccupations. So the child may only learn that he is 'nothing but a nuisance', 'a little pest', and 'always clumsy and careless' before he even gets to school. These labels are not only unmistakably negative in meaning, but they convey no information about what he should do in order to please people more; even if he tries to be particularly careful, this is likely to go unremarked by an exhausted mother, so his efforts are not rewarded or reinforced and are likely to die away. What the child has learned is a negative view of himself.

This process goes on throughout life; the fortunate children, whose view of themselves is positive when they go to school, are likely to have this view strengthened by teachers and neighbours: the unfortunate ones, whose view is predominantly negative, are likely to have this view strengthened too. Teachers, social workers and youth leaders are meeting all the time with children and young people who place distressingly low value on their own worth; the crucial thing is to recognize this under-valuing of themselves, and to take all possible steps to rectify this. For the 'self' is not fixed once and for all; people can learn to place more value on themselves and they do this, at least in part, by receiving respect, attention and consideration from others.

Coopersmith (1967) examined in detail what were the circumstances of early life which led to a favourable and constructive self-concept, and found that the following were directly linked antecedents:

(1) Affectionate relationships with parents within a cohesive family.
(2) Good communication with parents.
(3) The establishment of clear guidelines for behaviour by parents.
(4) Freedom of action allowed within those limits.
(5) The encouragement of self-reliance.
(6) The conveying of social skills—by teaching and modelling.

Michael Argyle, who has written extensively (notably in *Social Interaction*, 1969) on the concept of the 'self' and on interpersonal behaviour, has suggested that we continue to learn from other people the ways in which they categorize us, and these categories are either acceptable or not. For instance, we all usually accept without great difficulty the name, the sex, the age and the nationality assigned to us, even though these are in essence merely abstract descriptions coined because of their usefulness in general living. Most of us are less willing to accept other roles and descriptions given to us merely through tradition, or because we live in a specific social environment: 'peasant', 'housewife', 'immigrant'; and many of us also feel a good deal of conflict and resentment when we are categorized in ways which we feel to be inaccurate and incompatible with our own self-image: 'inexperienced', 'tactless', 'pompous' or 'pushing'. Most of us seek a reasonably positive view of ourselves, and to hear negative evaluations made of us or of our behaviour is painful, and calls forth self-protective responses. It is for this reason that criticisms of clients, adult or child, if they must be made—and sometimes they must—need to be made with extreme tact, and in the context of a generally supportive relationship.

'Why do they call me "Pakistani"?' asked the puzzled little Indian boy of the social worker. 'I know it's a calling word (a teasing word), but I don't know what it means.' Here was a little boy, struggling not just with the meaning of a word which he had met but did not understand, but also with the non-verbal implications of the tone in which it was said, and with the attempt to see how this description by others of himself could be accommodated in his self-concept. Several people were calling him by this term, not just one, so several people must think it fitted him, but how could he fit something he did not understand into his view of himself?

Those who work in psychiatric hospitals often find patients struggling with their self-concepts; attitudes to mental disorders are gradually changing, but many people, particularly older ones, are often deeply troubled by the mere fact of informal admission. Thus, in addition to the stressful conditions and emotions which precipitated admission to hospital, patients have to cope with all their feelings about being 'mental'.

> It's not too bad actually being here. . . . I mean, people are kind . . . but it's going out. When the doctor said I had to come here, I wanted to die. . . . I mean, how ever can I keep it from the neighbours?

Kuhn and McPartland (1954), two psychologists particularly interested in the self-concept and in means of investigating changes in it, devised the Twenty Statements Test, in which subjects are asked to give twenty answers to the questions 'Who am I?' They used this technique to examine the self-concepts of 100 patients admitted to a psychiatric hospital, and found that the self-concepts of patients were closely related to different types of ward behaviour, 'withdrawn', 'restless', 'socializing well' and so on, and also to the occurrence of grossly disturbed actions as well.

The implication is that any sudden alteration in the way in which a person views himself is likely to be accompanied by uncharacteristic and disturbed behaviour. Those who work in psychiatric hospitals, and in other institutions to which people are admitted suddenly, become so familiar with and habituated to the routines of their establishment that it may be well nigh impossible to retain the sensitivity desirable in order to understand the behaviour and anxiety of new admissions; it is perhaps in such circumstances that a social worker has a particular understanding and opportunity, provided that she can herself avoid becoming habituated.

The work of Carl Rogers and his development of 'client-centred therapy' is clearly intimately related to the increasing understanding of how the self and the sense of self comes about. Rogers was one of the earliest to investigate empirically the effects of the particular form of therapy which he had devised and published in *Client-centred Therapy* in 1951. In order to evaluate his approach Rogers obtained the agreement of those he was attempting to help to allowing their meetings to be recorded on film and tape; the contents of these were then analysed and classified in an attempt to establish exactly what was occurring in the interviews, and what the outcome was. The classification indicated three main types of transaction:

(1) Clients asked questions.
(2) They referred to other people.
(3) They made statements about themselves, positive, negative and ambivalent.

Subsequently, when clients had participated in a series of meetings in which Rogers employed his particular form of non-directive therapy, the contents of these later interviews were again classified. Analysis of the results showed two changes:

(1) The number of references to the client's own 'self' had decreased, while the number of references to other people had increased.
(2) The number of references to the client's self which were framed in a positive manner had increased, while the number framed in a negative or ambivalent manner had decreased.

Rogers reasoned that if during the course of this therapy clients had come to concern themselves to a greater extent with other people, and were furthermore adopting a more positive attitude towards themselves, this constituted an improvement in mental health. There have been a number of criticisms made about these criteria as indices of improved mental health, and a number of writers have pointed out that, as explained above, Rogers' clients were not necessarily 'growing' but perhaps more accurately 'were learning to feel positively and confidently about themselves' as a result of Rogers' consistently courteous and respectful manner towards them, which conveyed 'unconditional positive regard'. To be treated as worthy of esteem and regard was in itself restorative and curative and led to the client's increased self-respect, which in turn strengthened his ability to resolve some of his difficulties. Whatever theoretical position one chooses to adopt, there is ample evidence that many clients do 'feel better' when they are treated with positive regard, though whether that is of itself adequate to resolve more than minor problems is highly speculative.

Another specific and very engaging approach which psychologists have developed towards understanding how a person views himself was adopted by Kelly (1955). His ideas have been enlarged on by subsequent workers and a very readable summary both of the original theory and of later developments is available in *Inquiring Man* by Bannister and Fransella (1971). The essence of the theory proposed by Kelly is that there is no way in which we may be sure that we know ultimate reality, but that all of us are taught, and derive for ourselves, various ideas about 'how reality is.' Many of these ideas remain with us from early childhood, sometimes unmodified, but others are being tentatively formulated, adjusted, accepted or rejected.

If, as we hear, a piece of wood with four appendages is, from one point of view, largely empty space populated by whirling protons, electrons and neutrons, then the notion 'table' is a construct; how much more personal, individual and idiosyncratic then are constructs such as 'a good husband', 'a rewarding job' or 'a loving mother'. These are largely learned or deduced notions. Kelly (1955) saw man as 'in business to make sense of his world', and thus as experimenting from childhood onwards with possible interpretations of events, from which more general laws for living (i.e. meaning) could be deduced. The child learns, for example, 'Mummy gets cross when I bite pussy, but not when I bite teddy', and has to make sense of (to wrest meaning out of) such apparently inconsistent behaviour by his mother.

By repeated trial and error the child adopts or works out a self-consistent pattern of rules for living, which protect him from anxiety, and these tend to form his behaviour pattern throughout life. What Kelly was able to do was to develop a means, called the repertory grid technique, and described in the books mentioned above, of showing fairly reliably what are the main principles or constructs by which a person orders his life, such as 'Women are sympathetic and considerate: men are not'; 'Neither a borrower nor a lender be' and 'Blood is thicker than water.' What Kelly was seeking to do was to develop a means of demonstrating to the people who sought his help what were the main principles and assumptions by which they ordered their lives, and to show them how by accepting these constructs unquestioningly they were unwittingly limiting their freedom of action and thought. Put another way, Kelly was able to help people to become aware of the lessons they had learned, or the conditioning they had experienced, in early life and thus to reflect upon the validity and usefulness of those lessons for different circumstances in later life. Construct theorists nowadays make use of this approach to enable people to experiment with different ways of behaving, new ways of thinking and with untried, but potentially successful, strategies of living.

There is then a considerable body of evidence all pointing towards the notion that we do indeed 'learn' how to feel towards ourselves from the attitudes of other people towards us, and the way in which they treat us. The implications of this notion for parents, teachers, employers, social workers and indeed for all those whose work brings them into close contact with people are enormous; they are just beginning to be explored in a few professions, notably medicine and nursing. The difficulties are compounded by two psychological phenomena already explored in this book: perception and communication. Thus although a social worker intends to treat his client with consideration and respect, it is not his intention but the client's perception which counts; furthermore, it is often not what the social worker or counsellor says, verbally, which will carry his attitude and message: it is the non-verbal components which will convey the essence of his communication.

Some parts of the self-concept are particularly important to us

Certain aspects of the self-concept are of greater importance to us than others; some aspects are more central to our view of ourselves than are others, and more vital to our sense of identity. These central concepts have been described as core concepts.

A core concept to most of us is our sex; we usually do not doubt if we are a man or a woman, and for the most part we play the role assigned by our culture to a man or a woman without great conflict. Yet this is an extremely emotive area; the masculine woman and the effeminate man are traditional butts of mockery and amusement, and the popularity of drag witnesses to the fascination held for us by those who are willing to set aside a core concept which most of us hold dear.

> 'I can't understand it', said the young, newly married man, who found himself attracted to the thought of dressing in his wife's clothes; 'I've always thought of myself as quite a masculine type—I mean I play rugby, and I drink a lot . . . but now, suddenly, this awful feeling! It's frightening . . . . I'm not a queer, am I?'

Maleness, and the stereotypes that accompany it, ranked high in this young man's view of himself: to discover anything other than the stereotype was genuinely horrifying to him. Another man, with a different conception of maleness, perhaps one accommodating more receptiveness, might have been less distressed.

Core concepts are highly individual, but seldom discussed: not because they are necessarily private, but because it is not socially conventional in our culture to discuss the pivot of our sense of identity. It is more customary in Western society to discuss the manifestations of the self, behaviour, opinions and attitudes rather than to speak of the matrix from which these spring.

It has been suggested by Purkey (1967) that not only do we hold certain aspects of our self-concept as more central than others, but that we attach differing values, positive and negative, to these concepts:

> being a 'Negro' might be very close to the centre of Self, but could be valued negatively. For example, an individual might think: 'I am aware most of the time of being a Negro, being a

Negro is a central part of me, but it is not very good to be a Negro.' Thus, the Self is central to roles or tasks, and each role has its own value.

I would suggest that readers might find it an interesting experience to complete Kuhn and McPartland's (1954) Twenty Statements Test, mentioned on p. 154, and write down twenty answers to the question 'Who am I?.' Some core concepts are likely to emerge, and it may be useful to go further and examine the relative 'charges', positive and negative, which each concept carries.

Undoubtedly everyone's sense of their own worth varies to some extent according to their circumstances: a lone granny is likely to feel 'out of it' in a party composed mainly of teenagers, while the basic grade social worker, voluble in the general office, may not utter a word in a gathering primarily of seniors. After an uncomfortable experience, in which our self-value is endangered, we tend to hurry back to an environment which reassures us of our worth.

Another psychologist, Abraham Maslow (1954), who has been particularly aware of the importance of a positive self-concept, has suggested that we need minimal self-esteem in several fields, including personal and social relationships, employment and in the context of our own value-system. One danger is that we tend to compensate for lack of self-esteem in one area by over-involvement in another, as the following *cri de coeur* shows:

Oh yes, I know I've got a PhD and that I teach at the University. People think how marvellous that is, but what they don't know is that I'm losing my husband. . . he's going, I can feel it. He wants me to be a *mother*, and to look after him and the children, but I don't know how! The only thing I know anything about is computer programming, and they say they don't want a computer programmer—they want a mother! I don't know how to *be* a mother!

We can all sympathize with this woman's dilemma. Her sense of self-value was based on a very narrow role, ill-suited to the demands of marriage and parenthood, yet, as I shall suggest below, by using the techniques devised by psychologists, it would be possible to help her if she so wished. She could practise mothering behaviour.

The same is true of the person so frequently and readily written off as 'inadequate'; what a useless and valueless comment this is. A psychologist would want to know in exactly what respects the person was having difficulty in managing his life: in decision-making, in social relationships, in the management of financial affairs, in holding down a job, in his marriage or in what? When the main focus of trouble has been pinpointed, then it may be possible to plan a programme specifically designed to help that person learn new ways of managing that area of his life, either as an individual or in a group with others having the same difficulty. It helps no one to label a person as inadequate, or to allow him to acquire such a notion as part of his self-concept.

Clearly, core concepts, and the values attached to them, have considerable implications for social workers in their attempts to understand and assist the people they meet. These implications will be discussed later in the chapter.

Links between the self concept and behaviour

Several psychologists have claimed that the way in which an individual views himself is a vital key to understanding his behaviour. In particular, Combs and Snygg (1959) believe that the maintenance and enhancement of the perceived self is the motive behind all behaviour, while Jourard (1964) suggests that where experience is in accord with the way in which a person views himself, the implications of that experience are used and assimilated; where the experience is not in accord with the self-image, the implications appear alarming and unacceptable, and the person withdraws.

In addition, there are likely to be peak experiences or critical events in a person's life which change his view of himself in a dramatic fashion; these may be for the better or worse. For instance, one elderly lady said quietly:

It may sound funny, but the day I was elected 'the most popular girl in the school' was one of the best days of my whole life; it was only a tiny village school, and I suppose they wouldn't think that sort of thing was at all right these days, but I went home singing, 'They like me, they like me.' That little event has been with me all these years—has given me confidence, you might say. I can still feel the glow of it now.

By contrast, a man whose wife had left him very suddenly, said:

I suppose soon I'll have to consider myself as 'divorced': I never thought I should come to that . . . . I thought that was the sort of thing that only happened to other people . . . How can I face it?

This man, whose whole life and whose whole view of himself had been centred on his role as a husband, attempted suicide several times. However, with much unstinting support from his social worker, he was gradually able to accommodate other views into his self-concept, as well as that of deserted husband. For instance, he learned to see himself as having skills (in wood-work and metal-work) which other people were anxious to acquire; from there he developed an awareness of himself as having great potential for teaching, and his self-concept, from having been almost shattered by a bitter and overwhelming experience, began to develop in different directions.

How do people react to criticism? Take, for instance, student social workers. Suppose a tutor says, 'Mr Davis, this work is not good enough; you neglected to discuss your client's financial position with him at all, and you have not indicated in this report whether he has any job to return to after he leaves hospital.' Mr Davis, according to his view of himself as a potential social worker, is likely to respond with at least a justification of why he did not raise those particular topics. I am not for the moment interested in what the explanation might be: the point that I wish to illustrate is that if a person's self-esteem is at stake he is almost certain to defend it. More simply, *people do not like being criticized*. Secord and Backman (1974) have suggested that we all employ several 'stabilizing procedures' to defend and maintain our self-esteem:

(1) We choose as far as we can other like individuals with whom to interact; thus, we try to select as friends, working colleagues and companions, other people who have roughly the same set of values as ourselves.

(2) If criticism is made against us, we tend to devalue the person who made the criticism: in other words, his opinion is not worth listening to in the first place. Deutsch and Solomon (1959) found this response to criticism extremely frequent.

(3) Alternatively, we reject the criticism as unjustified; thus the student might respond, either aloud or under his breath, 'How could I ask those sort of mundane questions when he was telling me all about how afraid he was of dying?'

(4) Just occasionally, we accept the criticism as valid—or at least appear to do so.

If, as seems likely, we all use these 'stabilizing procedures', how vital it is that we should be alert to the same events in those whom we try to help. Almost certainly, the mere necessity of seeing a social worker carries with it some loss of self-esteem; the implication is that for one reason or another the person concerned has been unable to manage his life for himself—and managing one's life for oneself is a value much prized in our society.

Diggory (1966), for example, found that success and failure as perceived by the person concerned spread or generalized throughout that person's attitudes towards himself. Where people succeeded in one area, which was of importance to them, they felt more positive towards themselves in other, unrelated areas: conversely, where they failed in an important area they felt more negative towards themselves in other, unrelated areas. Thus one might expect loss of a job or desertion by a spouse to have the effect of lowering a person's confidence and competence throughout a wide range of activities.

How can social workers and counsellors make use of these findings?

I suggest that there are several focal questions relating to how a person feels about himself which a social worker might bear in mind when meeting those he is trying to help. The highly empathic counsellor will detect these without the aid of mental notes, but for counsellors in training or those who, habituated by a lifetime's acquaintance with unhappiness, have, through no fault of their own, become dulled to distress, an aid-to-memory may be useful. Such questions might include:

(1) How has this person learned to think of himself?
(2) How has what has happened to the client affected his core concepts?
(3) Is the importance of these core concepts understood by his family?
(4) How is the counsellor or social worker affecting these core concepts?

How has this person learned to think of himself?

A useful inquiry therefore, once it is established that the relationship between social worker and client is to continue, might be, 'Could you tell me a bit about how you see yourself?' If this is answered 'In what way do you mean?' the initial query might be elaborated, 'Do you feel that you're, say, a good person, or not?' or, 'Does it seem to you that people understand what you're really like?' The answers are often more illuminating, and give a much surer foundation for setting future goals, than a detailed description of day-to-day events since the last meeting.

One young woman, Sandra, who was of high intelligence but low self-esteem said of herself: 'I feel I am just not worth bothering about. . . . I'm no use to anyone—and anyone who spends any time on me isn't going to get anywhere. . . . I'm so useless it's hardly worth going on.' However, Sandra's behaviour, to the casual observer, gave exactly the opposite impression; she seemed not to care at all what anyone thought of her, gave up her job, tried drugs but gave them up because they frightened her, avoided her parents and former school associates, and sank more and more deeply into an almost clinically depressed state.

It will be apparent that the traditional approach of social workers, in terms of the principles expressed by Biestek (1957)—individual-ization, a non-judgmental approach and so on (or, if one prefers to think in Rogerian language, of 'unconditional positive regard')—is likely to be helpful in such a situation. If the social worker can be sensitive to the self-concept of such a young woman as Sandra, and perceive the isolated, self-condemning individual masked by the rebellious, and outwardly blustering personality, then one is well on the way to reaching that person. Then, having reached her it is important to be very clear what one is going to do next. For, whether we like it or not, we are from the standpoint of learning theory behaving and speaking in ways which our clients will find either rewarding or not, and they will respond accordingly.

If then, it becomes apparent to us that such a person as Sandra has a crippling low self-concept, I suggest we should examine what are Sandra's strengths, what qualities or personality traits she has which are perceived and appreciated by us, and we should convey our appreciation to her. People with low self-concepts have not, as we know from the work of Coopersmith (1967) which was mentioned on p.153, learned from their parents or form significant others to set any value on their natural endowments or their achievements; few positive features of their personalities or their behaviour have been singled out for mention (i.e. few have been reinforced) while several negative features have been persistently remarked on and grumbled about, so that the person readily comes to think of himself in primarily negative terms. However, in such cases we can plan with our clients how they may attain small but accumulating successes in living.

Some readers may object to this formulation, and say that one is 'flattering' or 'manipulating' the client, or perhaps being insincere if this is not one's natural mode of making contact with people. The point is, according to many psychologists' formulation, rewarding or non-rewarding exchanges are going on anyway, so it is vital to be quite clear which parts of a person's behaviour or self-concept one wishes to reward, and which one wishes to avoid reinforcing. It is when a person with a low self-concept finds himself appreciated and valued by a social worker or counsellor that he relaxes and becomes open to further attempts to gain his confidence and co-operation.

How has what has happened to the client affected his core concepts?

Once the initial contact has been made, a question uppermost in a social worker's mind might be, 'How does this person see himself as a result of what has happened?' The answers to this, either direct or indirect, are likely to be widely varying. As an example I include the differing attitudes towards their homosexual tendencies of two male patients. One said:

I don't know how this happened. . . . I took a wrong direction somewhere I suppose, but I don't know when or where. I never chose it deliberately—it just sort of arose in me. . . . I feel it's just something I've got to live with. . . . It makes me terribly lonely—but I don't have any worries about the thing itself. I've just got to accept it.

and the other:

I feel *terrible* about this; it's wrong and wicked and sinful, and I know I mustn't do it, but I can't help myself. Every time it happens I go out and get drunk, and every time I tell myself that I shall control myself next time, but I never can. . . . I'm in a torment about it.

The two patients were both admitted homosexuals but in terms of their self-concept found to be completely different. Methods of trying to help them had to be devised accordingly.

The counsellor has the opportunity, by aligning himself sensitively to the patterns of thinking and feeling of his client to tease out exactly what the events leading to their meeting mean to the client, and how it has affected his self-concept. The intact aspects, say, the record of regular employment, or the family affection can then be pointed out and appreciated, thus providing a foundation from which the client can work to rebuild the aspects of his self-concept which have been overthrown by past events. For example, one thing which may have remained intact from the storm resulting from the discovery that the son of the family is on drugs is that, when the truth came out, the young man in question asked his parents' help. To the mother and father who value family loyalty very highly, this may be the vital brick upon which the social worker can base her work of rebuilding relationships; but if she had failed to notice the concept 'families must hang together at all costs' held in that particular family, what an opportunity she would have missed.

Is the importance of an individual's core concepts understood by his family?

This may be just another way of saying 'One job of a social worker is to improve communication', because to focus on clarifying the core concepts of one individual to another may bring a surprising improvement in understanding and tolerance between people formerly at odds with each other. In such cases it may, for instance, be helpful for the social worker to say to the troubled parents of a difficult adolescent, 'Did you realize that he believes that whatever he does he'll fail in—he sees himself as David, the failure'; and conversely, it may be illuminating to say to David, if of course it is true, 'I've come to feel that your mother and father see themselves as hopeless parents; so many people have told them where they went wrong with you that they've lost sight of the fact that basically they care deeply about you, and did their best for you, as they saw it, for years and years.' Clearly, the timing of such attempts to interpret (not in the psychoanalytic sense of that word) the self-concept of one person to another has to be carefully thought out; it would not be appropriate early in an interview or a relationship, but this technique of exploring a person's self-concept with him, and then of drawing on what emerges as a means of making sense to those about him of behaviour which is unacceptable, difficult to understand or even frightening, can improve communication enormously.

How does the social worker affect a person's core concepts?

We are all affecting the self-concepts and the self-esteem of others by the way in which we treat them. What else is an insult but a contravention of a person's self-esteem, and what else is a compliment but an enhancement of the way in which we see ourselves? If we are insulted we feel threatened and diminished; we justify and defend ourselves; it is a most unrewarding experience which we take considerable pains to avoid in future. If we are complimented we glow and blossom; we relax and warm towards the person who not only perceived our worth, but thought fit to comment on it.

The lesson for social workers is clear; our clients, for the most part, will have suffered a considerable loss of self-esteem before we ever meet them. Our own manner, our tact, our courtesy and our considerateness will convey all the non-verbal messages about our attitude towards them; these will be the primary communications which those we attempt to help will receive, and which they will find rewarding or not. If the sum of these early communications, rewarding and otherwise, do not amount to some slight improvement in the self-concept, then the client is likely to be out when we call again.

It may, of course, be in order for us sometimes to attempt to re-shape quite deliberately the self-concept which a person has acquired about himself; as I have suggested above, those with an exceedingly depressed view of themselves are likely to require specific appreciation of what they have achieved, to prime the pump, as it were, for further effort. One woman, utterly ashamed of a court appearance for shop-lifting, and suicidal as well, was only able to take a positive view of herself again when it was pointed out that her behaviour was frequently that associated with a depressive illness following a bereavement; only when a doctor had spent a long session with her assuring her of this with unmistakable sincerity did this woman's self-esteem revive.

Occasionally, of course, it will be in order to convey to a client that his self-concept is inappropriately inflated, and that our responsibility to other members of his family, or to society in general, requires us to make this clear. The father, for instance, who, proud of his achievement in providing magnificent material surroundings for his family, has largely neglected their emotional welfare, may well be an example of this; but the chances are that, given an appreciative response by the social worker of what such a father *has* achieved, this sincere recognition will enable him to consider in what ways he may have been neglecting his children; if we feel we are fundamentally respected then we can tolerate an invitation to behave differently in some ways, but if our self-concept is wholly at risk then we are likely to become inflexible and hostile.

In conclusion, I am well aware that the self-concept is a 'construct' in just the way that Kelly (1955) himself meant and, as such, it will appeal much more to some readers than to others. Inasmuch as it can be used to describe certain learned patterns of feelings which people have about themselves, however, and inasmuch as there are recognized techniques now available of examining not only a person's self-concept *per se,* but also changes in it over time, then I suggest it offers a way of looking at people, and of how to help them, which may be useful. One particular advantage is that since the self-concept is a construct it is less likely to invite acrimonious dispute: this way of looking at people is offered as a tool, an approach, rather than as a dogma.

Chapter 9

Applying principles from social learning theory

I have already described, in previous chapters, some of the general ways in which social learning theory can be used; I wish now to describe and discuss their application to a small number of specific cases. Before embarking on this, however, it is important to distinguish between the various levels of rigour or exactness which it is possible to adopt when putting theory into practice; I have, arbitrarily, selected three levels:

(1) The level of the research study, whose rigour should be aspired to by all studies.
(2) The level of tight application within fieldwork.
(3) The level of general application within fieldwork.

It is also important at this point to explain the relationship between the term behavioural theory and social learning theory. Briefly, the terms are often used synonymously, but it has emerged from the research of the last few years that psychologists have had to take account of the multiplicity of other variables and influences which were operating when, as they had first thought, they were investigating a simple system of rewarding or penalizing behaviours. A very large number of variables, including the personality of the counsellor, his commitment to the client, his non-verbal communication, together with the client's expectations and his perception of what is taking place, have to be considered when trying to understand effective counselling and it is this complexity which theorists are having to accommodate.

In other words, although the strength of the original learning theory, i.e. the concepts of rewards and penalties, has been retained, 'pure' learning theory has now been broadened to include some of the other important influences mentioned above, particularly the social ones, and is thus now called social learning theory. To be clear about my meaning, the behavioural approach is now seen as contained within the social learning theory approach, and I have purposely adopted the latter expression throughout this book.

Let us now, then, consider the application of the principles of social learning theory at the three levels listed above.

Application at the level of the research study

This level represents the most rigorous and exact application of the principles, and is the model which practitioners should attempt to follow; it requires careful assessment, the specifying of areas in which client and therapist have agreed to work for change, accurate record keeping, the systematic application of principles from social learning theory and the recording of such changes as these principles take effect. Follow-up is also essential. This approach is characteristically employed in helping mentally handicapped children to gain skills, in helping sufferers from phobias to overcome their fears and in an increasing number of areas where people wish to be helped to change their own behaviours, such as over-eating, intense shyness, or agoraphobia.

Having become interested in the empirical approach to the study of human behaviour, my attention was caught by an article 'Behavioural approach to the treatment of child abuse', by Gilbert (1976). This seems at first an extremely improbable area for a behavioural approach, and yet of such immediate and urgent relevance to social work that I was obliged to read it. Once I had read it I could not deny the effectiveness of the approach. Since the case also illustrates the precise application of social learning principles at the level of the research study, I reproduce all of the text of that article below, with the author's permission.

Behavioural approach to the treatment of child abuse

The comparatively recently identified problem of baby battering (Kempe, 1962) has been the subject of intensive research over the past few years. This research has largely been directed towards finding the incidence of the problem, and in-depth examinations of the parents who assult their children (Skinner and Castle, 1969). In April 1974, the Department of Social Security issued a 'Memorandum of Advice' to the professions concerned with non-accidental injury to children. This pointed out the urgent need to check ands strengthen measures to prevent, diagnose and manage cases of child abuse.

Maltreatment of a child may bear no relation to the child's behaviour. More likely it relates instead to the parent's negative feelings about himself or his situation.

Abusive parents are found in all classes of society. They do not fall into any specific psychiatric category, but have many emotional and social problems. Often the parent has experienced rejection in his or her childhood and has learned to expect it.

The parent has a low self-esteem, feels inadequate, hopeless and despairs about his or her ability to improve the situation; and although the parent would like to do something about it, he or she just does not know how or where to start.

Most abusive parents feel they have no one to turn to when in need. Whether this isolation is emotional or realistic, there is a defective communication system, and no support within the patient's environment.

However, very little has been written concerning treatment. To some, a case of battering may be seen as an atrocious crime (which should deserve severe punishment) rather than a case of bad mothering. The battering parent needs educating, some sympathy and not punishment.

One would predict that blaming and judging a parent for his or her behaviour reinforces his/her lack of self-esteem and inadequacy. To call and see that 'everything is all right', count the bruises, or sympathise with a parent may be of little value, as it does not tell the parent how to cope with the siuation. Indeed it may add to the often reported feeling of futility and incompetence, and increase the damage already present in the relationship with the child.

This study illustrates a treatment approach, in the problem of child abuse, embodying the principles of behaviour psychotherapy.

Kathleen, aged 30, was referred to the department of clinical psychology on July 12, 1974. The consultant psychiatrist identified Kathleen's problems as frigidity and a strong aversion towards the first child, Sarah, aged 4, whom she could not even touch. Kathleen was afraid of ill-treating Sarah.

Parents' history

Although there was no family history of psychiatric illness as such the patient's family situation was relevant. Her father was a very successful businessman. Her mother was said to be 'emotional', had suffered from depression in the past and now drank heavily. Both parents lived in London.

Many of the factors identified by Kempe and Helfer (1968)

associated with the developmental history of abusive parents also apply to Kathleen.

Kathleen described an early life which sounded emotionally deprived. Her mother, she felt, had never had time for any of her children, and all were brought up by nannies.

Kathleen said she never mixed readily during her childhood. She had no interest outside the home and little contact inside it. At school, she was academically sucessful. She held several secretarial jobs with high responsibilities. She married in April 1968 a man two years younger and of a lower social class than herself. She considers herself to be more clever than her husband, and said so. Kathleen said she was suffering from 'depression' at the time of her marriage, but that she overcame it without medical help.

Problem

Kathleen's daughter, Sarah, was born in October 1970. Both parents wanted a girl. Until then Kathleen had been working and resented very strongly having to give up her established career. She became very depressed two weeks after Sarah was born, and wanted nothing to do with the baby. Kathleen started to smack her and shout at her.

When Sarah was three months old, Kathleen tried to suffocate her with a pillow. On another occasion she tried to drown her in a bath.

The GP had her admitted to a mental hospital in March 1971. Kathleen was diagnosed as suffering from a 'puerperal type of depression'. She was given a course of electro-convulsive therapy (ECT), but the case notes report that it was not beneficial. She was found to have a 'very neurotic personality' with 'numerous personality difficulties'.

Meanwhile the child was looked after by Kathleen's mother-in-law, whom she described as possessive and domineering. Kathleen said that she was critical of the way Kathleen behaved towards the child.

In July 1971, Kathleen was discharged home and it seems that her husband took over the care of the child. A second daughter, Lisa, was born in February 1973. Kathleen found that she enjoyed this child right from birth, and this made her more aware of the way she was behaving towards Sarah. She started feeling more guilty about it, and depressed in consequence. At the time I began to treat Kathleen, she could not cuddle or kiss Sarah, the sound of whose voice irritated her, and nothing Sarah did was right. She was smacking her again and also shouting at her. The relationship between her and her husband was deteriorating. The problem was not discussed properly and there were no sexual relations.

Because of the problems between Kathleen and the child, they bought a supermarket, so that Kathleen was never left alone with her. Kathleen then devoted most of her time to managing the shop and doing her housework. She used to get up every day at 4.30 am and worked practically non-stop until 11.00 pm. As a family they never went out and had no social life. Kathleen would not take the children out for a walk, they only went out with her husband. Sarah went to nursery school every morning.

Kathleen realised that she was avoiding any contact with Sarah, and that the child was noticing it. However, she just did not know how to change her behaviour and could not see any way of solving the worsening situation.

Treatment strategies

The patient realised that she was attempting to solve her problem by avoidance, in a manner similar to many people with phobias. Indeed it was possible to see Kathleen's problem as having much in common with a phobia.

One of the behavioural treatments of phobias requires that the patient be encouraged, in suitable circumstances, to expose herself to the feared situation while with the therapist. This is known as participant modelling. The therapist acts in the appropriate way and also prevents the patient acting in a manner liable to make her fears worse, that is, in avoidance.

Kathleen was afraid to harm Sarah by contact, but was also afraid of the harm the lack of emotionally warm contact might produce. The two main aims of the treatment were to:
(1) Prevent the sort of incident (physical harm) Kathleen feared.
(2) Present a 'good' model of how to handle the child in a warm, loving manner for Kathleen to imitate and learn.

The strategy was that once the appropriate child-handling was established with the therapist present, the therapist would then gradually 'fade out' of the scene. What follows is an account of the treatment.

Treatment

At the first interview on September 11, Kathleen was tense and depressed but could present her problems quite well. She was feeling guilty of what she was doing to Sarah. She wanted very much to change her attitudes towards her.

On October 8, Kathleen saw the clinical psychologist and myself and we explained the treatment approach to her.

On October 29, we visited Kathleen at home. We met her husband and the two children. She was talking quite sharply to Sarah and was much more friendly towards Lisa. Her husband was quiet, rather passive, making sure that nothing was done to upset his wife, so that she would not take it out on Sarah.

As outlined above, the treatment involved Kathleen being with Sarah and the therapist. In this setting Kathleen was encouraged to copy the therapist's interactions with Sarah. These actions would include games of increasing contact and intimacy with Sarah. While carrying out these actions Kathleen was encouraged to behave in a way that would indicate a warm regard for the child.

Kathleen said that as she could not 'feel anything' towards Sarah, she could not see how this approach would help 'because it was not natural', 'Sarah would know'. It was pointed out that, often, changes in behaviour precede changes in attitudes. In this case the aim was for Kathleen to change her behaviour towards Sarah, in the expectation that attitudes appropriate to the behaviour would follow. She would, by modelling on the therapist, learn new ways of behaving which then would become natural and she would, as a consequence, enjoy Sarah's company. This reward, enjoyment, would 'reinforce' the learning. Kathleen still felt that, at first, showing warm behaviour towards Sarah would be 'hypocritical'. She would only be 'pretending'. However she agreed to try this approach. It was felt at that time that Kathleen minimised her problem of frigidity, but was worried about her behaviour towards Sarah.

Treatment was carried out between October 29, 1974 and January 15, 1975. We visited Kathleen twice a week, during times when the children were at home.

Kathleen was required to sit next to Sarah at every mealtime, and Sarah's response was used as the positive reinforcer. If Sarah became too demanding, her father was encouraged to intervene. Gradually Kathleen became aware of the fact that she could actually enjoy Sarah's company; a feeling that had never happened up to then. She began to see how new 'good' habits could become established.

It appeared that Sarah noticed very quickly that her mother's behaviour towards her was changing. At all sessions Kathleen was reminded not to expect too much of herself or of the child.

Also she was reminded that some days would be better than others, and that outside events and circumstances would influence her behaviour. She was encouraged to make careful notes of these occasions.

As part of the initial behavioural analysis we outlined 'targets of treatment'. By targets, we meant the forms of behaviour she would like to show towards Sarah, but could not. These targets were put in order of terms of the anxiety they provoked, going from a low to a high level of anxiety—for instance talking to Sarah; praising Sarah; smiling at Sarah; sitting next to Sarah; picking Sarah up; kissing Sarah; cuddling Sarah and hearing Sarah's voice.

The targets were worked through with the therapist as a model. Between sessions Kathleen was encouraged to increase her involvement with Sarah, by practising what had been done in the previous session with her husband in attendance. Her husband took on the role of the therapist in these sessions.

The aim of this was to establish these new behaviours as being more under control rather than merely a function of the therapist's presence. By Christmas Kathleen could achieve the following targets without feeling at risk of anxiety:

(1) Cuddle Sarah at night, knowing that no demands that she was unable to meet would be made upon her by the child.
(2) Smile at Sarah in a natural way.
(3) Praise Sarah.
(4) Sit next to Sarah at mealtimes and also sit next to the child during the day, for instance sit on the settee while watching television.
(5) Talk to Sarah in a much warmer tone of voice, and build up a better relationship with the child.

We made Kathleen aware of the fact that she could achieve five of the eight targets we had set her.

In spite of the improvement she was making, we became aware that her depression was getting worse.

In January 1975, Kathleen agreed to see the referring psychiatrist and take the opipramol (Insidon) tab 1 *t d s* that he prescribed. As the depression lifted, she became more fully aware that she was really enjoying the child's company. So much so that from February 1975 she took two afternoons off from the shop during the week, and devoted that time entirely to the children.

It was felt that at that point that Kathleen was ready to start a programme of self-directed and self-maintained therapy. The programme consisted of targets already practised with the therapist. Emphasis was put on how much she would enjoy reaching the target. Rather than rate the 'anxiety' felt in relation to each target, she was encouraged to rate the enjoyment. A time limit of 1 to 30 minutes was set for each target. The programme was to cover 10 weeks and targets were arranged in random order of difficulty.

(1) Read to Sarah.
(2) Join in indoor games.
(3) Sit next to Sarah.
(4) Converse with Sarah.
(5) Sit down with Sarah on her knees.
(6) Take children out for walks.
(7) Put arms round Sarah.
(8) Hug Sarah in the morning.
(9) Cuddle Sarah in the day.

The basis of the self-control procedure was that, by keeping the records of the targets, with her husband's help she could see how she was progressing. Also Kathleen would become aware that she was gaining control of the situation. It was brought home to her that something positive was done to relieve the problem, and that she was instrumental in achieving this. Kathleen was regaining her self-esteem and self-confidence. Also she realised that most of the tasks were done quite naturally.

From Figures 1 to 6 we can see the steady progress Kathleen made. Figures 7, 8, 9 indicate slow progress. This was probably linked to Kathleen's depression, particularly Figure 8 which shows a target set for mornings.

Kathleen's depression showed a clear diurnal variation which was reflected in her better performance at cuddling Sarah later in the day (Figure 9). Also Kathleen was generally uncomfortable in situations involving physical contact.

By Easter 1975, her medication had been decreased and discontinued. By then Kathleen was allowing herself to learn and accept new behaviours. Her life was more meaningful, she was not feeling so guilty about Sarah, and was more optimistic about the situation.

Follow-up

I visited Kathleen at home on June 16, 1975 and July 21, 1975. The improvement in Kathleen's behaviour was maintained. Sarah does not hesitate to cuddle and kiss her mother. She appears to feel wanted and loved. Kathleen knows she can always contact the psychology department as she did on two occasions at Christmas.

Some ways in which people learn and change

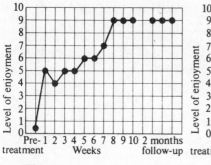

Figure 1
Read to Sarah

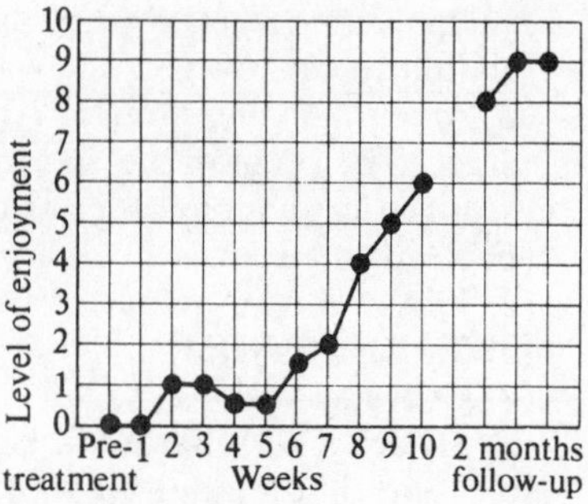

Figure 2
Indoor games

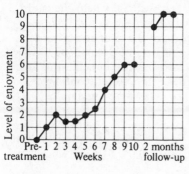

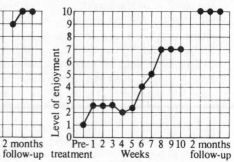

Figure 3
Sit next to Sarah

Figure 4
Converse with Sarah

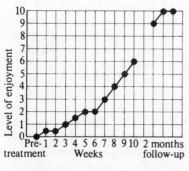

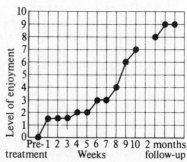

Figure 5
Sit down with Sarah on knees

Figure 6
Take children out for walks

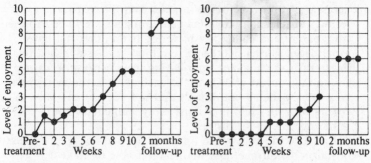

Figure 7
Put arm round Sarah

Figure 8
Hug Sarah in the morning

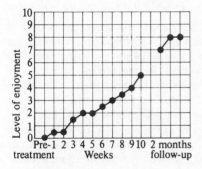

Figure 9
Cuddle Sarah during the day

Her change of attitude is reflected by the fact that she now spends much more time with the children and does not resent it. She now never gets up until after 6.30am. Kathleen knows that she must not build up her expectations and Sarah's too high. She has also learned to set her target in a realistic way, so that she has a better chance of success. She is seen at home or at the department of clinical psychology with Sarah every two months.

In the treatment of child abuse the emphasis is on preventing separation of the child from the parent. But in some circumstances separation may be necessary as a way of providing safety for the child. It may also be a way of helping the parents to work out their problems and seek help if necessary. It must be borne in mind that with separation, feelings of rejection, abandonment and guilt are to be expected from parent and child. The battering parent may not have experienced normal mothering, and not have established the basic trust which comes from having one's earliest needs met within the context of loving relationships. It is the therapist's task to help the parent directly and to teach her new ways of coping with the child in a satisfactory manner, without battering, anxiety or distress.

Kathleen was relieved to find that she had not been criticised or judged by anyone, and that she was able to make a contribution to solving her problems.

The level of tight application within fieldwork

Behavioural approaches and the rehabilitation of young offenders

One area in which research has been particularly urgent is that of attempts to rehabilitate young offenders. Although I know of no comparable work in this country I should like to draw the attention of readers to an American survey by Romig (1978) in which he reviews over 800 books and articles on the treatment of juvenile delinquents. Only about 170 of the studies met his primary criteria of having a matched or randomly assigned control group, and from a close scrutiny of these he derives two lists, one of approaches which have consistently failed to rehabilitate and another of approaches which have consistently achieved favourable rehabilitation. I paraphrase these below.

Summary of approaches that have consistently failed to rehabilitate:

(1) Casework.
(2) Direct services.
(3) Diagnosis and recommendations only.
(4) Discussion groups.
(5) Use of behaviour modification for performance of complex behaviours.
(6) Manipulating what teachers expect of their pupils.
(7) School attendance alone.
(8) Job placement.
(9) Vocational training.
(10) Occupational orientation and work programmes.
(11) Field trips: camping.
(12) Group counselling.
(13) Individual psychotherapy.
(14) Family therapy.

Summary of approaches that consistently achieved favourable rehabilitation results:

(1) Behaviour modification for simple behaviours.
(2) Involving the youths in setting their own goals.
(3) Differential reinforcement.
(4) Specificity for rehabilitation goals.
(5) Education when it utilized:
    (a) Individualized diagnosis.
    (b) Specific learning goal.
    (c) Individualized programme based on relevant material.
    (d) Basic academic skills.
    (e) Breaking complex skills into simpler ones.
    (f) Rewarding attention and persistence initially.
    (g) Differential reinforcement of learning performance.
(6) Job training with supportive educational training.
(7) Training in job advancement skills.
(8) Training in systematic career decision-making skills.
(9) Educational programmes that culminate in a qualification.
(10) Follow-up help after job placement.
(11) Group therapy with a teaching focus.
(12) Individual counselling that included the following ingredients:
    (a) Counselling to get input from youths on problems.
    (b) Diagnose the problem and the problem setting.
    (c) Set behavioural goal.
    (d) Practise new behaviour in the problem setting.
    (e) The staff member who provided the counselling directly observing the youths in the problem setting.
    (f) Evaluate and modify goals in subsequent counselling sessions.
(13) Family treatment that focused on improving the communication skills of the family.
(14) Parent training in problem-solving and disciplining skills.

It will be apparent from the above lists that the approaches which Romig (1978) found to be consistently effective can in many cases be best described in terms of social learning theory and a behavioural approach. This has clear implications for practice.

Behaviour modification

These principles of social learning are of course also those employed in behaviour modification settings, both the specific units established to help, for example, severely handicapped children to learn to extend their speech, to feed themselves, to dress and to become more mobile as well as those being increasingly employed in schools for maladjusted children. In the latter, the principle is that just as maladaptive patterns of behaviour can be learned, for example by inconsistency of management, so these patterns can be replaced by other patterns, by first establishing consistency, and seeing that it is maintained.

Thus, for example, Brown (1977) compared the progress of twelve children with severe behaviour disorders who were treated by behavioural methods with that of twelve other children matched one to one for age, educational ability, socio-economic background and type of disorder, who were treated by drugs, psychotherapy and general social work intervention. By a process of establishing base-line behaviours they were then able to set target behaviours and to explain these to the children intellectually or cognitively: it was explained that they would be rewarded both tangibly and with approval as they achieved these targets—for instance getting through a whole day without being involved in a fight. The outcome was that it was possible to discharge the children treated behaviourally after 3.8 months, while the children in the control group were not discharged before 6.8 months had passed. Moreover, at follow-up six months later, nine of the behaviourally treated children (whose parents and teachers had been taught how to employ the same principles of social learning theory) were still in the settings to which they has been discharged, while only four of the control children were still in their post-treatment settings.

Herbery (1978) examines this important area of conduct disorders in childhood and adolescence in detail.

Richard: an aggressive pre-school child

The case I wish to use to illustrate the employment of learning theory and behavioural principles in fieldwork is that of a small boy who came to the notice of health visitors in the area and with whom our department worked closely. This boy, aged nearly four, had always been lively but since the birth of his younger brother he had become increasingly difficult to manage. At first this had been confined to the home, where he would irritate the little brother unceasingly, but latterly he had begun to prove unmanageable outside the home also. He would bite other children, pull their hair, take toys from them and hit them to such an extent that the playgroup leaders found him a threat to other children and were asking that he should not be brought to the group.

It was this last event which proved the final straw to a harassed and over-worked mother; if Richard was able to go to playgroup each morning she could cope with the baby, the washing and the house, but the prospect of having him at home all day every day, particularly when it was not possible to leave the baby and him together in the same room, made her feel completely unable to cope. It was at this point that the health visitor called upon our department.

The first thing to be done was, of course, to help this mother get off her chest her distress and unhappiness about Richard. She was angry with him, frightened by his behaviour, embarrassed by the way in which other mothers would not allow him to come to their house to play, and aware of neighbourhood attitudes towards the family as a result of his behaviour. Her husband was equally upset, for he had backed up his wife in her efforts to manage their wild little boy, but felt that things were deteriorating rather than improving. Both parents were sensible, concerned people, and although I took a social history as our department required I neither expected nor found anything remarkable about either the family or Richard. 'He has always been a handful, ever since he was born', said his mother, 'but things are getting much worse.'

It was not difficult for me to sympathize with Richard's parents. I, too, had found it extremely difficult to manage two small children, one of whom did not welcome the arrival of the other, and I recalled also the relief I experienced as in due course they grew old enough to go to playgroup for a few hours each morning. So I deliberately spent time in helping this mother to 'ventilate' a good deal of very hostile and rejecting feelings towards her little boy, together with her sense of failure that her child was proving such a source of public embarrassment. In due course we reached the end of the usefulness of exploring feelings, for Richard's mother, though easier in herself through finding her emotions understandable and acceptable to me, was still having problems in managing him. I therefore asked her to pinpoint which were the items of Richard's behaviour which caused her and her husband most anger and trouble. She selected three:

(1) Richard's behaviour at meal-times, when he would throw food, refuse to eat or deliberately eat slowly. If she removed his plate, however, Richard would protest loudly and demand it back.

(2) His attacks upon the baby, sometimes direct, when he would hit or bite the baby. and sometimes indirect, when he would take his toys or pull the covers from him.

(3) His pattern of coming downstairs when he had been put to bed, asking for drinks or complaining that he felt lonely. This also sometimes occurred in the middle of the night, when he would wake his parents by repeatedly calling out.

Of these three, the one which naturally concerned the parents most was the attacks Richard made on the baby, since these were genuinely dangerous and caused the mother great anxiety. The next most irritating was his behaviour at mealtimes and the third was his coming downstairs after being put to bed. We therefore addressed the problems in that order.

Once I had assessed that an approach based upon social learning theory was appropriate, and we had specified the particular areas of difficulty which Richard's parents were complaining of, it was important to gain a record of these behaviours against which to measure future progress. (The technical term for this record is base-line data, and in the child-abuse case described earlier in the chapter this is represented by the pre-treatment level recorded on each of the small graphs.) I therefore asked them to keep a note during the next week of the number of instances each day of the three key or target behaviours on which we had agreed to focus. Richard's parents were understandably disappointed at not being given some immediate guidance about 'what to do about Richard', but inasmuch as they had gained a good deal of relief merely by unburdening their feelings towards him, and since I explained my reasons for asking for the records to be kept, they were willing to comply. We agreed that three separate sheets, one for each target behaviour, should be used, and that the number of instances of each behaviour day by day should be recorded in the form of a simple bar chart. When I went a week later the charts were ready, and we began to talk of how Richard's parents could begin to cope with the most urgent problem: Richard's behaviour towards his baby brother.

Management of Richard's attacks on the baby

I asked Richard's mother to bear in mind several principles (based on learning theory—though I did not call it that):
  (1) Initially, if Richard and the baby were together, she should try to be with them as much of the time as she could. For four to five days, or it might need to extend to a week, she should be present whenever possible to give consistent and continuous warning (penalty) to Richard whenever she saw that he was giving signs of intending to harm the baby.
  (2) This should take the form of a sharp 'No!', angry in tone, and accompanied by a fierce facial expression, each time that she saw Richard intended harm. She should then lift him bodily away from the baby and try to find something to distract him.
  (3) If he persisted in pestering the baby to the extent of making him cry he should be excluded briefly but completely from the room and obliged to spend about five minutes alone. This might be in a bedroom, a bathroom or a passage, but the point was that no one should pay the slightest attention to him during this time, i.e. he should be deprived of all social rewards. If he damaged

things in the room to which he was sent he would have to stay longer. (A small portable kitchen timer is excellent to signal the passing of the exclusion time, and Richard's mother placed it where Richard could hear it when he was sent out.)

(4) Richard's mother should, however, make a point of giving Richard her full attention for a regular period each day, say twenty or thirty minutes, when the baby was asleep. This would be his 'special time' for which baby was 'too young'.

(5) Richard's mother should differentially reinforce other behaviour, i.e. whenever Richard did anything at all considerate towards the baby, e.g. give him a toy, rock his pram gently, bring his nappy, then his mother should praise him warmly for these actions and thank him for helping her look after the baby. She should tell neighbours and relatives about such growing helpfulness, too, so Richard might receive a further source of encouragement for kindness to the baby.

When I called a week later, Richard's mother reported a great change in Richard's behaviour towards the baby; she felt more confident, which was probably attributable to her having unburdened herself of so much ambivalent feeling towards her little boy, but she now also had clear guidelines from me on which to work, in addition to a sense of being backed up in what she was doing rather than floundering from day to day. She reported that the first three days after my first visit had been exceptionally difficult, because she had tried to be on hand most of the time when the two children had to be together, and in addition to using the verbal reprimand of 'No!' and the angry expression, she had had to exclude Richard five times on the first day and four on the second.

Richard, for his part, had apparently hated being put outside the living room into a cold passage and being prevented from joining the family again until the timer rang at the end of the five minutes. On the very first occasion he had laughed defiantly and turned the lights on and off persistently but subsequently he had cried and begged not to be put outside. His parents, mindful of my injunction to be consistent, had persisted and on any occasion when Richard made the baby cry he was excluded. The chart showed a drop from four or five instances daily to only one in the two days prior to my visit. The speed of the effectiveness of this measure had astonished his parents, but I was able to assure them that this was characteristic of the way in which consistent application of these principles often worked— though it frequently does take rather longer. This change was maintained.

Richard's parents had also played their part in praising him for any kindness shown to the baby, and had involved the grandparents in the scheme. They felt Richard was still jealous of the baby, so his mother tactfully did as much of the feeding and tending as she could when Richard was out of the way, but she managed to involve him in mixing cereal and trying to feed the baby—for which she had praised him and had him 'show Nana how helpful he was being.' Nana had played her part warmly, and Richard, from being much disapproved of, was now, on occasion, the centre of attention for helping with the baby.

Management of Richard's meal-times

The management of the little boy according to principles of social learning having proved useful, I recommended that the parents should continue to follow these consistently, but that in addition we could turn our attention to the second main source of difficulty — Richard's eating habits. Meal-times were a constant source of tension within the household, as Richard managed to dominate these by demanding to be fed, asking for special dishes, throwing unwanted food about and deliberately eating slowly. The recommendations I made may sound completely obvious, and inasmuch as principles of learning theory are in operation all the time in everyday life, so they are: yet many people are unaware of this, and so are unable to draw upon what to many parents is intuitive knowledge.

(1) If Richard threw food, he should be told 'It looks as though you've had enough' and his plate should be removed. However much he protested, it should not be returned.

(2) If Richard refused to feed himself (he was nearly four, and regularly fed himself when at his grandparents, who refused to feed him) he should be told cheerfully 'Sorry, we're busy eating our dinner. You can manage.' If he would not then his plate should be taken away and should not be returned.

(3) If Richard ate very, very slowly in a deliberate fashion, he should be told, 'I shall be clearing the plates away when Daddy has finished his dinner; I'll be taking yours too then, so that I can serve the pudding.' If Richard had not finished, then his plate should be removed.

With my support, Richard's mother could see the simplicity and obviousness of these ideas; she really only needed the reassurance that Richard was not going to become under-nourished if she did not give way to his demands, and the confidence to try out the ideas. Her husband and the grandparents supported her whole-heartedly and, as the chart showed, these principles were effective: a week later Richard's eating habits had improved to the point where he was eating well and regularly with the family, one eye on his mother's hand.

182

Management of Richard's habit of coming downstairs at bedtime and waking at night

The next week I called I heard that Richard had had to be excluded only once at the beginning of the preceding week and once at the end, and I encouraged his parents to continue to be firm and consistent with him and not to 'soften up'. (In learning theory terms I encouraged them to continue intermittent penalizing responses to maintain the improved behaviour in existence.) Meal-times were now agreeable for everybody, though Richard had lost his dinner on two occasions. The morale of both parents was high, however, and it therefore seemed appropriate to turn our attention to Richard's refusing to settle to sleep and disturbing his parents by repeatedly coming downstairs and calling out.

By now the parents were perceiving the straightforward quality of the principles I was suggesting, and they themselves were able to see what had been going wrong. In effect they had been rewarding or positively reinforcing Richard's habit of coming downstairs by attending to him *sometimes*: in other words by giving him occasional attention on some evenings, but sending him straight back upstairs on others they had been maintaining in existence the very behaviour they had been intending to stop, i.e. they had been giving him intermittent reward. What they saw they now had to do was to provide him with consistent penalizing responses: every single time he came downstairs looking for attention, he was instead to be angrily received and sent straight back to bed. The same practice was to be followed if he disturbed his parents for no good reason in the middle of the night: he should not be taken into their bed, as had been their practice, but should be led firmly back to bed.

Richard responded to these management techniques as expected: the chart showed his trips downstairs in the evening lasted only two nights, and his calling out for attention at 2 am. lasted another two. After that his parents reported no further sleeping problems. Since the parents now understood the principles I was employing they were soon able to use them themselves with, as it were, only intermittent reinforcement from me. When I made a follow-up visit some weeks later things were progressing smoothly, and both parents felt they 'now had a different child.' They had discussed with the playgroup leaders the need for very firm handling whenever Richard became aggressive towards another child; the leaders had taken the point and responded immediately; if Richard hurt another child he had to sit alone on a special chair for five minutes and no one was to take the slightest notice of him however hard he sought attention. When he was considerate to another child, however, he was made much of and openly praised. The playgroup leaders were no longer asking for

Richard to be withdrawn from the group. There are several points to be made here:

(1) The principles which I was clarifying with Richard's parents are not particularly original: confident and intuitive parents have been acting on them for thousands of years, but psychology has contributed some of the detail and subtlety of the underlying theory.

(2) I was drawing on a wide range of theoretical material in my efforts to help Richard's parents: in a sense my encouraging Richard's mother to ventilate her anger and resentment towards her little boy was essential in order to give her the equanimity to try new methods of handling him, while her giving of special time to Richard while the baby was asleep could be seen from the psychodynamic standpoint as primary reassurance to the little boy that his aggressive feelings had not deprived him of the comfort and love of his mother also. In other words, social learning theory provided the core of the approach on this occasion but used within an eclectic framework.

(3) The adjustment of rewards and penalties, or positive and penalizing responses, have to be matched to the individual and couched in terms of what has meaning for the person concerned. The use of social learning theory in the management of difficult older children or of adolescents would require the adoption of rather different rewards and penalties. It is usually safe to assume that people respond to social approval and appreciation, but even that is not an infallible principle; it may depend on the role or perceived sincerity of the approver; as a rule of thumb though, people seem to be crying out for appreciation (call it 'love', if you will) and the expression of this is a powerful source of pleasure to most of the human race.

(4) The role of non-verbal communication seems to have been particularly important here; not only did Richard's mother report that Richard seemed to be particularly aware of her angry tone of voice and disapproving expression, but also said that she could tell when Richard was 'up to something' from the way he kept an eye on her. I have no doubt also that my own enthusiasm for the ideas which I was explaining to them, stemming from my having been able to use them predictively in the past, as well as from my identification with these parents who were having such a difficult time with their youngster, played a considerable part in enlisting their co-operation and willingness to try out what I was suggesting. In other words some of the success of this case derived from my being (unwittingly) 'high in persuasiveness.'

The level of general application within fieldwork

Learning theory, and social learning theory, have given birth to a large number of techniques and ways of working; these include behaviour modification, desensitization to fearful situations, contract making and self-modification. A result of the variety of resources available and of the difficulty which social workers and counsellors have in using these approaches in a 'tight' way because of the intensely varied and demanding nature of their work has been the emergence of a number of general applications of social learning theory. These do not meet strict theoretical criteria, but they nevertheless appear to have a useful contribution to make to social work and counselling practice. I give below three instances where principles from social learning theory have been applied in a fairly general way within ordinary fieldwork practice.

Principles of social learning theory within family therapy

I am aware, of course, of the great popularity of 'family therapy' among social work practitioners, and I feel it appropriate that any book written for social workers and counsellors should take this popularity into consideration. I feel it important to be open to as many varied ways of helping people as prove effective, and if family therapy is effective then I have no wish to be other than positive towards this fairly new approach. I hope, however, that we may soon look for some empirical evidence that family therapy generates theories which can be used predictively; for example, that working with the family together produces significantly better results (for everybody) than working with individuals, or that using the techniques of family therapy has results which can be clearly distinguished from the effects of the therapist's personality.

Experimental psychologists are, however, taking family therapy seriously, as they do many of the other approaches put forward in an attempt to promote human happiness; what they seem to be finding is that many of these approaches are employing the same concepts but are developing their own terminology and jargon to express them. This leads to much confusion. Since, however, my wish is to establish common ground between practitioners rather than to be divisive, I have been glad to discover and to be able to describe something of how social learning theorists have applied their understanding to the concepts of family therapy producing, as it seems to me, a happy marriage. Liberman (1970) writes of the application of learning theory to family therapy as providing three areas of particular concern for the therapist. They are:

Creating and maintaining a positive therapeutic alliance

This is our old friend, the good relationship. The implication is that by demonstrating concern and empathy for *all* the members of the family, the counsellor or therapist conveys his respect for them both as individuals and as part of a family 'system'. In other words, by his attitudes and actions, as well as by his words, he reinforces and models the harmonious and rewarding aspects of family life, so that these grow stronger. This is not to suggest that he should ignore the difficulties—of course he should not; but if, as I suggest, the principles of reinforcement are in operation throughout our everyday life, then what the counsellor attends to (reinforces by attending to it) is of great importance: in so much of counselling by far the greater part of the interview seems to be devoted to discussing the problems of a relationship, while almost no time is given to the successful aspects or strengths. This, of itself, reinforces the client to preoccupy himself with negatives rather than positives. Liberman suggests that without this 'positive alliance' between the therapist and those he is helping, there is likely to be little successful intervention, and explains that in learning theory terms it is this relationship

> which permits the therapist to serve as social reinforcer and model: in other words, to build up adaptive behaviours and to allow maladaptive behaviours to extinguish. The therapist is an effective reinforcer and model for the patients to the extent that the patients value him and hold him in high regard and warm esteem.

Making a behavioural analysis of the problem(s)

This consists, Liberman suggests, of the therapist, in collaboration with the family, asking two major questions:
(1) What behaviour is maladaptive or problematic—what behaviour in the designated patient should be increased or decreased? Each person in turn is asked:
   (a) What changes would you like to see in others of the family?
   (b) How would you like to be different from the way you are now?
   Answering these questions forces the therapist to choose carefully *specific behavioural goals*.
(2) What is maintaining undesirable behaviour or reducing the likelihood of more adaptive responses? The mutual patterns of social reinforcement in the family deserve special scrutiny in this analysis since their deciphering and clarification become central to an understanding of the case and to the formulation of therapeutic strategy.

The suggestion that the patterns of social reinforcement in the family are deserving of special scrutiny I particulary endorse: often an adolescent's unacceptable behaviour, for example, is being maintained by inconsistent management: Dad says he should be in by 11 p.m. but Mum stays up and lets him in quietly at 1 a.m. whenever Dad is on night-shift; a primary school child learns with astonishing skill to play off one parent against another; a toddler manages effectively to break up a marriage by screaming unless his mother always sleeps in his bed rather than with her husband. When what is happening is understood in terms of what is being reinforced, then the specific behavioural goals, together with how they can be achieved, often become infinitely clearer.

Choosing and implementing of therapeutic strategy and tactics

In this area it is the counsellor's responsibility to draw up what one might call a 'contract', i.e. a series of small-scale goals which the members of the family can agree to reach, and to help each other to reach, together.

It is particularly important that the earliest small-scale goals should be easily attainable, so that members of the family readily achieve them, and thereby not only enjoy the satisfaction of so doing but are reinforced to attempt the more difficult goals in the series by their earlier success. For example it might be important for success or failure to avoid a goal such as 'Dad to take more interest in the children, and the children to help more in the house' in favour of simpler and specific activities. For example, for a given week, the goals might be:

(1) The children to clear the table after meals.

(2) Mum to cook Dad's favourite meal every Friday.

(3) Dad to take the children out to give Mum a rest on Saturday afternoon.

In this specimen week each person is involved in a bargain or contract which has the effect of rewarding another or other members of the family by changing his own behaviour; but in return each member of the family is also rewarded by the changes in the behaviour of the others. The principles, which may seem obvious, are rooted in social learning theory but lend themselves readily to social exchange theory and to the family therapy approach. The role of the therapist is both to enable the family to achieve small but regular success in attaining the small-scale goals which are established from week to week, both by limiting the objectives of each weekly contract so as to be reasonably sure that they can be achieved, and to offer encouragement and reinforcement as small gains are made. Sometimes a written form of the weekly contract, signed by the family members (devised by the counsellor in discussion with the family) helps enlist involvement, and acts as an index of what has already been achieved when things become difficult at later stages.

As Liberman writes, these tactics can be conceptualized as 'behavioural change experiments.' Another writer, Ballentine (1968), who takes the same approach sees these behavioural change experiments, starting with small but well-defined successes, as leading to, and conducive of, a number of positive factors:

(1) A shift towards more optimistic and hopeful expectations.

(2) An emphasis on doing things differently, while giving the responsibility for change to each family member.

(3) Encouragement of an observational outlook, which encourages family members to look closely at themselves and their relationships with one another, rather than looking 'inside' themselves with incessant whys and wherefores.

(4) The generation of empirical data which can be instrumental to further change, since they often expose sequences of family action and reaction in particularly graphic and unambiguous fashion.

An example of the social learning or behavioural approach to family difficulties is given by Liberman (1970) who describes the case of Mrs D., a 35-year-old housewife and mother of three, who had a fifteen-year history of very severe headaches. Frequent hospital investigations had found no organic problems, and eighteen months of intensive, psychodynamically oriented psychotherapy had also given her no relief; her practice had therefore been to retire to bed for several days at a time, and so on those occasions her husband, who was an extrovert and liked to be up and doing rather than being involved in conversation, would become very solicitous and concerned and give her a great deal of attention. In his behavioural analysis of this relationship, the therapist gently explained the role which Mrs D.'s headaches were playing: only when Mrs D. was ill did she receive the reward of her husband's attention; it was therefore to her advantage, as she perceived it, to become ill frequently. The therapist was able to form a close, noncritical and supportive relationship with both members of this partnership and gradually, by keeping a detailed record of their occurrence, to show them the pattern which existed between periods of illness experienced by Mrs D. and her husband's gratifying changes in behaviour.

Liberman reports that he was able to build a close and trusting relationship with both partners, and was able to teach the husband how to be more demonstrative to and appreciative of his wife on a day-to-day basis, so that he took a deeper interest in the management of the children and his wife's activities in general. Similarly he was able to teach the wife how to be responsive to her husband's efforts, to tell him how much she liked his inquiring about the events of the day, and how much she enjoyed the evening outings they began to make together. Liberman goes on:

On the other hand, Mr D. was instructed to pay minimal attention to his wife's headaches. He was reassured that in so doing he would be helping her decrease their frequency and severity. He was no longer to give her medication, cater to her when she was ill, or call the doctor for her. If she got a headache, she was to help herself and he was to carry on with his regular routine insofar as possible. I emphasised that *he should not, overall, decrease his attentiveness to his wife, but rather change the timing and direction of his attentiveness.*

Within ten sessions, both were seriously immersed in this new approach toward each other. Their marriage was different and more satisfying to both. Their sex life improved. Their children were better behaved as they quickly learned to apply the same reinforcement principles in reacting to the children.

It is reported that a year later a follow-up call to Mr and Mrs D. found them continuing to progress.

Principles of social learning theory as the basis of a contract with an adolescent who wouldn't go to school: Wendy

Wendy had a great many difficulties: she was an adopted girl of fourteen, who, unlike the son who had subsequently been born to her adoptive parents, 'was a handful from the moment she arrived'. As a toddler she had been strong-willed, and would demand her own way, throwing a tantrum if this were denied. Her parents had coped somehow, but it was inevitable that the arrival of their placid, and easy-going son should throw Wendy's turbulence into greater relief, and make her both understandably jealous and even more difficult to manage. Wendy's aggressiveness meant that she had few friends and those she had would not put up with her for long; she had considerable academic ability, but found school unrewarding. This was not due to lack of concern on the part of her teachers, but because as soon as Wendy was checked or reprimanded in any way—and she gave many occasions for reprimand—she would become insolent and truculent, blaming others for all her difficulties, and shouldering no responsibility at all herself. She spent more days at home than at school.

Wendy came to the notice of our department both because of non-school attendance and at the invitation of the school counsellor who, while very anxious to help Wendy, realized that her parents were in great need of support as well. They were, as I subsequently found when I met them, both unhappy and distressed people, genuinely fond of and concerned for Wendy and aware of the girl's unhappiness.

There was no need to point out to them her low opinion of herself, her sense of inadequacy by comparison with the son of the family, her attempts to win attention by acting outrageously: they saw it all and in a sense had seen it coming during the tempestuous years following their son's birth. These were people to be in no way condemned or criticized; they had throughout acted in good faith hoping for a gradual softening of Wendy's rejection of them, and they were still prepared to continue trying. We drew up the following two main priorities.

Getting Wendy back to school

After it had been agreed that the school counsellor continue to see Wendy while I try to help the parents, we all sought to establish the most urgent problem. From everybody's point of view, including the legal one, it was the matter of school attendance: the school authorities were protesting, her parents knew that it was both illegal and unhelpful to her school career and her future to remain at home, and even Wendy agreed that she was bored. Looked at in terms of social learning theory, however, Wendy was obtaining reward and reinforcement for staying at home in terms of the fuss and attention this brought to her, and in terms of social exchange theory the benefits of staying at home as she perceived them outweighed the costs.

My role, therefore, was to redress this balance, and try to make it more rewarding for Wendy to go to school than to stay at home. As things stood, Wendy was staying home almost every day and going out with her friends most evenings; these outings she enjoyed very much. These circumstances seemed to offer the basis for a contract—which is really no more than a regulated balance of agreed and reciprocal rewards between two individuals or parties: 'I will reward you in return for your rewarding me'. The contract is thus a concept derived and derivable directly from social learning theory. What actually happened on this occasion was that after discussion with Wendy and her parents and with the full co-operation of the school, it was agreed that Wendy might go out four evenings per week, being home by a specified time, on condition that she went to school every day. Should she not go to school, or should she return home late, then she would not be allowed to go out with her friends the evening next appointed for an outing. This 'contract' was written down in fairly formal and explicit terms and agreed by all concerned.

The contract was kept; Wendy returned to school where the school counsellor made a point of keeping regular contact with her, and the staff encouraged her in her particular interests. Her parents, bolstered by me, practised the principle agreed on of not allowing Wendy to go out if she had not either been to school or been back on time from the previous outing. The objective of getting Wendy back to school was achieved.

Coping with Wendy's temper tantrums and violent outbursts

In this respect there was less success. As explained earlier, Wendy had apparently had a violent temper since she was a toddler (I have often wondered how many of today's 'difficult adolescents' have not in fact had a history of being hard to handle as had the little boy described earlier, and whether intervention at that stage might not have avoided grave problems later). This temper had intensified rather than diminished as she grew older. As I acknowledged earlier, the rewards and penalties have to be appropriate to and meaningful to the people who receive them, and one cannot exclude a fourteen year old in the garden or in the bathroom with much hope of success. One can, however, usually find some particular aspect of their behaviour or their self-concept to commend, as a spring-board from which better communication and more positive interactions can start, and Wendy's mother could praise in all honesty the quality of her daughter's cooking and home-craft—and did, to good effect. The improvement which this practice brought about was counter-balanced by the strength of the jealousy which Wendy felt (and expressed to the counsellor) about her brother, as well as by the physical violence which she employed. Pots and pans and furniture were thrown about and her mother was the object of both physical violence and a torrent of verbal abuse on several occasions.

To this extent, I feel that both I and the theory I was able to employ failed in these circumstances, and an application for reception into care was eventually made. I wish that I had known at that time of another development which I mentioned briefly in a previous chapter (p. 129) as a further branch of social learning theory: the self-modifying of behaviour. This, it may be recalled, takes into account the notion that we ourselves are a major source of approval or disapproval of our own behaviour; that we are, in essence, self-evaluators. Now Wendy, as I subsequently learned, at the very same time as she was shouting and abusing her parents and her brother, both hated and condemned herself for behaving in that way. She recognized that a great many people were actively working to help her, and that her lack of self-control was causing intense unhappiness in her home as well as considerable strain for the staff responsible for her school. I believe, since the research literature is now beginning to report on this aspect of social learning theory, that had we, between us, been able to recognize Wendy's condemnation of herself we could have helped her to better effect. Had I known, for instance, about Bergin's (1969) work on self-regulation techniques for impulse control disorders, or about Goldiamond's (1965) work on self-control procedures in personal behaviour problems, then that application for reception into care might not have been needed. (The essence of this work indicates that people who, at heart, dislike their behaviour, their ill temper, their violence, their over-eating or their social ineptness can, if they so wish, be helped to change their ways. The same principles of social learning can be used: very simple, very short-term goals can be set initially, which are relatively easy to attain; on the basis of these successes further goals are set, and so on). Had I known of this approach I might have been able to draw on it to help this family, but I did not. This is why it is so important to keep in touch with the research literature emerging month by month from psychology, particularly from social and applied psychology.

Principles of social learning theory to promote better relationships

Social workers often find themselves in situations where no individual and specific behaviour is complained of: there seems to be just a cycle of poor relationships with many general complaints from each member of the family about the other members. Typically, one youngster has been made the subject of a supervision order and his parents state that he is a 'difficult boy' who is 'in with a rough lot' and that they've 'tried everything with him', to no effect. 'Everything' often seems to include sterner discipline, keeping the boy in, allowing no pocket-money and sometimes thrashing; in my experience it almost never includes praise or encouragement for areas in which the boy is pleasing or attempting to please his parents.

For example, when asked to visit one particular family where the youngster, Steve, aged eleven, was kicking over the traces, getting involved in petty theft and behaving objectionably at home, I found it necessary first to listen at some length to his parents' account of the boy's shortcomings in order to relieve some of the intense emotion and anxiety which these had caused. My sympathy for the family in such a case was always genuine; they had often been intensely provoked, let down and disappointed by their son or daughter, and it was vital to allow them to express these powerful feelings and for me to empathize with them. Even if it did appear, in psychodynamic terms, that they were using Steve as a scapegoat, this diagnosis, while just possibly accurate, did not help them in managing relationships any better in the future.

What did prove helpful, when the ventilation of emotion was over, was to ask them what they liked about Steve; at first they could think of nothing at all (!) but gradually his mother remembered that he did occasionally give her a bit of help in the house. My role, then, was gently to teach these parents to comment appreciatively upon Steve's help whenever it occurred and to reward or reinforce these gestures on his part. I found one suggestion given to me by Mrs Alice Sluckin of Leicester School Psychological Service and Child Guidance Clinic particularly effective: to teach parents the practice of keeping a daily diary of some aspect of their son's or daughter's behaviour or attitude which they had been able openly to commend. Parents sometimes found the idea of using praise and encouragement as a means of coping with their children extremely difficult, sometimes because they had received so little encouragement themselves, and sometimes because they felt it was a form of bribery and that 'children ought to behave properly anyway.' Often, however, they had tried other approaches without success, so in desperation and with my encouragement they were willing to try this approach. They were often surprised at its effectiveness.

In Steve's case, his mother first of all thanked him for giving a hand with the washing up, and the next day told him that he looked good in his new shirt; on the third day Steve changed a plug, and his father told him he had made a good job of it; on the fourth day Steve played in a football match and his father went to watch and cheer him on; and on the fifth his mother was touched to find a birthday card and a box of chocolates awaiting her downstairs. All these incidents were duly written down in the notebook I had left with them for the purpose, and when I called after a week it was very easy for me to reinforce with my own real pleasure this increase in considerate behaviour and kindness of each member of the family towards the other. Once 'considerate behaviour' had become established, and things were going better in general (though I asked that the use of the notebook should be still continued), it became possible to talk of areas of specific difficulty which still persisted, but in a very much better atmosphere than formerly. It was essential to help the parents to see the continuing need which we all have for recognition and appreciation and to support their efforts to go on giving it.

In this type of situation the principles of social learning theory are only very loosely and generally applied, but it is often surprising how consistent and sincere encouragement will bring about positive change within families and within personal relationships. This same principle holds good not just in formal social work and counselling situations, but within schools, factories, residential and community centres: it is probably the main message that I hope to leave with readers of this book: people need appreciation.

Reflections on the application of social learning theory

In addition to illustrating several fundamental principles from social learning theory, and their application to social work or counselling situations, there are other key ideas involved which it is important to highlight.

Offering clients something to do

While in no way under-valuing the importance of 'insight' (understanding of the origins and maintenance of interpersonal difficulties) the social learning approach does not regard this as indispensable to change. Rather, by offering clients a means of doing something to improve a situation, it places a different emphasis on the process of change. For it often seems to be assumed by theorists of the various approaches which stress 'insight' that change, in terms of improved relationships and greater happiness, accompanies the new understanding brought by insight in an almost inevitable way, and that emotional growth in the desired direction occurs in an almost spontaneous fashion. Many psychologists would, however, question this assumption, and while agreeing that investigation of the reasons for troubled relationships may provide a useful explanatory framework, suggest that this understanding does not seem to lead to change for the better automatically. They suggest that insight and changes in feeling often *follow* changes in behaviour, not precede them.

In some complex situations the simplicity of the social learning approach is particularly useful; rather than spending lengthy sessions exploring the origins and tortuous detail of a deteriorating relationship, two simple questions can be borne in mind:
(1) In terms of social learning theory (or by extension, social exchange theory) in what areas and in what individual ways do these people want to be more fully rewarded by each other?
(2) Knowing this, how can I help them to behave more rewardingly to each other, each in a way which is important to him or her personally?

For we cannot assume that what is rewarding for one person will be perceived as such by another: as I have said (p. 184), appreciation, approval and thanks are almost universally welcome and even if a few shy away from public expression of such attitudes we all are alert to some kind of reward; it is the counsellor's role to discover within the family situation what is important to each individual, and to help the members to practise rewarding each other.

Circumscribing the problem rather than extending it

In the case of Mrs D. described on p. 188, the therapist deliberately circumscribed the problem of Mrs D's headaches by focusing on the behaviour and what maintained it rather than on the possible and speculative origins of her choice of headache as a means of obtaining attention. Some readers may object that his method of treatment was a treatment of the symptom rather than the cause, and I would have no hesitation in agreeing; for here, as in hundreds of similar cases, the headache is both symptom and cause.

In traditional therapy, the counsellor might well have (and indeed from the account, a previous therapist actually did) spend many months on attempting to understand, and give Mrs D. insight into, the nature of her headaches and to help her work through these; in therapy based on principles of social learning the main focus of attention is the behaviour itself, and what maintains it in existence; thus instead of involving the client in much introspective examination of and great preoccupation with her feelings, thereby intensifying the problem, the counsellor is able to emphasize the relatively limited nature of Mrs D's disability, making her feel more normal rather than less.

Highlighting the client's strengths rather than his weaknesses

This circumscribing of a family's or an individual's difficulties gives the counsellor a further advantage: that of being able to draw attention to, and thus automatically to reinforce, the many ways in which the family or the individual is proving successful. If we, as social workers, allow ourselves to spend all our time with a family dwelling on the problems they are experiencing with, say, a difficult teenager, without highlighting the ways in which things are going well, or have gone well in the past, are we aware of what we are doing? In terms of social learning theory we are reinforcing gloom and despondency.

It is very rare, for instance, that one encounters the total rejection of a child or adult by a parent or partner; usually there is ambivalence and our agency or department becomes involved because of a court appearance or the likelihood of a divorce. Our responsibility is to recognize this ambivalence, and to give quite as much attention and reinforcement to the positive aspects of the relationship as to the negative. This has the double effect of putting the difficulty into genuine perspective, and of offering great reassurance to the family or individual involved. Thus, where a young person is in trouble with the courts one can usually, with genuineness, remark on the distress which the parents are experiencing—which is in itself a mark of their concern for him: if they really didn't care about him they wouldn't show distress. One can then ask to hear about times when things were going well for the family, achievements on the part of the youngster in question, times when the family or the relationships were a successful concern; one can ask to hear, then, about things which are still good for the family, school achievements on the part of the children, sporting interests, aspects of relationships between members which have been overshadowed by the present difficulties, common interests, continuing bonds of affection, things that the counsellor picks up about the positive ways people feel about each other despite all the negatives which have arisen. It is fitting to draw attention to these strengths, and inasmuch as they are often strengths which continue despite much bitterness and resentment, their being highlighted by the counsellor can give new hope and motivation to families who have almost abandoned the struggle to co-operate with each other. If the counsellor ignores these strengths, however, and dwells solely on the problems, what an opportunity has been lost both of establishing a warm relationship with people in need and of reinforcing the very strengths which people require to rebuild their own relationships.

Use of an eclectic approach

Although I have deliberately emphasized the strengths of the approach to clients based on social learning theory, I am far from imagining that such an approach is adequate to deal with the enormous range of difficulties which are encountered by counsellors and social workers. I have chosen to devote so much time to it both because it is rooted in principles of psychology which, as I have said before, are to be found in most basic psychology text-books but which are seldom included within the syllabus of many social work or counselling training courses, and because it seems to me that other approaches, particularly that rooted in psychodynamic theory, are already very adequately represented in reading lists and on the social work shelves of libraries.

Thus although it is true that for many situations social learning theory and the predictions which it may generate offer a powerful model and technique of helping to those who have been adequately trained in its principles, it is also true that a fully competent counsellor needs to be familiar with other models as well, so that he may select 'theory for practice', as Olive Stevenson (1976) suggests. After a good deal of experience I suspect, one can tell which approach is going to help most, but until one has had this amount of experience then the counsellor needs to be able to conceptualize a person's or a family's difficulties in several different ways so that he may choose the best 'match'.

Part four

Review

Chapter 10

An attempt at integration: the eclectic approach

Models of man within psychology

Before making any attempt to integrate some of the main ideas discussed in previous chapters, it seems appropriate to devote a little space to considering the ways in which the 'fragments of theory' to which I referred in the first chapter of this book are beginning to be grouped together by psychologists. There are, of course, a wide number of ways in which the fragments could be grouped; one common way is often found in psychology text-books where the available evidence concerning, say, memory is assembled within a chapter. In this book I have attempted to group some fragments of theory round themes which seem particularly salient for social workers and counsellors, but this, it will be appreciated, is not a 'natural' grouping—just as a book on psychology for nurses or psychology for teachers would not be 'natural'.

There is, of course no fundamentally 'natural' way of presenting the fragments, and yet there are now a considerable number of them, and some kind of order has to be imposed to make them coherent. What is therefore tending to happen is that, in some circles at least, the notion of several 'models' of man is being introduced, in order to accommodate the diversity of the available material. (A 'model' is really an 'approach' or a 'viewpoint', a way of looking at man so that certain aspects of his being are highlighted, since it is no longer possible to claim that a single view of man, such as 'a social animal', is adequate.)

There are of course a wide range of models of or approaches to man, but for the purposes of this book I wish to draw attention to five of these:

(1) The physiological approach.
(2) The psychoanalytic and psychodynamic approach.
(3) The social learning and behavioural approach.
(4) The cognitive approach.
(5) The humanistic approach.

The physiological approach

This approach is grounded in the unmistakably biological and neuro-physiological nature of man. It is based on the central fact that we are born, with a physical body which functions in accordance with certain laws associated with chemistry and physics, which develops and which eventually dies. The meaning which we attach to all that happens between birth and death is usually intensely personal but during what we call human life we are grounded in our bodies and in the way they function.

There is a vast amount of material available within this approach, much of it obtained by physiologists, biochemists and the many workers in medical research. Recently, however, other inquirers have contributed to this approach, notably the ethologists, such as Lorenz (1966) and Eibl-Eibesfeldt (1970), who are particularly interested in what can be learned from a comparative study of man and animals, and the physiological psychologists, such as Olds and Olds (1965) and Penfield (1969), and a host of others, who have turned their investigations to mapping out the areas of the human brain which, when stimulated electrically, produce sensations of pleasure and pain or of past memories. This approach to the study of man appears to be almost inexhaustible; we have barely embarked upon it. Included within its scope are genetics and the vast field of developmental processes, as well as the interactions between these.

The psychoanalytic and psychodynamic approach

While, in a sense, the biological and physiological approach has always been central in man's attempts to understand himself, the psychoanalytic or psychodynamic approach is of relatively recent origin; for while great writers and thinkers may have used themes or expressed emotions which we can now formulate in psychodynamic terms, it was Freud and his collaborators and disciples who first explicitly set out the ideas and hypotheses which we now call psycho-analytic theory. Many of the original ideas, concerning Freud's views on psychosexual development and the implications of these for subsequent personality are now very seriously questioned: readers interested in pursuing this subject are referred to the study by Kline (1972). However well or badly psychoanalytic ideas stand up to rigorous investigation, the particular contribution of Freudian thought and that of his followers has been to draw attention to the intensely powerful role of emotion and feeling, constructive as well as aggressive, not only in the obviously dramatic situations of which we read in the papers and which we see on television, but in the round of everyday life, at home, at school, in the factory and in the high street. Yet it has always seemed to me rather a pity that counsellors and social workers are so frequently invited to direct their attentions primarily towards problems when discussing cases, so that the psychopathology of the family has claimed, to my mind, far more than its share of intensive case work. It might well have been better to make it clear that strong feeling can be loving and caring as well as hostile, and to give the former due weight; we can dwell on and reinforce the love and care within the situations about us just as readily as we can explore and reinforce the hostility.

The psychoanalytic and psychodynamic approach to man has generated a great many so-called therapies; most readers will know something of the techniques employed by psychoanalysis, but I would refer them to the findings discussed in chapter 1, which examined research into effective psychotherapy and counselling, before they accept uncritically the claims of psychoanalysis. The effectiveness of 'therapies' stemming from the psychoanalytic tradition requires, to my mind, equal investigation; until we know whether the 'therapy' itself has anything to offer, as distinct from the personality and/or experience of the 'therapist', it seems appropriate to be sceptical.

The social learning and behavioural approach

This approach, which has already been dealt with in some detail in chapter 9 conceptualizes man not in terms of hypothesized psychosexual stages and as primarily torn by conflict, whether conscious or unconscious, but as having to a great extent learned to become much of what he is. He has learned this in several ways: by direct training during childhood, so that he grows up to be broadly acceptable and understood by his family, community and sub-culture, and by observing other members of his culture and modelling himself on them. Some of the sets of circumstances which bring about speedy, enduring or ineffective learning are known in considerable detail, as well as those which bring about learning which is almost impossible to unlearn.

The social learning model does not, however, exist as a discrete entity; the understanding which it offers is enriched by drawing on other understandings drawn from different and overlapping models, such as the biological or the cognitive: as is so often the case, it is by drawing on several approaches or appreciating the interactions between approaches that enables us to understand and offer help in a particular situation. The social learning model is proving particularly fruitful in providing new therapeutic approaches, since it is much easier to make predictions on the basis of learning theory, but it appears that this model is not effective alone: it also requires the offering of a warm and genuine relationship for maximum therapeutic effectiveness.

The cognitive approach

This model takes account of the indications that man is not merely tossed by unconscious stress, nor under the sway of stimulus-response conditioning, but that he actively plans, thinks about and judges various strategies in the conduct of his life, and in his attempts to make sense of his own personal life. This model sees man as an information processor, as a creature who perceives — so the chapter on perception in this book draws heavily upon the cognitive model — remembers, compares, judges, assesses and decides. Social-exchange theory is thus also rooted in cognitive activity, though it draws on social learning theory as well.

The cognitive model has also given rise to its own forms of therapy.

The humanistic or personal growth approach

The humanistic viewpoint, which again arose as a counter-balance to other approaches and is, historically, the youngest model, attempts to re-establish the importance of the subjective experience of individuals as a valid and fitting study. This seems entirely appropriate and may appeal especially to readers of this book whose work testifies to their conviction of the worth of the individual and of the personal nature of the meaning found in life by those individuals. This model emphasizes the innate potential possessed by man for learning and for new growth, and sees man as capable of controlling his own destiny and of achieving far greater levels of fulfilment than is usually the case.

This optimistic and positive approach to man is very appealing and has given rise to the 'growth movement' which is apparently much more powerful in the USA than it is (yet) in this country. A number of therapies are also associated with the approach; it is in a sense grounded in client-centred therapy, which has had a powerful impact on social casework and counselling theory in this country. However, there is no notable indication that such theory has proved an adequate tool to the task, it is perhaps time that the limitations of the theory on its own as a single model should be recognized, and that an approach based on knowledge and approaches from several models should be more readily available.

The proliferation of 'therapies'

As described in the Introduction one of the more confusing developments to occur in the field of human relationships within the past
few years has been the multiplicity of new 'therapies' which have
arisen in this country or, more accurately, have been brought here
from the USA. Some of these have gained earnest adherents, and
some of them are becoming fairly influential in the fields of counselling and even in the more conservative field of social work. In an
attempt to make sense of the astonishing range and variety of these
so-called therapies in Figure 6 I have allocated them in a very general
way to the field or model of psychology with which they seem to me to

Physiological	Psychoanalytical and psychodynamic	Social learning and behavioural	Cognitive	Humanistic
	Psychoanalysis	Behavioural therapy	Rational–emotive therapy	Client-centred therapy
	Gestalt	Strategic therapy	Reality therapy	Existential psychotherapy
	Transactional analysis			Logotherapy
	Primal therapy			Family therapy
	Psychodrama			
	Transpersonal psychosynthesis			

Figure 6 *An overview of 'therapies'*

belong, and in whose general tradition they appear to be. It will be
apparent to many readers that this allocation is over simplistic, and
that many therapies span two or even more models, but I have attempted to link them with the model which seems most central to the
approach. It is to be hoped that even if the reader did not have
doubts about the proven efficacy of some of these approaches before
he read this book, he will now.

There are several points to be made arising from Figure 6.
First, that the range of different approaches is probably much

broader than many readers had realized. In my efforts to bring some of the findings emerging from psychology to the attention of counsellors and social workers one particular objective I have selected is to enable them to step back, as it were, from their own individual training or experience and to appreciate that there is a very much broader perspective than they may have realized. Frequently, when we have been taught or trained in the methods of working of one particular approach, we identify very closely with that approach, perceive events and interactions through the filter of that approach and even feel anxious or troubled when we meet another counsellor or worker who has been trained in a different way. There is almost a danger of sectarianism within the helping professions: we have seen how the challenges and counter-challenges about the effectiveness of different methods of psychotherapy led to the psychoanalyists, the traditional high-priests of therapy, losing their exclusive role as therapists when the effectiveness of their methods was called in question; and we have seen how, under attack, adherents to the original teaching fell away and established their own protest movement, although there remained sufficient of the original adherents for the traditional approach to be maintained, still claiming exclusive knowledge and understanding. There is an engaging parallel to be drawn here between the claims to exclusiveness and what happened to them of the Roman Catholic Church and those of the psychoanalytic persuasion. Further, once credibility has been effectively undermined, there follows another familiar pattern: the seekers after truth, no longer united under a common banner, begin to fragment into sects, each claiming to have found a closer approximation to the 'truth' than their fellow-claimants; these are the Protestants and Non-conformists of the Christian tradition, and the transactional analysts, the gestalt therapists and the psychodramatists of the therapeutic tradition. In both cases, this proliferation of approaches leads to confusion among the faithful.

What appears to happen is that enthusiasts for, say, gestalt therapy, attend training sessions, are introduced to the patterns of thinking of that particular sect, learn its norms and jargon, and begin to identify themselves with that approach because of the comfort and cosiness of belonging. They associate with other enthusiasts for the gestalt approach, so that a great deal of mutual reinforcement occurs and awkward questions are out of place; an in-group, which is self-rewarding and self-sustaining, becomes established, books and articles are written and key people become elders to whom points of unclear doctrine may be referred for elucidation. The disciples, trained in these approaches, go out perceiving and interpreting situations in the light of what they have been taught, and may well be in danger, because of the nature of their conditioning, of relying over-exclusively on this viewpoint. They may neglect, or even be unaware of, what is available from other approaches.

Second, as an important paper by Patterson (1977) indicates, these new approaches in counselling may indicate healthy diversity or may be actively anti-therapeutic. He writes:

> Anything goes now in psychotherapy. The field *is* a mess. . . . Every few months we have a new technique or approach being advocated in books and journal articles. But what is discouraging—and disturbing—is the lack of, or the inadequacy of, theory and concepts supporting the new methods or techniques; the ignoring, or ignorance of, the research supporting what have come to be known as the core conditions; the evangelistic fervour with which many of the approaches are advocated; the lack of concern for any evidence of their effectiveness except possibly testimonials; the failure to recognize that what is called counselling or psychotherapy can be for better or worse—that people can be hurt as well as helped; and finally the eagerness with which the approaches are commercialized. Many of the originators of new approaches are not satisfied with publishing books and articles, and then waiting for their ideas to be subjected to critical scrutiny, evaluation and research before eventually being accepted or rejected, or modified and revised and finally incorporated in the teaching and training programmes of universities. Instead, many of these methods are being promoted by advertising and workshops and short-term training courses, or are the basis for institutes or organisations which issue diplomas and certificates, all resembling the development of a cult (e.g. scientology, EST, transactional analysis (T.A.) primal scream therapy, and even Gestalt therapy.)

It is true that Patterson is writing of the situation which prevails in the USA, but I suggest that Britain is already witnessing the beginning of the phenomenon which disturbs him so much, and that counsellors and social workers are sometimes caught up in these 'sects'. In the USA, he reports, charges for malpractice are being brought to the courts; in this country social workers and counsellors are perhaps under sufficient scrutiny already to prevent these excesses, but let us at least be on our guard against uncritical acceptance of a new approach. It is, after all, the social workers who become the focus of a public inquiry in the event of scandal or tragedy, and not their trainers.

Third, as Patterson reminds us, and as this book has attempted to show, the ultimate criterion by which the effectiveness of a particular technique should be assessed is that of research evidence. As far as I am aware, and my knowledge is of course limited, there is evidence for the *consistent usefulness* of only two of the fourteen therapies listed in Figure 6: client-centred therapy, and therapy based on principles of social learning, of which behaviour therapy is part. The usefulness of these approaches is attested in numerous research programmes and reviews of the literature, and it is for this reason that I have drawn so heavily on them in this book. In many instances it is possible to draw on these theories for predictive purposes; they may be improved on, or refined, but it is unlikely that the fundamental principles will be overturned.

This is not to say that the other twelve approaches are valueless, or that we cannot draw a great deal from them; it is rather that the critical appraisal which we should make of any ideas presented to us as useful for effective intervention in the lives of other people should be intensified when ideas which have not been validated are presented. What, it is reasonable to inquire of any trainer, is the evidence supporting the effectiveness of the ideas you are now describing?

A possible model for an eclectic approach to casework and counselling

In attempting to devise such a model I have tried to take into account a number of factors:

(1) Social casework and counselling, though different in some respects, share a common core of theory and practice.

(2) There is no good reason for making counselling or casework mysterious; it is a skill which may be learned, and although some people seem to have a natural aptitude for it which is of great use to them, it appears that non-professionals given appropriate training can be just as helpful as professionals.

(3) Ideas about effective counselling which have emerged from repeated research studies should have a prominent place.

(4) While 'sectarianism', or strict adherence to the principles of one or other of the new therapies, is undesirable the model should allow selective use of such approaches where there is research evidence of their usefulness, when the client is agreeable and where the practitioner is trusted.

(5) That while client-centred therapy is of proven value in many situations, (perhaps particularly those in which some decision has to be taken, as in pregnancy counselling or in having to decide whether to allow a severely handicapped child to go into residential care, or indeed in situations where a great deal of support is needed) it is apparent that this alone is far from adequate in many others. It will not usually resolve problems,

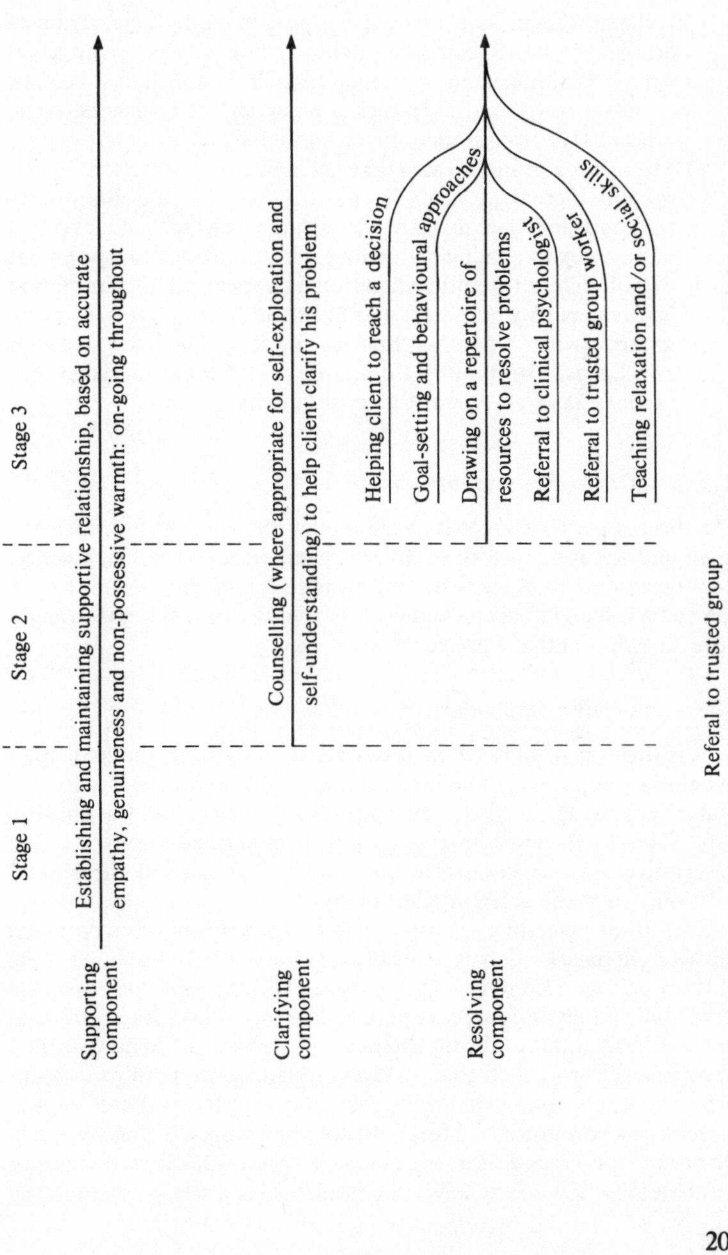

Figure 7 *The supporting, clarifying and resolving components of the approach to eclectic helping*

it will not enable a mother having difficulties in coping with a wildly aggressive four-year-old to manage him better; and it will not help a person with a violent temper to stop beating his wife.

(6) If the indiscriminate use of one approach alone is clearly inappropriate, then the model should, while retaining the great strengths of the client-centred approach, enable the counsellor to draw discriminatingly upon a repertoire of resources, some practical and some theoretical, on behalf of his client.

(7) The approach should also take account of the objection, which is being increasingly raised, that traditional counselling practice tends to locate many of the difficulties which a client or his family is experiencing within that client; the objectors point out that often his difficulties stem from injustice and discrimination on the part of others, and that to expect him to 'grow' to come to terms with this is less than appropriate. The book by Lewis and Lewis, *Community Counselling: A Human Services Approach* (1977), sets out this position clearly.

Aspects of the eclectic approach

The three main components of the model, the supporting, the clarifying and the resolving strands, are complementary to each other; they represent what seem to be key features of any attempt by a counsellor, social worker, voluntary befriender or just a good neighbour to help another person.

The supporting component

This is the core of the model. It derives directly from the principles of helping, empathy, genuineness and warmth, established by Rogers and his colleagues in 1951, and confirmed by Truax and Carkhuff in 1967. These principles have already been described in chapter 3 in descriptive and behavioural terms, and in this section therefore I wish only to make a few further points.

First, these principles are, up to a point, the very ones that common sense might have guided us to select as important. The teachers whom most of us found helpful when we were children were the ones who were kind, understanding and patient, the ones who took an interest in us as individuals and who listened to us—without being soft and letting us get away with things. When we are ill we tend to look for compassion and patience and expect that people will perceive and understand how unwell we feel, and act accordingly. Similarly, when we are in trouble and need the help of a social worker or counsellor we are temporarily extremely vulnerable, just as when we are children or when we are ill; we are temporarily very dependent on the way we are treated by those from whom we seek, or are instructed to seek, help. If we meet with kindness, compassion, respect and consideration, and continue to meet those attitudes, we lose our sense of vulnerability, our anxiety diminishes and we are able to perceive events and situations with a vision less clouded by self-protective emotion. Thus any person who consistently treats another with respect and consideration adds to that person's sense of worth and dignity, and hence to his capacity to manage his life effectively. This appears to be true whether one is considering the parent-child, doctor-patient, teacher-pupil, counsellor-client or merely neighbour-neighbour relationship.

Second, if, as I have suggested in chapter 4, a person's behaviour usually makes sense to himself, however outrageous or unacceptable it may appear to others, then the empathic counsellor is soon able, by means of lending himself to the way his client perceives events, also to make sense of that behaviour. In other words, an effective counsellor or social worker is an extremely understanding person— but able to be understanding not only of his client but also of all those who interact with his client; since everybody's behaviour makes sense to himself the counsellor is enabled by his empathy to enter the perceptions of the several persons interacting within a situation and also to make sense of the behaviours of each.

Third, the counsellor often can then genuinely understand how situations of bitter conflict, depression and violence have come about, and can convey his understanding to each participant. This conveying of understanding by both verbal and non-verbal means to both individuals and to participants within a dispute is as I have said elsewhere, very reassuring; it has the effect of allaying anxiety and self-defensiveness and of thereby gradually promoting willingness to consider what each participant's own role has been in heightening tensions within a relationship, or how that role has been perceived by others. I expect most counsellors will have had the experience of listening to a tirade of invective against a husband, wife or child lasting for an hour or perhaps more, as the bitterness of months or years is released within an accepting atmosphere; they may then also have had the experience at the next meeting of hearing their client say, 'I suppose the fault hasn't been only on his side'. This second stage, however, may never be reached unless the supporting and accepting aspects of the relationship are present throughout.

Fourth, this supportive component may sometimes be all that is wanted to meet the needs of the person seeking help at that time; often we seem to make too much of a mystery of counselling, and it has therefore been one of my objectives to devise a way of looking at what goes on when one person helps another which is just as relevant to the confidential chat over a cup of coffee in the corner of the youth club as it is to the formal visit to the marriage-guidance counsellor. In essence, the person is received kindly, his story is listened to with patience and consideration, he is not condemned or overtly criticized for his role in events and he obtains emotional relief from sharing in confidence something which has been causing him stress and anxiety. This can be seen simply as getting things off one's chest or, letting off steam as well as, in the jargon of psychotherapy, abreacting or ventilating emotion. Let us not make a mystery of a human relationship which is as old as humanity itself: that of caring, compassion and concern.

Because most of us would wish to be perceived as possessing these personal characteristics and behaviours which have been found to be useful in this core component of the counselling role, I list below some of these features—but translated into behavioural terms. Friends and colleagues can tell us how they perceive our behaviour in a given situation—for only by obtaining feedback on our own behaviour do we learn. For much is often made by trainers of counsellors of self-awareness, a nebulous concept which is readily confused with self-consciousness, and little guidance is given on how this state of self-awareness should be arrived at. Many of the games and consciousness expanding exercises claim to achieve this goal on behalf of those who participate in them, but often make too much of a mystery of what is occurring. Although some fairly complicated things often happen; one thing which does is that people are enabled to receive feedback from others on how they are perceived and on the attitudes they stimulate in others; not in just one other but in a variety of others.

There seem to me to be two particularly relevant areas which might be discussed by tutors or trainers, or by any supportive colleague, with people learning to work with people. There is no reason of course why this should not be a reciprocal arrangement, with the student or trainee giving information to the tutor or trainer.

(1) How one is perceived by a wide range of people

    (i) What do people (a wide range of people) assume

                        from my appearance?
                        from my style of dress?
                        from my voice/accent?
                        from my age?
                        from my manner?

    (ii) What is my non-verbal style: effusive? or withdrawn?
                                  cold? or warm?
                                  challenging? or passive?
                                  aggressive or defensive?

    (iii) Am I seen as approachable?

We know from the research described in chapter 2 what characteristics appear to be useful to others; do we possess them? Perhaps we can only learn this type of information from others, or by audio-visual techniques, using role-play situations which can be filmed and re-run for our benefit.

(2) How we behave as counsellors or social workers, and even as friends

(i) Can I recognize when people have something worrying on their minds?

(ii) If appropriate, can I help them bring it into the open?

(iii) Am I a good listener, helping the other person to do most of the talking?

(iv) If they are not very articulate, can I help by tentatively putting into words what they seem to be trying to say?

(v) Can I talk about difficult and personal subjects without embarrassment?

(vi) In such matters as, for example, arriving at a decision, do I avoid imposing my own solution?

(vii) Do I, however, give all relevant information which is available—such as other sources of help for a given person?

The clarifying component

It is clear, however, that support, acceptance and compassion are not enough. Although they offer hope and dignity to the individual, strengthening his capacity to manage his life and its difficulties, there is little evidence that they of themselves remove depression, enable wives to decide whether to leave or remain with a husband who beats them or resolve sexual difficulties. If the offering of a relationship characterized by empathy, genuineness and warmth on the part of the caseworker or counsellor does not meet the client's needs, then it is probably appropriate to move to a further stage of the relationship helping him explore and clarify the key features of his difficulty and the specific needs for which he wants help.

There are several points which it is appropriate to make. First, if it has not already been done, then the client's expectations concerning his relationship with the social worker or counsellor should be clarified as soon as possible. Limitations of time, resources and counsellor availability can be brought into the open, but the commitment of the counsellor to the client within those limitations can be emphasized; both these clarifications seem to act to engage the client's own motivation when they are offered in a supportive and concerned way.

Second, it is appropriate at this stage to help the client to explore some of the issues of the many which he often brings to the counsellor in order both to give some shape or structure to the meetings between them, and to pinpoint which are the most urgent of the matters with which he wants help. People in trouble are sometimes extremely uncertain which of many pressing problems to attempt to cope with first, and if they cannot tell then it falls to the social worker or counsellor to help them focus on key issues; if the counsellor can list or specify a number of possible foci of discussion, then a client is often able to distinguish which to him is the most pressing.

Third, some of the traditional models of counselling, particularly counselling for decision-making, as offered by the British Pregnancy Advisory Service, as well as 'client-centred therapy' can be seen in terms of these components, support and clarification of the eclectic model. Thus in counselling for decision-making the client, supported by the understanding and empathy of the counsellor, is enabled to explore her ambivalence towards her pregnancy, to generate and discuss possible courses of action and the consequences thereof; this clarification is often extremely valuable in helping people weigh up the advantages and disadvantages of several possible courses of action and to arrive at a clear view of what they want to do. Similarly, in client-centred therapy, the client, in the words of Truax and Carkhuff (1967), 'spends much of his time in self-exploration—attempting to understand and define his own beliefs, values, motives and actions—while the therapist, by reason of his training and knowledge, is attempting to facilitate this process.'

It is possible to conceptualize a great deal of counselling and social casework within this eclectic model; caseworkers will be very familiar with the supportive and self-exploratory aspects of social work when they discuss with parents whether to ask for a child to be taken into care, or to relinquish a baby for adoption; they will be drawing on it, too, when they avoid advising elderly people about giving up their homes, since what has meaning and importance for one indivudal may have none for another, and to give advice where matters of personal values are concerned neglects the intensely personal nature of our cost-benefit analyses.

Nevertheless, a great deal of help can be offered at this stage by the act of giving information; to learn for example that a particular organization exists to help people with the same difficulty as oneself, be it childlessness, some form of sexual irregularity, agoraphobia or depression, can be extremely reassuring and helpful; whether clients use this information is up to them.

The resolving component

This third strand of what I am calling the 'eclectic approach' goes beyond the traditional boundaries of counselling. It does so because traditional counselling is based primarily on the client-centred approach, and this approach has been assumed to be adequate to resolve a host of difficulties which are in fact far beyond its scope. Client-centred therapy will not, of itself, stop violent youngsters from beating up old ladies, will not pay the rent and will not stop a depressed and lonely housewife from resorting to alcohol. People almost certainly need the respect and individual attention offered to them by the client-centred approach, and almost certainly benefit from the opportunity to clarify their needs and wishes in a supportive but realistic way, which takes into account the needs and wishes of others, but they also need a great deal more.

To this end the counsellor or social worker can usefully act as a resource person, either possessing or having access to a wide repertoire of means of taking action to resolve a client's difficulties. There is no reason why, contrary to convention within 'traditional' counselling, the counsellor should not himself help to implement some of the strategies which have been devised.

I propose to discuss below some of the possible resources of which any social worker or counsellor should be aware.

Need for medical intervention A number of people who seek the help of a social worker or counsellor are unwell; they may be physically exhausted, suffering from an unrecognized illness or from a clinical depression. Although the way we behave towards them and the kindness and consideration we show may be comforting to them, the way in which we can best help may well be to encourage them to seek the help of a doctor, and if necessary, accompany them to the surgery.

Need for intervention by a clinical psychologist Great advances have been made over the last few years within the field of clinical psychology, and although there is a great shortage of these practitioners there is a service offered by them within the National Health Service in every area health authority. Clinical psychologists will usually seek the agreement of a patient's general practitioner before undertaking to see or offer treatment to someone in need, and that is usually forthcoming. Such psychologists all have had at least an honours degree in psychology, followed by another two years of training in the application of understanding derived from empirical research to problems within mental health and personal development.

Areas in which clinical psychologists have made great progress are in the treatment of phobias, such as agoraphobia and the fears of particular objects or events, passing dogs, going in buses, carving knives, and the like, which disrupt the lives of many sufferers, and in the treatment of obsessions, such as hand-washing, ritualistic counting, sequencing of activities and checking of light switches and so on. Many of these disorders, although they have disabled people for many years, can be simply and effectively dealt with by the careful and sensitive application of basic principles derived from research in psychology. These psychologists can also be asked for help in making detailed assessments of patients with mental disorders and in, for example, establishing parents groups for families with handicapped children. They share this role with their colleagues, the educational psychologists.

Clinical psychologists are now beginning to apply their skills to helping people who suffer from acute shyness, lack of social skills and from sexual difficulties; their success in these fields is receiving wide attention. Clearly it is appropriate for social workers and counsellors to know what this relatively new profession has to offer, so that clinical psychologists can be invited to participate in training sessions and so that clients can be referred to them for help with specific problems.

Helping clients to set goals specifying ways in which he would like to change It has been suggested that when a client comes to see a counsellor the traditional question, 'What is your problem?' could often be very profitably replaced by 'How would you like to behave differently?' Such a phrasing of the question may enable a person to move very swiftly from the stage of describing and cataloguing his difficulties to a consideration, supported by the counsellor, of what he is going to do about his difficulties. If, for instance, a parent complains about the behaviour of his child, we would clearly expect a social worker to listen in a concerned and supportive way to the account of the parent's troubles, but since from the work of Phillips (1960) described on p. 101, there was indication that parents gained more help by being given simple instructions about how to manage their child than from in-depth interviews, then it is likely that a similar approach would be found helpful again. Thus, for example, when a parent has finished letting off steam about his troublesome son, it may be possible for the social worker to say in essence, 'A lot of people have found that paying a bit less attention to a child's faults while paying a lot more attention to his qualities, has had very valuable effects. Since you've asked my help, could we work out some ways in which you might handle him a bit differently?'

If the father is willing, it may then be possible to set simple behavioural goals, based on principles of social learning as described on p. 166-93. If the child is older, or if the other contender in a dispute is a husband, wife, or another adult, then a shared understanding of objectives, the basis of which would be along the lines of a contract, might be appropriate. The point is that unless people are clear about what they are trying to achieve, they have no guidelines to work on and no objectives towards which to work; once the issue of what the objectives are have been clarified, it is possible to devise means of achieving them.

If one carries the same principle over into the management of one's case load it should surely be possible for every social worker to say, at a given time, when asked by his senior, what objectives he is trying to attain in his work with each family or individual. For if he doesn't know what he is trying to do, in fairly specific terms, how can he be sure when he has done it, or when he should give up trying? If, for example, Mr Jones, social worker, can say when he goes for his weekly supervision to his senior, in respect of the Smith family, 'I am trying to achieve the following ends with this family:

(1) That Mrs Smith will see a doctor as she seems very ill.

(2) That Mr Smith should realize that he is entitled to more benefit than he has been claiming. If he then chooses not to claim it that is up to him, but he should realize he is entitled to it.

(3) That their handicapped child, James, should have the riding lessons he longs for.

(4) That the local Mencap Society volunteer visiting service might be asked to visit this family, as the Smiths have asked.'

When a worker's objectives can be clarified in this way, having already been discussed with and agreed with the Smith family, everyone knows where they stand and what they are working for. The achievement of even one of these goals can then be a matter of some satisfaction to everyone, and offer incentive to achieve the next. But people need to know clearly what they are trying to do. These are fundamental principles of effective management as well as fundamental principles of psychology.

Referral to a trusted group worker The meaning of the term group worker is as nebulous and ill-defined as the term counsellor; rather than attempt to limit its meaning by specifying what constitutes group work and what does not—an impossible task anyway—I use the term to refer to anyone who spends regular time with a group of people to achieve desired objectives. The term therefore includes people as far apart as the leader of the local action group striving for better facilities for unemployed immigrant youngsters and the leader of the personal growth workshop which meets each Friday to reflect on the meaning of dreams.

My point is that, as was found to be the case by Truax and Carkhuff (1967), the helpfulness of the group may be closely related to the personality of the leader, as perceived by the group members. It is no good merely referring people with problems to a new therapy group, of whatever complexion, unless one can be sure that they are going to be helped; this certainty is most likely to stem from evidence given by a number of people who have used the group and report that they respect the leader, value his skills and who confirm that they have found the experience to be helpful. Ideally, social workers and counsellors should try to meet and observe the methods of working of as many of the local groups and their leaders who try to help others as possible, but if this is not possible then some evidence of effectiveness should be sought before one refers one's clients to unknown groups.

Initiating or supporting efforts to gain better facilities for one's clients Among one's repertoire of activities as a social worker there should be the capacity to promote activities which further the interests of one's clients. It seemed to me, when visiting families with severely handicapped children, that in addition to or even instead of my supportive role as social worker, what I ought to be doing was to work actively on their behalf for the setting up of better day-care facilities for holidays and weekends rather than attempting to help them to come to terms with their situation. Similarly, the promotion of day-centres for the recovering mentally ill or for the elderly has seemed a much more valuable, and cost-effective procedure than the occasional call from a social worker — however anxious he may be to offer support.

For the trend to locate the problem within the client or within the family has been effectively checked by the sociologists; the desperate mother with three young children living in a block of flats needs playgroup facilities for her children and other mothers to talk to, rather than a fortnightly visit from her social worker; the time spent on those fortnightly visits could often be spent just as well in enlisting the mothers as colleagues and helpers in finding a room big enough to offer play space to six or eight toddlers and in working out a rota of whom to regard as responsible for the children two or three mornings a week. Social workers need not confine their activities to 'maintenance work' with families: they can act as resource people, catalysts for activity, enthusiasts for developments which will materially affect the day-to-day lives of their clients.

Involvement in social action to further the lawful interests of one's clients If, as sometimes happens, a social worker or counsellor finds himself meeting with a succession of distressed people, be they unemployed young immigrants, homeless young people, single-parent families or people discriminated against because of colour or creed, then it seems appropriate for that social worker to campaign actively to promote the lawful interests of such people. It is impossible, for instance, to locate the problems of thousands upon thousands of unemployed young West Indians within these young people; the perspective one is obliged to take of their difficulties must veer towards the sociological rather than the psychological, towards the macro- rather than the micro-model. This is not to say that psychologists have nothing to offer to those trying to help such young people; to offer them consistent respect and consideration may go some way to fostering a positive attitude towards themselves, but they need more than respect and consideration; they need work, freedom from discrimination and decent living standards; it may be that only active campaigning on their behalf by social workers, community workers and even counsellors will draw sufficient public attention to the plight of these and similar minority groups. I am suggesting that such activity should figure clearly as a possible course of action in this third stage of attempting to resolve a client's difficulties. The helping professions have conceptualized their help rather narrowly in the past; perhaps it is time to broaden it in order to accommodate the founding or supporting of pressure or social action groups.

I have been able to expand on only six possible ways of meeting a client's needs and thus of attempting to resolve his problems; these are but six among what should be an enormously wide repertoire of resources and ways of working available to any social worker or indeed, any counsellor. For any person working within the helping professions to have narrow allegiance to one or other of the various 'therapies' and thus to see his clients through the filter of that therapy, its assumptions and its jargon seems nowadays inadmissable; if one has a preferred approach, one should know both the evidence for the effectiveness of that approach, and its limitations as a way of helping. I am aware that my preference for the social learning model, while I feel it to be based on sound evidence, must not be carried too far; I must be alert to situations which would be alleviated much more readily by, for instance, an approach based primarily on medical intervention or, indeed, on purely sociological principles. Sometimes the provision of some new furniture, and sending mother for a holiday while the children go to a holiday scheme, does more for a family's morale than hours of conventional casework.

If I have been able to broaden the perspective of practising or intending counsellors or social workers a little, and to show that an eclectic approach to our clients' difficulties is now essential on both psychological and practical grounds, then I shall have accomplished something of my objective. One of the main messages from all the psychological research into means of helping people is astonishingly simple: people in trouble need a great deal of kindness, understanding and consideration from others; they need consistent respect and support and this respect needs to be sincere. Another message is that if this kindness and support alone is not enough, then people in the helping professions need as wide a repertoire of skills and resources as they can possibly achieve; they do indeed need 'theory for practice'; the time for the eclectic approach has arrived.

Bibliography

Allen, K. E., Hart, B. M., Buell, J., Harris, F. R. and Wolf, M. M. (1964), 'Effects of social reinforcement on isolate behaviour of a nursery school child', *Child Development,* vol, 35, pp. 511-18.

Argyle, M. (1969), *Social Interaction,* London, Methuen.

Argyle, M. (1972), *The Psychology of Interpersonal Behaviour,* Harmondsworth, Penguin.

Argyle, M. (1975), *Bodily Communication,* London, Methuen.

Argyle, M., Lalljee, M. and Cook, M. (1968), 'The effects of visibility on interaction in a dyad', *Human Relations,* vol. 21, pp. 3-17.

Argyle, M., Salter, V., Nicholson, H., Williams, M. and Burgess, P. (1970), 'The communication of inferior and superior attitudes by verbal and non-verbal signals', *The British Journal of Social and Clinical Psychology,* vol. 9, pp. 221-31.

Aronfreed, J. (1969), 'The concept of internalisation', in D. A. Goslin (ed.), *Handbook of Socialisation Theory and Research,* New York, Rand McNally.

Aronson, E. and Linder, D. (1965), 'Gain and loss of esteem as determinants of interpersonal attractiveness', *Journal of Experimental Social Psychology,* vol. 1, pp. 479-95.

Asch, S. E. (1946), 'Forming impressions of personality', *Journal of Abnormal and Social Psychology,* vol. 41, pp. 258-90.

Ballentine, R. (1968), 'The family therapist as a behavioural systems engineer—and a responsible one'. Paper presented at Georgetown University Symposium on Family Psychotherapy, Washington DC. Quoted in G. Erickson and T. Hogan, *Family Therapy: An Introduction to Theory and Technique,* Monterey, Calif., Brooks Cole.

Bandura, A. (1965), 'Influence of models' reinforcement contingencies on the acquisition of imitative responses', *Journal of Personality and Social Psychology,* vol. 1, pp. 589-95.

218

Bandura, A. (1973) *Aggression: A Social Learning Analysis,* Englewood Cliffs, New Jersey, Prentice-Hall.

Bandura, A. and Walters, R. H. (1963), *Social Learning and Personality Development,* New York, Holt, Rinehart & Winston.

Bannister, D. and Fransella, F. (1971), *Inquiring Man: The Theory of Personal Constructs,* Harmondsworth, Penguin.

Barnes, G., Charbon, R. and Hertzber, L. (1974), 'Team treatment for abusive families', *Social Case Work,* Family Service Association of America, December.

Beck, A. T. and Rush, A. J. (1975), 'Cognitive model of anxiety formation and anxiety resolution', in I. Sarason and C. Spielberger (eds), *Stress and Anxiety,* Washington, DC, Hemisphere.

Becker, W. C. (1964), 'Consequences of different kinds of parental discipline', in M. L. Hoffman and L. W. Hoffman (eds), *Review of Child Development,* vol. 1, New York, Russell Sage Foundation.

Bednar, R. L. (1970), 'Persuasability and the power of belief', *Personnel and Guidance Journal* vol. 48, pp. 647-52.

Bergin, A. E. (1969), 'A self-regulation technique for impulse control disorders', *Psychotherapy: Theory, Research and Practice.* vol. 6, pp. 113-18.

Bergin, A. E. and Garfield, S. L. (eds) (1971), *Handbook of Psychotherapy and Behaviour Change: An Empirical Analysis,* New York, Wiley.

Betz, B. J. and Whitehorn, J. C. (1956), 'The relationship of the therapist to the outcome of therapy in schizophrenia', *Psychological Research Reports,* vol. 5, pp. 89-105.

Biestek, F. (1957), *The Casework Relationship,* Chicago, Loyala University Press.

Blau, P. (1964), *Exchange and Power in Social Life,* New York, Wiley.

Bowlby, J. (1951), *Maternal Care and Mental Health,* Rome, World Health Organization.

Bowlby, J. (1953), *Child Care and the Growth of Love,* Harmondsworth, Penguin.

Brackbill, Y. (1958), 'Extinction of the smiling response in infants as a function of reinforcement schedule', *Child Development,* vol. 29, pp. 115-24.

Brammer, L. M. (1969), 'Eclecticism revisited', *Personnel and Guidance Journal,* vol. 48, pp. 192-7.

Brammer, L. M. and Shostrom, E. L. (1964), *Therapeutic Psychology: Fundamentals of Counselling and Psychotherapy,* Englewood Cliffs, New Jersey, Prentice-Hall.

Brossard, L. and Decarie, T. G. (1968), 'Comparative reinforcing effects of eight stimulations on the smiling response of infants', *Journal of Child Psychology and Psychiatry,* vol. 9, pp. 51-60.

Brown, B. J. (1977), 'A social learning programme for behaviour disordered children in a day-patient psychiatric setting', *The Journal of the Association of Workers for Maladjusted Children,* vol. 5, no. 1.

Brown, D. G. (1956), 'Sex-role preference in young children', *Psychology Monograph,* vol. 70, no. 421, pp. 1-19.

Bibliography

Bruner, J. S. and Goodman, C. C. (1947), 'Value and need as organising factors in perception', *Journal of Abnormal and Social Psychology*, vol. 42, pp. 43-4.

Bundza, K. A. and Simonson, N. R. (1973), 'Therapist self-disclosure: its effects on impressions of therapist and willingness to disclose', *Psychotherapy: Theory, Research and Practice*, vol. 10, pp. 215-17.

Byrne, D. (1971) *The attraction paradigm*, New York, Academic Press.

Cabeen, C. W. and Coleman, J. C. (1962), 'The selection of sex offender patients for group psychotherapy', *International Journal of Group Psychotherapy*, vol. 12, pp. 326-34.

Cameron, N. (1963), *Personality Development and Psychotherapy. A Dynamic Approach*, Boston, Houghton Mifflin.

Campbell, J. P. and Dunnette, M. D. (1968), 'Effectiveness of T-group experiences in managerial training', *Psychological Bulletin*, vol. 70, pp. 73-104.

Carkhuff, R. (1969), *Helping and Human Relations: A Primer for Lay and Professional Helpers*, vols 1 and 2, New York, Holt, Rinehart & Winston.

Carkhuff, R. and Berenson, B. (1967), *Beyond Counselling and Therapy*, New York, Holt, Rinehart & Winston.

Carkhuff, R. and Truax, C. B. (1965), 'Lay mental-health counselling: the effects of lay group counselling', *Journal of Consulting Psychology*, vol. 29, pp. 426-31.

Caudill, W. and Weinstein, H. (1966), 'Maternal care and infant behaviour in Japanese and American urban middle class families', in R. Konig and R. Hill (eds), *Yearbook of the International Sociological Association*.

Clarke, Ann and Clarke, A. D. B. (1976), *Early Experience: Myth and Evidence*, London, Open Books.

Cooley, C. H. (1902), *Human Nature and the Social Order*, New York, Scribner's.

Combs A. W. and Snygg, D. (1959), *Individual Behaviour*, New York, Harper.

Coopersmith, S. (1967), *The Antecedents of Self-Esteem*, San Francisco, Freeman & Co.

Danziger, K. (1976), *Socialization*, Harmondsworth, Penguin.

Davie, R., Butler, N. R. and Goldstein, H. (1972), *From Birth to Seven*, London, Longman, in association with the National Children's Bureau.

Dell, D. M. (1973), 'Counselor power base, influence attempt, and behaviour change in counseling', *Journal of Counseling Psychology*, vol. 20, pp. 399-405.

De Lucia, L. A. (1963), 'The toy preference test: A measure of sex-role identification', *Child Development*, vol. 34, pp. 107-17.

De Risi, W. J. (1975), *Writing Behavioural Contracts: Case Simulation Practice Manual*, Illinois, Champaigne.

Desharmes, R., Levy, J. and Wertheimer, M. (1954) 'A Note on attempted evaluations of psychotherapy', *Journal of Clinical Psychology*, vol. 10, pp. 233-5.

Deutsch, M. and Solomon, L. (1959), 'Reactions to evaluations by others as influenced by self evaluations', *Sociometry,* vol. 22, pp. 93-111.

Diggory, J. C. (1966), *Self-evaluation: Concepts and Studies,* New York, Wiley.

Dion, K. and Berscheid, E. (1972), 'Physical attractiveness and social perception of peers in pre-school children', Unpublished paper. University of Minnesota.

Dollard, J. and Miller, N. E. (1950), *Personality and Psychotherapy: An Analysis in Terms of Learning, Thinking and Culture,* New York, McGraw-Hill.

Doman, G. (1965), *Teach your Baby to Read: The Gentle Revolution,* London, Cape.

Douvan, E. and Adelson, J. (1966), *The Adolescent Experience,* New York, Wiley.

Egan, G. (1975), *The Skilled Helper: A Model for Systematic Helping and Interpersonal Relating,* Monterey, Calif, Brooks Cole.

Eibl-Eibesfeldt, I. (1970) *Ethology,* New York, Holt, Rinehart & Winston.

Ellis, A. (1959), 'Requisite conditions for basic personality change', *Journal of Consulting Psychology,* vol. 23, pp. 538-40.

Erickson, G. D. and Hogan (1972), *Family Therapy: An Introduction to Theory and Technique,* Monterey, Calif., Brooks Cole.

Exline, R. V. (1963), 'Explorations in the process of person perception: visual interaction in relation to competition, sex and the need for affiliation', *Journal of Personality,* vol. 31, pp. 1-20.

Eysenck, H. J. (1952), 'The effects of psychotherapy: an evaluation', *Journal of Consulting Psychology,* vol. 16, pp. 319-24.

Eysenck, H. J. (1955), The effects of psychotherapy: a reply, *Journal of Abnormal and Social Psychology,* vol. 50, pp. 147-8.

Fiedler, F. E. (1950), 'The concept of an ideal therapeutic relationship', *Journal of Consulting Psychology,* vol. 14, pp. 239-45.

Fogelman, K. R. (1976), *Britain's Sixteen Year Olds.* Research feedback on National Children's Bureau's National Child Development Study (1958 cohort), London, National Children's Bureau.

Folkard, M. S., Smith, D. E. and Smith, D. D. (1976), *IMPACT: Intensive Matched Probation and After-Care Treatment, vol. II, The results of the experiment,* London, Home Office Research Study.

Frank, J. D. (1961), *Persuasion and Healing,* Baltimore, John Hopkins Press.

Frank, J. D. (1965), 'The role of hope in psychotherapy'. Paper read at Kentucky Centennial Psychotherapy Symposium, University of Kentucky.

Frank, J. D., Gliedman, L. H., Imber, S. D., Stone, A. R. and Nash, E. H. (1959), 'Patients' expectancies and relearning as factors determining improvement in psychotherapy', *American Journal of Psychiatry,* vol. 115, pp. 961-8.

Gazda, G. M., Ashbury, F., Balzer, F., Childers, W. and Walters, R. (1973), *Human Relations Development: A Manual for Educators,* Boston, Allyn & Bacon.

Gilbert, M. (1976), 'Behavioural approach to the treatment of child abuse', *Nursing Times,* 29 January 1976.

Goffman, E. (1959), *The Presentation of Self in Everyday Life,* New York, Doubleday.

Goldiamond, I. (1965), 'Self-control procedures in personal behaviour problems', *Psychological Reports,* vol. 17, pp. 851-68.

Goldstein, A. P. (1973), *Structured Learning Therapy: Toward a Psychotherapy for the Poor,* New York, Academic Press.

Goldstein, A. P. and Shipman, W. G. (1961), 'Patients' expectancies, symptom reduction, and aspects of the initial psychotherapeutic interview', *Journal of Clinical Psychology,* vol. 17, pp. 129-33.

Guerney, B. G. (ed.) (1969), *Psychotherapeutic Agents. New Roles for Non-professionals, Parents and Teachers,* New York, Holt, Rinehart & Winston.

Hadley, R., Webb, A. and Farrell, C. (1974), *Across the Generations,* London, Allen & Unwin.

Halmos, P. (1965), *The Faith of the Counsellors,* London, Constable.

Hargreaves, D. (1972), *Interpersonal Relations and Education,* London, Routledge & Kegan Paul.

Hartup, W. and Zook, E. (1960), 'Sex-role preferences in 3-and-4-year-old children', *Journal of Consulting Psychology,* vol. 24, pp. 420-6.

Heine, R. W. and Trosman, H. (1960), 'Initial expectations of the doctor—patient interaction as a factor in continuance in psychotherapy', *Psychiatry,* vol. 23, pp. 275-8.

Herbert, M. (1978), *Conduct Disorders of Childhood and Adolescence. A Behavioural Approach to Assessment and Treatment,* London, Wiley.

Herbert, M. (1981), *Behavioural Treatment of Problem Children,* Academic Press.

Hilgard, E., Atkinson, R. C. and Atkinson, R. L. (1975), *Introduction to Psychology,* New York, Harcourt, Brace & Jovanovich.

Hoffman, M. L. and Saltzstein, H. D. (1967), 'Parent practices and the child's moral orientation'. Paper presented at meeting of the American Psychiatric Association.

Holmes, S., Barnhart, C., Canton, L. and Reyner, E. (1975), 'Working with the parent in child abuse cases', *Social Case Work,* Family Service Association of America, January.

Homans, G. (1961), *Social Behaviour: Its Elementary Forms,* London, Routledge & Kegan Paul.

Jehu, D. (1967), *Learning Theory and Social Work,* London, Routledge & Kegan Paul.

Jourard, S. M. (1964), *The Transparent Self: Self-Disclosure and Well-Being,* Princeton, New Jersey, Van Nostrand.

Jourard, S. M. (1971), *The Transparent Self,* New York, Van Nostrand, Reinhold.

Kelley, H. H. (1950), 'The warm-cold variable in first impressions of persons', *Journal of Personality,* vol. 18, pp. 431-9.

Kelly, G. A. (1955), *The Psychology of Personal Constructs,* vols 1 and 2, New York, Norton.

Kempe, C. and Helfer, R. (1968), *The Battered Child,* University of Chicago Press.

Kempe, C. and Henry, C. (1962), 'The battered child syndrome', *Journal of the American Medical Association,* July.

Kendon, A. (1972), 'Some relationships between body motion and speech: an analysis of an example', in A. Siegman and B. Pope (eds), *Studies in Dyadic Communication,* New York, Pergamon.

Kline, P. (1972), *Fact and Fantasy in Freudian Theory,* London, Methuen.

Kuhn, M. H. and McPartland, T. S. (1954), 'An empirical investigation of self-attitudes', *American Sociological Review,* vol. 19, pp. 68-76.

Lambert, M., De Julio, S. and Stein, D. (1978), 'Therapist interpersonal skills: process, outcome, methodological considerations and recommendations for future research', *Psychological Bulletin,* vol. 85, no. 3, pp. 467-89.

Lamonica, E., Carew, D., Winder, A., Hassie, A. and Blanchard, K., 'Empathy training', *Nursing Mirror,* 25 August 1977, pp. 22-5.

Legge, D. (1975), *An Introduction to Psychological Science,* London, Methuen.

Lerner, B. and Fiske, D. (1973), 'Client attributes and the eye of the beholder', *Journal of Consulting and Clinical Psychology,* vol. 40, pp. 272-7.

Levinson, D. J. (1962), 'The psychotherapist's contribution to the patient's treatment career', in H. H. Strupp and L. Luborsky (eds) *Research in Psychotherapy,* vol. 2, Washington, DC, American Psychological Association.

Lewis, J. and Lewis, M. (1977), *Community Counselling: A Human Services Approach,* New York, Wiley.

Liberman, R. (1970), 'Behavioural approaches to family and couple therapy', *American Journal of Orthopsychiatry,* vol. 40, no. 1, pp. 106-18. Also published in Erickson, G. B. and Hogan (eds) (1972), *Family Therapy: An Introduction to Theory and Technique,* Monterey, Calif, Brooks Cole.

Lipkin, S. (1954), 'Clients' feelings and attitudes in relation to the outcome of client-centred therapy', *Psychological Monographs,* vol. 68, no. 372.

Lorenz, K. (1966), *On Aggression,* New York, Harcourt, Brace & Jovanovich.

Lott, R. E., Clark, W. and Altman, I. (1969), *A Propositional Inventory of Research on Interpersonal Space,* Washington, Naval Medical Research Institute.

McMahon, J. T. (1964), 'The working class psychiatric patient: a clinical view', in F. Riessman, J. Cohen and A. Pearl (eds), *Mental Health of the Poor,* New York, Free Press.

Martin, D. (1972), *Learning-Based Client-centred Therapy,* Monterey, Calif., Brooks Cole.

Maslow, A. H. (1954), *Motivation and Personality,* New York, Harper.

Mayer, J. and Timms, N. (1970), *The Client Speaks: Working-Class Impressions of Casework,* London, Routledge & Kegan Paul.

Menninger, K. (1963), *The Vital Balance: The Life Process in Mental Health and Illness,* New York, Viking.

Bibliography

Mischel, W. (1973), 'Towards a cognitive social learning reconceptualisation of personality', *Psychological Review,* vol. 80, pp. 252-83.

Mischel, W. and Grusec, J. (1966), 'Determinants of the rehearsal and transmission of neutral and aversive behaviours', *Journal of Personal and Social Psychology,* vol. 2, pp. 197-205.

Morea, P. C. (1972), *Guidance, Selection and Training,* London, Routledge & Kegan Paul.

Mussen, P., Conger, J. and Kagan, J. (1969), *Child Development and Personality,* New York, Harper & Row.

Mussen, P. and Distler, L. (1959), 'Masculinity, identification and father-son relationships', *Journal of Abnormal and Social Psychology,* vol. 59, pp. 350-6.

Newcomb, T. M. (1931), 'An experiment designed to test the validity of a rating technique', *Journal of Educational Psychology,* vol. 22, pp. 279-89.

Newcomb, T. M. (1961), *The Acquaintance Process,* New York, Holt, Rinehart & Winston.

Olds, J. and Olds, M. E. (1965), 'Drives, rewards and the brain', in F. Barron, C. Dement, W. Edwards, H. Lindman, L. Phillips, J. Olds and M. E. Olds, *New Directions in Psychology,* vol. 2, New York, Holt, Rinehart & Winston.

Packer, A. (1974), 'Developments in counselling: what views should social workers hold?', *British Association of Social Workers' News,* 3 October 1974.

Parry, J. (1967), *Psychology of Human Communication,* University of London Press.

Patterson, C. (1973), *Theories of Counselling and Psychotherapy,* New York, Harper & Row.

Patterson, C. (1977), 'New approaches in counselling: healthy diversity or anti-therapeutic?', *British Journal of Guidance and Counselling,* vol. 5, no. 1.

Peine, H. and Howarth, R. (1976), *Children and Parents: Everyday Problems of Behaviour,* Harmondsworth, Penguin.

Penfield, W. (1969), 'Consciousness, memory and man's conditioned reflexes', in K. Pribram (ed.) *On the Biology of Learning,* New York, Harcourt, Brace.

Phillips, E. L. (1960), 'Parent-child psychotherapy: a follow-up study using two techniques', *Journal of Psychology,* vol. 29, pp. 195-202.

Piaget, J. (1951), *Plays, Dreams and Imitation in Childhood,* London, Heinemann.

Pringle, M. Kellmer, Butler, N. R. and Davie, R. (1966), *11,000 seven year olds,* London, Longman, in association with the National Children's Bureau.

Purkey, W. W. (1967), 'The self and academic achievement', Forida Educational Research and Development Council, *Research Bulletin,* vol. 3, no. 1.

Rank, O. (1958), *Beyond Psychology,* New York, Dover.

Rogers, C. R. (1951), *Client-centred Therapy,* Boston, Houghton Mifflin.

Rogers, C. R. (1957), 'The necessary and sufficient conditions of therapeutic personality change', *Journal of Consulting Psychology*, vol. 21, pp. 95-103.

Rogers, C. R. (1970), *On Becoming a Person. A Therapist's View of Therapy*, Boston, Houghton Mifflin.

Romig, D. A. (1978), *Justice for our Children*, Lexington, Mass., Lexington Books.

Rommetveit, R. (1960), *Selectivity, Intuition and Halo Effects in Social Perception*, Oslo University Press.

Rosenfeld, H. M. (1967), 'Non-verbal reciprocation of approval: an experimental analysis', *Journal of Experimental Social Psychology*, vol. 3, pp. 102-11.

Rosenfeld, H. and Baer, D. (1969), 'Unnoticed verbal conditioning of an aware experimenter by a more aware subject. The double agent effect', *Psychological Review*, vol. 76, pp. 425-32.

Rutter, M. (1972), *Maternal Deprivation Reassessed*, Harmondsworth, Penguin.

Sanford, N. (1954), 'Clinical methods: psychotherapy', *Annual Review of Psychology*, vol. 5, pp. 311-36.

Schofield, J. (1964), *Psychotherapy: The Purchase of Friendship*, Englewood Cliffs, New Jersey, Prentice-Hall.

Secord, P. F. (1958), 'The role of facial features in interpersonal perception', in R. Tagiuri and L. Petrullo (eds), *Person Perception and Interpersonal Behaviour*, Stanford University Press.

Secord, P. and Backman, C. W. (1974), *Social Psychology*, New York, McGraw-Hill.

Shaw, J. (1975), 'Consumer Opinion and Social Policy', *Journal of Social Policy*, vol. 5, pp. 19-23.

Shoben, E. J. (1949), 'Psychotherapy as a problem in learning theory', *Psychological Bulletin*, vol. 46, pp. 366-92.

Skinner, A. and Castle, R. (1969), '78 battered children: a retrospective study', NSPCC, September.

Slater, E. (1968), 'A review of earlier evidence on genetic factors in schizophrenia', in D. Rosenthal and S. Kety (eds), *The Transmission of Schizophrenia*, London, Pergamon.

Smale, G. G. (1977), *Prophecy, Behaviour and Change. An Examination of Self-Fulfilling Prophecies in Helping Relationships*, London, Routledge & Kegan Paul.

Smith, S., Hamon, R. and Noble, S. (1974), 'Social aspects of battered baby syndrome', *British Journal of Psychiatry*, vol. 125, pp. 568-82.

Sommer, R. (1965), 'Further studies of small group ecology', *Sociometry*, vol.28, pp. 337-48.

Spock, B. (1962), *Baby and Child Care*, New York, Pocket Books.

Steiner, I. D. and Johnson, H. H. (1963), 'Authoritarianism and "tolerance of trait inconsistency"', *Journal of Abnormal and Social Psychology*, vol. 67, pp. 388-91.

Stevenson, O. (1976), quoted in 'Ambitious Keele gains the social workers' friend', *The Times Higher Education Supplement*, 9 April 1976.

Bibliography

Strong, S. R. (1968), 'Counseling: an interpersonal influence process', *Journal of Counseling*, vol. 17, pp. 388-99.

Strupp, H. (1955), 'Psychotherapeutic technique, professional affiliation and experience level', *Journal of Consulting Psychology*, vol. 19, pp. 97-102.

Sullivan, H. S. (1954), *The Psychiatric Interview*, New York, Norton.

Swensen, C. H. (1972), 'Commitment and the personality of the successful therapist', *Psychological Bulletin*, vol. 77, pp. 400-4.

Task Force Report, (1973), *Behaviour Therapy in Psychiatry*, Washington, American Psychiatric Association.

Teuber, H. L. and Powers, E. (1953), *Evaluating therapy in a delinquency prevention programme, proceedings of the Association for Research into Nervous and Mental Disease*, vol. 31, pp. 137-47, Baltimore, Williams & Wilkins.

Thibaut, J. and Kelly, H. (1959), *The Social Psychology of Groups*, New York, Wiley.

Thomas, A., Chess, S. and Birch, H. G. (1970), 'The origin of personality', *Papers on Socialization and Attitudes Selected from Scientific American*, Reading, Freeman.

Thorne, F. C. (1944), 'A critique of non-directive methods of psychotherapy', *Journal of Abnormal Psychology*, vol. 39, pp. 459-70.

Thorne, F. C. (1957), 'A critique of recent developments in personality counselling theory', *Journal of Clinical Psychology*, vol. 13, pp. 234-44.

Thorne, F. C. (1969a), 'Editorial opinion: Towards a better understanding of the eclectic method', *Journal of Clinical Psychology*, vol. 25, pp. 463-4.

Thorne, F. C. (1969b), 'Editorial opinion: Value factors in clinical judgment', *Journal of Clinical Psychology*, vol. 25, p. 231.

Timms, N. (1973), *The Receiving End: Consumer Accounts of Social Help for Children*, London, Routledge & Kegan Paul.

Truax, C. and Carkhuff, R. (1967), *Towards Effective Counselling and Psychotherapy*, Chicago, Aldine.

Truax, C., Carkhuff, R. and Douds, J. (1964), 'Towards an integration of the didactic and experiential approaches to training in counseling and psychotherapy', *Journal of Counseling Psychology*, vol. 11, pp. 240-7.

Truax, C., Fine, H., Moravec, J. and Millis, W. (1968), 'Effects of therapist persuasive potency in individual psychotherapy', *Journal of Clinical Psychology*, vol. 24, pp. 359-62.

Truax, C., Tunnell, B. T., Fine, H. and Wargo, D. (1966), *The prediction of client outcome during group psychotherapy from measures of initial status*. Arkansas Rehabilitation Research and Training Centre, University of Arkansas.

Underwood, W. J. (1965), 'Evaluation of laboratory method training', *Training Directors' Journal*, vol. 19, pp. 34-40.

Varah, C. (1973) *The Samaritans in the 70s: To Befriend the Suicidal and Despairing*, London, Constable.

Vaughn, C. and Leff, J. P. (1976), 'The influence of family and social factors on the course of psychiatric illness: a comparison of schizophrenic and depressed neurotic patients', *British Journal of Psychiatry*, vol. 129, pp. 125-37.

Veness, T. and Brierley, D. W. (1963), 'Forming impressions of personality: two experiments', *British Journal of Social and Clinical Psychology*, vol. 2, pp. 11-19.

Warr, P. and Knapper, C. (1968), *The perception of people and events*, New York, Wiley.

Watson, D. and Tharp, R. (1972), *Self-directed Behaviour: Self-modification for Personal Adjustment*, Monterey, Calif, Brooks Cole.

Wedge, P. J. and Prosser, H. (1973), *Born to Fail?*, London, Arrow Books.

Weigel, R. G., Dinges, N., Dyer, R. and Straumfjorn, A. (1972), 'Perceived self-disclosure, mental health and who is liked in group treatment', *Journal of Counseling Psychology*, vol. 19, pp. 47-52.

Wheldall, K. (1975), *Social Behaviour*, London, Methuen.

Whiteley, J. (1967), *Research in Counseling*, Columbus, Ohio, Merril.

Williams, W. S. (1956), 'Class differences in the attitudes of psychiatric patients', *Social Problems*, vol. 4, pp. 240-4.

Wolberg, L. R. (1967), *The Technique of Psychotherapy*, New York, Grune & Stratton.

Wood, E. C., Rakusin, J., Morse, E. and Singer, R. (1962a), 'Interpersonal aspects of psychiatric hospitalisation. II Some correlations between admission circumstances and the treatment experience', *Archives of General Psychiatry*, vol, 6, pp. 39-45.

Wood, E. C., Rakusin, J. M., Morse, E. and Singer, R. (1962b), 'Interpersonal aspects of psychiatric hospitalisation. III The follow up survey', *Archives of General Psychiatry*, vol. 6, pp. 46-55.

Woody. R. (1971), *Psychobehavioural Counselling and Therapy*, New York, Appleton Century Crofts.

Wootton, B. (1959), *Social Service and Social Pathology*, London, Allen & Unwin.

World Health Organization (1962), *Deprivation of Maternal Care. A Reassessment of its Effects*, Geneva.

Index